A CHRISTIAN'S SECRET OF A HAPPY LIFE 2.0

A Victorious Path to Faith-filled Living

Dr Michael H Yeager

THE CHRISTIAN'S SECRET OF A HAPPY LIFE
By Hannah Whitall Smith

Chapter 1 Introductory. -- God's Side and Man's Side
Chapter 2 The Scriptural Ness of This Life
Chapter 3 The Life Defined
Chapter 4 How to Enter In
Chapter 5 Difficulties Concerning Consecration
Chapter 6 Difficulties Concerning Faith
Chapter 7 Difficulties Concerning the Will
Chapter 8 Is God in Everything?
Chapter 9 Growth
Chapter 10 Service
Chapter 11 Difficulties Concerning Guidance
Chapter 12 Concerning Temptation
Chapter 13 Failures
Chapter 14 Doubts
Chapter 15 Practical Results
Chapter 16 The Joy of Obedience
Chapter 17 Oneness with Christ
Chapter 18 "Although" and "Yet"
Chapter 19 Kings and Their Kingdoms
Chapter 20 The Chariots of God
Chapter 21 "Without Me Ye Can Do Nothing"
Chapter 22 "God with Us";

Preface: I must admit, this is not a theological treatise. I have not been schooled in the halls of theology, nor do I claim to comprehend their intricate methods and terminology. Yet, the Lord has graciously instructed me through practical and experiential lessons gleaned from His Word, the Bible, which have greatly enriched and brought joy to my Christian walk. I yearn to share this precious secret with you, dear reader, so that you too may discover a life of happiness and fulfillment.
I am not seeking to alter the theological perspectives of anyone.

Many of my readers, I presume, possess far more theological knowledge than I, and might even detect numerous perceived errors. However, I humbly implore you to overlook these shortcomings, and instead, focus on the experiential essence of what I endeavor to convey. If you find these insights beneficial and practical, I ask that you kindly forgive the imperfect manner in which they are presented.
My pursuit has been to unveil the unadulterated truth that serves as the

bedrock for all creeds and beliefs, guiding the soul into a personal relationship with God that transcends the disparities in religious expression. As it is written in the Bible, *"But without faith it is impossible to please him: for he that cometh to God must believe that he is, and that he is a rewarder of them that diligently seek him."* *(Hebrews 11:6)*

I have entrusted this work to the Lord, beseeching Him to nullify any erroneous content and permit only the truth to resonate within the hearts of my readers. This message emanates from a place of tender sympathy and ardent love for all those who are weary and burdened within Christ's Church. From the depths of my heart, I extend this offering to you.

In my sincere attempt to provide guidance, I have given the best I have to offer, and can do no more. May the blessed Holy Spirit employ these words to unveil the true secret of a joyous life for some of my readers. As the Scripture says, *"But the Comforter, which is the Holy Ghost, whom the Father will send in my name, he shall teach you all things, and bring all things to your remembrance, whatsoever I have said unto you."* *(John 14:26)*

ISBN: 9798397077569

DEDICATION

All of the Scriptures used in this book on **"A Christian's Secret of a Happy Life   2.0"** is from the original 1611 version of the King James Bible. I give thanks to God the Father , Jesus Christ and the Holy Ghost for the powerful impact the word has had upon my life. Without the word Quickened in my heart by the Holy Ghost I would've been lost and undone. To the Lord of Heaven and Earth I am eternally indebted for his great love and his mercy, his protections and his provisions, his Divine guidance and overwhelming goodness, the **Price He PAID for His Glorious Church**! To him be glory and praise for ever and ever: Amen .

CONTENTS

Acknowledgments   i

Chapter One   9

Chapter Three   47

Chapter Five   84

Chapter Six   101

Chapter Eight   136

Chapter Ten   173

Chapter Twelve   215

Chapter Fourteen   253

Chapter Sixteen   281

Chapter Eighteen   310

Chapter Twenty   362

ACKNOWLEDGMENTS

*To our heavenly Father and His wonderful love.

*To our Lord, Savior and Master — Jesus Christ, Who saved us and set us free because of His great love for us.

*To the Holy Spirit, Who leads and guides us into the realm of truth and miraculous living every day.

*To all of those who had a part in helping me get this book ready for the publishers.

*To my Lovely Wife, and our precious children, Michael, Daniel, Steven, Stephanie, Catherine Yu, who is our precious daughter-in-law, and Naomi, who is now with the Lord.

Important Introduction

Unveiling a dynamic reimagining of the influential classic, **"A Christian's Secret of a Happy Life,"** the original book was highly successful with over 10 million copies flying off the shelves. This compelling narrative encapsulates the awe-inspiring journey of Hannah Whitall Smith (1832-1911), a woman whose faith refused to be extinguished by the darkest nights.

Hannah's life was far from serene. She bore the devastating loss of four children and endured the betrayal of an unfaithful husband. As a pioneering female in the realm of ministry, she confronted the daunting challenges of a patriarchal society. Yet, she emerged from her crucible of trials with an unshakeable faith and deep wisdom.

Hannah's profound experience of navigating life through the lens of faith rather than sight provides invaluable insights for Christians today. With a tenacious spirit and unyielding faith, she forged a blissful existence centered on an intimate relationship with the ultimate Parent, Savior, Protector, and Friend. Smith's timeless teachings offer a beacon of hope to contemporary Christians wrestling with their own trials and yearning for joyous living.

CHAPTER ONE

INTRODUCTORY GOD'S SIDE AND MAN'S SIDE

As I begin to discuss the life and walk of faith, I am eager to clarify a common misunderstanding that often arises when exploring this subject, and which can obstruct a clear comprehension of the teachings. This confusion stems from the fact that the two aspects of the subject are seldom considered simultaneously. People tend to focus on one aspect, neglecting the other, which leads to distorted views. To truly understand the subject, it is essential to keep both perspectives in mind. I am referring to God's side and man's side, or, in other words, God's role in the work of sanctification and man's role. These two aspects are distinct and even contrasting, but they are not contradictory, although they may appear so to a casual observer.

This was illustrated to me in a striking way not long ago. Two teachers of the higher Christian life were holding meetings in the same location at alternating times. One focused solely on God's role in the work, while the other emphasized man's role. Both teachers were in complete harmony with one another, recognizing that they were teaching different aspects of the same profound truth. Many of their listeners also understood this.

However, some attendees were confused. One woman expressed her bewilderment, saying, "I cannot understand it at all. Here are two preachers claiming to teach the same truth, yet they seem to contradict one another." I realized that her confusion was shared by many sincere seekers of truth.

Consider the words from the Bible, in *Philippians 2:12-13: "Wherefore, my beloved, as ye have always obeyed, not as in my presence only, but now much more in my absence, work out your own salvation with fear and trembling. For it is God which worketh in you both to will and to do of his good pleasure."* This passage beautifully captures the delicate balance between God's part and man's part in the process of sanctification.

Imagine two friends who visit a renowned building and return home to describe it. One has seen only the north side, and the other only the south side. The first friend explains, "The building was constructed in a certain way, with specific stories and decorations." The second friend interrupts, "No, you're mistaken! I saw the building, and it was built differently, with unique ornaments and stories."

In reality, both friends are right, for they have observed different aspects of the same building. Just as the building has multiple sides, the life and walk of faith also encompasses both God's role and man's role. By weaving in scriptural references, I hope to provide a clearer understanding of the life and walk of faith, emphasizing the significance of considering both aspects in harmony.

To fully grasp the life and walk of faith, we must delve

deeper into both aspects, acknowledging that they are equally important and complementary to one another. As the Apostle Paul states in *1 Corinthians 3:9 (KJV), "For we are labourers together with God: ye are God's husbandry, ye are God's building."* This verse highlights the collaborative nature of our spiritual growth, with both God and man working together in the process of sanctification.

On God's side, we find His divine grace and power that enable us to overcome our sinful nature and grow in holiness. As stated in *2 Corinthians 12:9 (KJV), "And he said unto me, My grace is sufficient for thee: for my strength is made perfect in weakness."* God's grace is the very foundation of our spiritual progress, and without it, we are incapable of achieving true sanctification.

On man's side, we have our responsibility to actively participate in the process by submitting to God's will and seeking His guidance. As *James 4:7-8 (KJV) says, "Submit yourselves therefore to God. Resist the devil, and he will flee from you. Draw nigh to God, and he will draw nigh to you."* We must make a conscious effort to draw closer to God and resist the temptations that can lead us astray.

To maintain balance in our spiritual walk, we need to give due attention to both aspects. Neglecting either God's role or man's role can result in stagnation or even regression in our spiritual growth. For instance, if we rely solely on God's grace without making any effort on our part, we run the risk of becoming passive and complacent. On the other hand, if we rely only on our own efforts without seeking God's grace, we may end up striving in vain, as our strength is insufficient to overcome our inherent weaknesses.

The key to a successful and fruitful life of faith lies in embracing both aspects and understanding that they are intertwined in a divine partnership. As we seek to grow in our walk with God, let us keep in mind the words of *Philippians 4:13 (KJV), "I can do all things through Christ which strengtheneth me."* Through the power of Christ, we can strive to become more like Him, knowing that our efforts are supported by His boundless grace and love.

In conclusion, the life and walk of faith is a beautiful journey that requires the harmonious interplay of God's grace and our active participation. By holding both aspects in view and drawing on the wisdom found in the of the Bible, we can navigate the path of spiritual growth with confidence and assurance. I hope to encourage a deeper understanding of the life and walk of faith, inspiring others to seek a closer relationship with God and pursue the higher Christian life.

TWO SIDES TO FAITH

A spirited debate may arise concerning the accuracy of each person's description, until the two friends realize that they have been describing different aspects of the same building, and suddenly everything becomes clear. I want to express my thoughts on what I perceive to be the two distinct aspects of this matter, demonstrating how considering one without acknowledging the other can lead to misconceptions and erroneous views of the truth. To put it succinctly, our role is to trust, while God's role is to work. It's easy to see how contrasting these two roles can be, yet they are not necessarily contradictory. Let me explain.

There is a specific task to be achieved. We are to be freed from sin's power and made perfect in every good work to fulfill God's will. As it says in *2 Corinthians 3:18 (KJV)*, *"But we all, with open face beholding as in a glass the Glory of the Lord, are changed into the same image from Glory to Glory, even as by the Spirit of the Lord."* We are to be transformed by the renewing of our minds, proving what is good, acceptable, and perfect according to God's will *(Romans 12:2, KJV)*. Genuine change must be wrought within and upon us.

Besetting sins must be conquered, evil habits overcome, and wrong dispositions and feelings eradicated. In their place, holy attitudes and emotions must be cultivated. The Bible teaches that a genuine transformation must occur. Now, someone must accomplish this. Either we must do it ourselves, or someone else must do it for us. Many of us initially attempt to do it ourselves, only to fail miserably. Eventually, we learn from the Scriptures and our experiences that we are utterly incapable of performing this task on our own. Instead, we discover that the Lord Jesus Christ came to accomplish this purpose, and He will do it for all who wholly entrust themselves to Him and rely on Him to achieve it.

Under these circumstances, what roles do the believer and the Lord play? Clearly, the believer can do nothing but trust, while the Lord, in whom they trust, carries out the work entrusted to Him. Trusting and doing are indeed contrasting actions and can sometimes be contradictory, but is that the case here? Evidently not, since two different parties are involved. If we were to say that one party trusts another with a task but then takes care of it themselves, we would be stating a contradiction and an impossibility. However, when we say that one party trusts another to complete a task and that the other then proceeds to carry it out, we are presenting a perfectly coherent and harmonious statement.

Thus, when we say that in this higher life, our part is to trust and that God accomplishes the task entrusted to Him, we are not presenting a particularly difficult or perplexing problem. A preacher discussing our role in this matter can only speak of surrender and trust, as that is genuinely all we can do. We all agree on this point. Nevertheless, such preachers are often criticized for supposedly implying that there is no other role, and therefore nothing but trust is required. Yet, as we have seen, trust and surrender are our responsibilities, while God's role is to work and accomplish the transformation within us.

When we focus solely on trust and surrender, we must also remember that it is only half of the equation. Trusting God is essential, but it is equally important to recognize and emphasize the work that God performs within us. Trusting in God means surrendering our will to Him, acknowledging our inability to bring about the transformation we desire.

As *Proverbs 3:5-6 (KJV)* states, *"Trust in the Lord with*

all thine heart; and lean not unto thine own understanding. In all thy ways acknowledge him, and he shall direct thy paths."

Our trust in God allows Him to work powerfully within us, molding us into the image of His Son, Jesus Christ. It is God who works in us *"both to will and to do of his good pleasure" (Philippians 2:13, KJV).* As we trust and yield to Him, He empowers us to overcome sin, resist temptation, and grow in spiritual maturity. Our lives begin to bear the fruits of the Spirit, as described in *Galatians 5:22-23 (KJV): "But the fruit of the Spirit is love, joy, peace, longsuffering, gentleness, goodness, faith, meekness, temperance."*

In this journey, it is crucial to maintain a balanced perspective. We must not fall into the trap of believing that trust and surrender are all that is required of us, thereby neglecting the transformative work that God performs within us. Likewise, we must not become preoccupied with our efforts and self-improvement, forgetting that it is God who accomplishes this work in us. Understanding the harmony between our trust and God's work is vital for a healthy, growing relationship with Him.

In conclusion, while it may seem that trust and God's work are contrasting elements, they are not contradictory when we consider the different roles each party plays in our spiritual transformation. Our part is to trust and surrender, while God's role is to work within us, bringing about the change we so desperately need. Recognizing this balance helps us grow in our faith, deepening our relationship with God, and enabling us to become more

Christlike in our thoughts, words, and actions.

THE PROCESS OF SANCTIFICATION

As I cried out, it seemed that the doctrine of faith could be misunderstood as removing all realities. Some might assume that souls are simply instructed to trust, and that's the end of it. They may then envision themselves sitting in a religious easy-chair, dreaming away a life devoid of any actual results. Of course, this misapprehension arises from either the preacher failing to explain or the listener failing to comprehend the other side of the matter. The truth is that when we trust, the Lord works, and much is accomplished not by us, but by Him. Our faith leads to actual results because our Lord takes on the tasks entrusted to Him and brings them to fruition. We may not do anything, but He does it, and it is all the more effective because of this.

As it is written in *Philippians 2:13 (KJV)*, *"For it is God which worketh in you both to will and to do of his good pleasure."* This clarifies the puzzle of preaching faith. When we focus on God's side of the equation, we understand that His role is not to trust but to work. The Lord carries out the tasks entrusted to Him, shaping and training our souls through inward exercises and outward circumstances. He utilizes all the resources of His wisdom and love to refine and purify our souls, making everything in our lives serve the purpose of helping us grow in grace and gradually conform to the image of Christ.

As *Romans 8:29 (KJV)* states, *"For whom he did*

foreknow, he also did predestinate to be conformed to the image of his Son, that he might be the firstborn among many brethren." The Lord guides us through a transformation process that varies in length based on our individual needs, actualizing the results for which we have trusted. For instance, when we dare, according to **Romans 6:11 (KJV)**, by faith to reckon ourselves *"dead unto sin,"* the Lord makes this a reality by leading us to victory over self through His daily and hourly providential discipline. Our reckoning is only possible because God makes it real.

However, a preacher who emphasizes this practical aspect and speaks of God's processes for making faith's reckonings experiential realities might be accused of contradicting faith's teachings. Critics may argue that such preaching only presents a gradual sanctification by works, setting before the soul an impossible and hopeless task.

Sanctification is, in fact, both a sudden step of faith and a gradual process of works. It is a step-in terms of our responsibility and a process in relation to God's role. *Ephesians 2:8 (KJV)* affirms this: *"For by grace are ye saved through faith; and that not of yourselves: it is the gift of God."* By a step of faith, we enter into Christ; through a process, we grow up unto Him in all things. By a step of faith, we place ourselves in the hands of the Divine Potter; through a gradual process, He molds us into a vessel unto His own honor, fit for His use, and prepared for every good work.

THE POTTER AND THE CLAY

Imagine that I am describing to someone entirely unfamiliar with pottery how a lump of clay becomes a beautiful vessel. First, I will explain the clay's role in the process, which is simply to be placed into the potter's hands and remain passive, submitting to the potter's manipulations. There's not much more to say about the clay's part in this transformation. However, my listener cannot assume that nothing else happens, simply because the clay's role is limited.

If my listener is perceptive, they will ask, "I understand the clay's part, but what does the potter do?" To this, I reply, "Ah, now we come to the essential aspect. The potter takes the clay, which has been surrendered to his craftsmanship, and begins to mold and shape it according to his vision. He kneads and works the clay, tearing it apart and pressing it together again, moistening it and allowing it to dry. Sometimes he labors over it for hours, while at other times he sets it aside for days without touching it."

Throughout these processes, the potter renders the clay completely pliable in his hands. He proceeds to fashion it into the vessel he has envisioned. The potter spins the clay on the wheel, smoothing and refining it, drying it in the sun, and baking it in the oven. Ultimately, the potter unveils his creation, a vessel that honors him and is suitable for his use.

This analogy is reminiscent of a passage from the Bible, found in *Isaiah 64:8 (KJV),* which says, *"But now, O*

Lord, thou art our father; we are the clay, and thou our potter; and we all are the work of thy hand." In our spiritual journey, we are the clay, and God is the potter. Our role is to submit ourselves to God's will and allow Him to mold and shape us into vessels of honor, fit for His divine purposes. In doing so, we trust that God, in His infinite wisdom, will transform us into the people He has called us to be.

FROM GLORY TO GLORY

As I share this illustration, my listener might wonder if I am contradicting myself. They might think that earlier, I said the clay had nothing to do but remain passive in the potter's hands, and now I am placing a great responsibility on the clay that it cannot perform, making it seem like an impossible and hopeless task. However, such confusion would be misplaced.

My listener should understand that when I spoke of the clay's role, I was emphasizing its passivity and surrender to the potter. Now, I am highlighting the potter's role in shaping the clay. These two aspects are contrasting but not contradictory. The clay is not expected to do the potter's work but only to yield itself to his craftsmanship. There is a perfect harmony between these seemingly opposing teachings on the subject.

Regarding humanity's role in this great work, what more can be said than that we must continually surrender ourselves and trust in God? When we explore God's role, we discover countless remarkable ways He carries out the tasks entrusted to Him. This is where growth occurs.

A lump of clay would never transform into a beautiful vessel if it remained in the clay pit for thousands of years. However, once placed in the hands of a skilled potter, the clay quickly takes shape into a vessel of honor.

Similarly, when we surrender our souls to the Heavenly Potter, we are rapidly transformed from **Glory** to **Glory** into the image of the Lord by His Spirit. This transformation is reflected in *2 Corinthians 3:18 (KJV)*, which states, *"But we all, with open face beholding as in a glass the Glory of the Lord, are changed into the same image from Glory to Glory, even as by the Spirit of the Lord."* Thus, our role is to trust and surrender to God's will, allowing Him to mold us into vessels fit for His divine purpose.

"Through the Potter's Hands"

Having made a leap of faith and committed myself fully and unreservedly to God's hands, I anticipate the divine work to commence. However, the way in which God executes the task entrusted to Him may not align with my expectations. It's important to remember that His wisdom surpasses mine, and I must find contentment in this knowledge.

I recall a lady who ventured into this life of faith accompanied by a tremendous surge of the Holy Spirit and an overwhelming flood of light and joy. Naturally, she thought this spiritual awakening was a precursor to some significant service, expecting to be immediately deployed into God's harvest field. But life took a surprising turn. Her husband lost all his money, confining her to her home, swamped with numerous domestic chores. With no time or energy left for any gospel work, she found herself facing a different kind of service.

In the face of this unexpected challenge, she embraced her circumstance, devoting herself to sweeping, dusting, baking, and sewing as fervently as she would have to preaching or praying. Through her faithful acceptance and dedication, she became a vessel *"meet for the Master's use, and prepared unto every good work" (2 Timothy 2:21, KJV).*

Another lady, who had likewise embraced this life of faith amidst tremendous blessings, also assumed she was destined for some remarkable mission. Instead, she found herself tending to two petulant, sickly nieces, catering to their whims and providing comfort. Unfortunately, unlike the first woman, she resisted this unexpected assignment. She complained, fussed, and eventually rebelled. In her resistance, she lost her blessing and regressed into a state of chilling despair and sorrow.

The lady understood the initial aspect of trusting but failed to grasp the divine process of fulfilling the trust she had placed. She withdrew herself from the Heavenly Potter's hands, resulting in a marred vessel *(Jeremiah 18:4, KJV).* I believe that many vessels have been similarly damaged due to a lack of understanding of these spiritual realities.

Christian maturity isn't a momentary achievement but the

outcome of God's Holy Spirit's labor. It is the Holy Spirit who, through His invigorating and transformative power, nurtures us to grow into the fullness of Christ. As Ephesians 4:15 (KJV) reminds us, "But speaking the truth in love, may grow up into him in all things, which is the head, even Christ."

In conclusion, the journey of faith is not without trials and unexpected turns. Our expectations may not align with God's plan, but in faithfully surrendering to His divine process, we allow ourselves to be shaped and prepared for service. As we yield to the work of the Holy Spirit, we mature in our faith, growing closer to Christ in all aspects of our lives. Our role is to trust and submit to His divine process, allowing ourselves to be shaped into vessels for His use. Remember, it is in the hands of Heavenly Potter that our transformation truly unfolds.

Journey of Faith, Transformation, and Divine Timing

Once I decided to take a leap of faith, entrusting my life entirely to God, I was certain that He would begin to manifest His workings. His methods, however, could be quite different from my expectations. But God, in His divine wisdom, knows best. This realization compelled me to remain contented and patient.

Let me share with you a story of a woman who embarked on this journey of faith, fueled by a powerful outpouring of the Spirit and an overwhelming sense of joy. Initially, she assumed that her spiritual awakening would lead her to serve in some grand capacity in the Lord's vineyard.

But life had different plans. Her husband lost all their wealth, and she found herself confined to her home, consumed by domestic chores. There wasn't any time or energy left for the Gospel work she had anticipated.

But instead of resisting, she embraced her circumstances. She devoted herself to her household tasks — sweeping, dusting, baking, and sewing — with the same zeal as she would have for preaching, praying, or writing for the Lord. And this very training molded her into a vessel ready and fit for the Master's use, as described in *2 Timothy 2:21 (KJV): "If a man therefore purge himself from these, he shall be a vessel unto honour, sanctified, and meet for the master's use, and prepared unto every good work."*

Contrarily, there was another woman who, like the first, stepped into this life of faith under equally blessed circumstances, but her path diverged significantly. She was confined to caring for her two irritable, ailing nieces, a role that required constant patience and compassion. Unlike the first lady, she resisted and grew frustrated with her situation, which culminated in rebellion. Consequently, she lost her blessing and returned to a state of regrettable indifference and sorrow.

This woman had initially grasped the concept of trusting in God, but she failed to comprehend the divine process of fulfilling the faith she had committed to. She withdrew herself from the heavenly Potter's hands, and her spiritual vessel was marred in the process, much like the metaphor in *Jeremiah 18:4 (KJV),* which says, *"And the vessel that he made of clay was marred in the hand of the*

23

potter: so he made it again another vessel, as seemed good to the potter to make it." I've come to believe that many have faltered similarly due to a lack of understanding of these spiritual dynamics.

The full blossom of Christian experience cannot be achieved instantly; it evolves from the transformative power of God's Holy Spirit. As described in *Ephesians 4:15 (KJV), "But speaking the truth in love, may grow up into him in all things, which is the head, even Christ,"* we grow in the likeness of Christ through the energy and transformative power of the Holy Spirit.

In conclusion, every believer's journey is unique, paved with trials and triumphs. It requires surrender, patience, understanding, and an unwavering faith in God's wisdom and timing. As we entrust ourselves to Him, we must recognize that His methods of shaping and preparing us for His service may differ from our expectations. Yet, in His divine wisdom and timing, we become vessels fit for the Master's use, reflecting Christ in all we do.

Our Role and God's in the Plan of Salvation

Have you ever found yourself caught in a seeming paradox, asking, "How can we be called to trust implicitly while also being asked to accomplish what appears impossible?" To answer this question, imagine the carpenter's shop. Here, a saw is employed to cleave a log in two. Who is responsible for this feat - the saw or the carpenter? The saw, although an integral instrument, merely carries out the work. The real power and intent behind this task belong to the carpenter.

In a similar vein, we offer ourselves to God, our talents and abilities in His service, to be instruments of righteousness for His purpose. We find God working in us, enabling us to desire and carry out His divine plan. It is as the Apostle Paul profoundly said, *"I have labored more abundantly than they all: yet not I, but the grace of God which was with me" (1 Corinthians 15:10, KJV).*

We are meant to be God's handiwork, not our own. As stated in *Ephesians 2:10 (KJV), "For we are his workmanship, created in Christ Jesus unto good works, which God hath before ordained that we should walk in them."* Truly, only God, our creator, can re-create us. He alone comprehends the workings of His creation.

Striving to create ourselves only leads to our vessel's distortion. No soul can ever reach its ultimate potential except through the workings of the Almighty, who according to His perfect wisdom *"worketh all things after the counsel of His own will" (Ephesians 1:11, KJV).*

While this discourse will primarily focus on our part in this great divine work, as it is meant to guide believers towards fulfilling their roles, it is important to underline a central truth. Without my unwavering belief in God's effective action in this grand scheme, I wouldn't have put pen to paper. This recognition of God's role gives my words meaning and depth, breathing life into the pages of this book.

In conclusion, the journey of faith involves both complete trust in God's sovereign work and diligent effort on our part. It's a delicate balance, akin to a dance where we move as He leads. Let's continually yield ourselves to His perfect will, remembering always that we are the work of His hands, reshaped and refined for His **Glory**. Remember, in God's carpentry shop, He is the Master Craftsman, and we are His instruments.

Chapter Two
THE SCRIPTURALNESS OF THIS LIFE

Discovering True Christian Life in the Light of Christ

Every time I ponder upon the profound subject of the true Christian life, a life tucked away with Christ in God, I find myself caught in a whirlwind of thoughts, so many that they leave me on the brink of speechlessness. I find myself grappling with questions such as, where should I commence? What is the most crucial message to impart? How can I inspire people to read, absorb, and believe? The topic is simply awe-inspiring, and human vocabulary seems meager and impotent in its wake. Yet, I am propelled to share, to divulge this secret.

This secret, my friends, pertains to the victory that triumphs over the world, the assured deliverance from all our adversaries, the liberation that every child of God craves and prays for, but which seems persistently elusive. May the Lord equip me with the right words and wisdom so that every believer who engages with these reflections might have their eyes opened to the truth embodied in Jesus and may be stirred to take hold of this splendid life for themselves.

For I am utterly convinced that every soul born anew in Christ thirsts for victory and tranquility. Almost every individual, at various moments, intuitively discerns these to be their divine entitlement. Reflect, for a moment, on the joyous cries of triumph your soul exclaimed when you first encountered the Lord Jesus and perceived a hint of His formidable saving grace. Do you remember how confident you were of impending victory? How effortless it seemed to be more than conquerors, through Him who loves you.

You marched under the banner of a Captain who had never known defeat. How could you even fathom the prospect of failure? Nevertheless, many of you may have found that your actual experience diverged from this optimism. Your victories may have been sparse and transient, your defeats numerous and ruinous.

The Apostle Paul reminds us in *Romans 8:37-39, "Nay, in all these things we are more than conquerors through him that loved us. For I am persuaded, that neither death, nor life, nor angels, nor principalities, nor powers, nor things present, nor things to come, Nor height, nor depth, nor any other creature, shall be able to separate us from the love of God, which is in Christ Jesus our Lord."* Therefore, let us recall that defeat is not our destiny in Christ, but victory, a victory which is our birthright as children of God.

In conclusion, the true Christian life is a journey fraught with challenges, but it's a journey under the banner of a victorious Captain. As believers, we are assured of victory, not because of our prowess, but due to His love for us. Even when we face defeat, our faith is not futile, for the victory that we yearn for is not of the world but is found in the life hidden with Christ in God. When we fully embrace this truth, our defeats will be transformed into triumphs, and we will find the rest and peace that our souls long for in Christ.

A Journey Beyond Doctrinal Understanding

As a child of God, I often find myself reflecting upon my life's journey, recognizing that I have not lived as profoundly as one would expect from a believer. I've found my existence teetering on a precipice where there's a sharp divide between possessing a clear understanding of doctrinal truth and earnestly pursuing its power and life.

Yes, I have rejoiced in the knowledge of the sacred teachings, the scriptures, as they unravel truth after truth. Yet often I've been left yearning for a living realization of these truths, a conscious sensation within my soul. It's as if I've been tapping the surface of a great lake, but never plunged into its depths.

Christ, my Savior, my Master, is constantly in my thoughts, my conversations, my service. Still, His divine presence as my very life, an eternal fixture within me, a perpetual revelation of His grace, remains elusive.

Indeed, I have found the divine in Jesus, strived to serve Him, and committed myself to propelling His kingdom forward. I've devoted countless hours to studying the Holy Scriptures, unearthing gems of precious truth, which I've then sought to embody faithfully. However, even amidst this profound knowledge and active service for the Lord, I find my soul clandestinely yearning for nourishment, echoing a repeated plea for the promised bread and water of life.

"The LORD is my shepherd; I shall not want. He maketh me to lie down in green pastures: he leadeth me beside the still waters. He restoreth my soul..." (Psalm 23:1-3, KJV). Yet in the very core of my being, I sense a disconnect between my experience and the true, Scriptural experience.

The words of an ancient writer haunt me, suggesting that my faith is but a shadow compared to the luminous reality lived and possessed by early Christians. With each passing day and year, my early visions of spiritual triumph seem to fade, growing dimmer. I find myself succumbing to the belief that my faith journey can be nothing more than a life of alternating failure and victory. One moment I'm sinning, the next repenting, only to fall once again into the same cycle.

But surely, this cannot be the entire picture.

"Being then made free from sin, ye became the servants

of righteousness" (Romans 6:18, KJV). Is it plausible that our Lord Jesus, who sacrificed His precious life to liberate us from the oppressive chains of sin, intended for us only a partial deliverance? Was it His plan to leave us staggering under the weight of perpetual defeat and discouragement?

In conclusion, the yearning for a deeper connection with Christ, the thirst for divine sustenance, is indeed a call to examine our spiritual journey. It beckons us to rise above mere doctrinal understanding and strive for a living, breathing faith. Let us remember, *"Jesus said unto them, I am the bread of life: he that cometh to me shall never hunger; and he that believeth on me shall never thirst" (John 6:35, KJV).* This promise encourages us to seek and know Jesus as our very life, our eternal soul's companion, and the continual revelation of divine beauty in our lives.

Unveiling God's Absolute Salvation

Have you ever pondered, "Could the Lord worry that His unending victory might somehow dishonor Him or bring shame to His holy name?" When the sacred proclamations regarding His advent and His mission were made, did they only signify the experiences we have encountered so far? Did each promise carry a hidden clause, limiting its complete fulfillment?

For instance, when He spoke of "delivering us out of the hands of our enemies," did He only mean a select few of our foes? Did "enabling us always to triumph" indicate only occasional victories, or did being "more than conquerors through Him that loves us" imply constant defeat and failure? Absolutely not! A resounding no echoed a thousand times! God is fully capable of saving to the utmost, and it's His intention to do so.

As the Scripture in *Hebrews 7:25 KJV* reads, *"Wherefore he is able also to save them to the uttermost that come unto God by him, seeing he ever liveth to make intercession for them."* This promise, fortified by His oath, states, *"That we should be saved from our enemies, and from the hand of all that hate us;" (Luke 1:71 KJV).* It's no small task, but our Deliverer is fully capable.

He descended to demolish the devil's works, and would we dare to consider for a moment that He lacks the ability or the will to realize His purposes? At the outset, firmly establish this belief: the Lord has the power to fully save you here and now, in this life, from the authority and dominion of sin, and to entirely deliver you from the clutches of your adversaries.

If doubts persist, I urge you to scour your Bible, assembling every announcement or assertion regarding the purpose and aim of His crucifixion. You'll be astonished to discover their magnitude. Unfailingly, His mission is said to be to deliver us from our sins, our bondage, and our impurity. Not once is there a suggestion that this deliverance should be anything less than the comprehensive one, we sometimes settle for within the Church.

Let's turn to a few Biblical passages on this topic. The angel of the Lord appeared to Joseph in a dream and announced the forthcoming birth of the Savior, stating in *Matthew 1:21 KJV, "And she shall bring forth a son, and thou shalt call his name Jesus: for he shall save his people from their sins."*

Later, upon the birth of his son, Zacharias, filled with the Holy Spirit and prophesying, declared that God had visited His people to fulfill the promise and the oath He had made to them. This promise, as recorded in *Luke 1:74-75 KJV*, was, *"That he would grant unto us, that we being delivered out of the hand of our enemies might serve him without fear, In holiness and righteousness before him, all the days of our life."*

In conclusion, we are invited to embrace the limitless scope of God's promise for our deliverance and salvation. His promise is not partial, not limited. It is total and absolute. Let's not limit the infinite capability of our Savior, for He is willing and able to save us fully and to deliver us completely from our adversaries. God's promise of deliverance is unbroken and enduring - it signifies the absolute salvation He offers us.

"Sanctification: The Divine Purpose of Salvation"

Paul in the revered courtyard of the temple, found himself, akin to Peter, standing before a throng of curious Jews. As if channeling his words, I declared, *"Unto you first, God, having raised up His Son Jesus, sent Him to bless you, in turning away every one of you from his iniquities" (Acts 3:26, KJV).* The purpose of Christ's coming, his love, was not merely for redemption but also transformation.

When Paul, the tireless advocate for Christ, unraveled the truth to the Ephesian church, he stated a profound purpose: *"That He might sanctify and cleanse it with the washing of water by the word, that He might present it to Himself a glorious church, not having spot or wrinkle, or any such thing; but that it should be holy and without blemish" (Ephesians 5:26-27, KJV)*. Paul emphasized that Christ's sacrifice was for our purification, to form us into His holy and unblemished church.

Just as Paul explained the grace of God to his spiritual son, Titus, I share that same grace with you today. He taught that this grace urges us to deny *"ungodliness and worldly lusts" and live "soberly, righteously, and godly in this present world" (Titus 2:12, KJV).* He further expressed the reason for this: Christ *"gave Himself for us that He might redeem us from all iniquity, and purify unto Himself a peculiar people, zealous of good works" (Titus 2:14, KJV).* The beauty of Christ's sacrifice is that it not only redeems us but also purifies and empowers us to engage in good works.

In the same vein as Peter, Paul implore every Christian to aspire to a life that is holy and mirrors Christ. Peter reminded us that Christ *"did no sin, neither was guile found in His mouth" (1 Peter 2:22, KJV).* He stressed, *"who His own self bare our sins in His own body on the tree, that we, being dead to sins, should live unto righteousness; by whose stripes ye were healed" (1 Peter 2:24, KJV).* Christ's exemplary life and sacrifice were meant to inspire us to live righteously.

When Paul contrasted the life of a Christian with the life of an unbeliever in his letter to the Ephesians, he encouraged them to *"put off concerning the former conversation the old man, which is corrupt according to the deceitful lusts; and be renewed in the spirit of your mind; and that ye put on the new man, which after God is created in righteousness and true holiness" (Ephesians 4:22-24, KJV).* This transformation, from the old man to the new, is the crux of our Christian walk.

And in Romans, Paul declared, answering once and for all the question about continuing in sin, *"God forbid" (Romans 6:2, KJV).* The idea of persisting in sin is entirely at odds with the spirit and aim of Jesus's salvation. His sacrifice has facilitated not only our redemption but also our transformation and sanctification.

In conclusion, we understand that the divine purpose of Christ's sacrifice extends beyond redemption. It is meant for our sanctification, transforming us into His image. As Christians, we are called to not only receive the grace of God but also live a life marked by righteousness and holiness. We must cast off the old man and put on the new, radiating the righteousness and true holiness of our new creation in Christ. The act of salvation isn't merely a ticket to heaven, but a call to an entirely new way of life. It requires our participation, our willingness to be changed, and our resolve to strive for holiness.

Like the Ephesians, we should take heed of Paul's advice and be constantly *"renewed in the spirit of our mind" (Ephesians 4:23, KJV),* so that we might fully embrace this new life. His words echo with as much relevance today as they did in the early church. The transformation we seek is not a superficial one, but a deep, inward change that begins in our hearts and minds, and permeates our entire being.

Moreover, the lessons of Peter and Paul speak volumes about the life we are called to live. Peter's teachings remind us that we were chosen because Christ suffered for us, leaving an example for us to follow. Paul further illuminates this by reminding us of our obligation to reject sin in its entirety, to live a life that is befitting of our salvation.

And so, it becomes evident that the path of sanctification is one of conscious denial of ungodliness and worldly lusts. It's about willingly picking up our cross daily, dying to self, and following Jesus. It's about being zealous for good works, not out of a sense of duty or obligation, but out of a transformed heart that mirrors the heart of Christ.

Christ's sacrifice not only saved us from sin, but it also paved the way for us to be sanctified and purified. His stripes healed us, and His love transformed us. The salvation of Jesus is not an invitation to continue in sin, but a powerful call to live unto righteousness. This understanding should be the driving force behind our journey as Christians. We are redeemed, yes, but we are also transformed and sanctified, molded into His likeness, and set apart for His **Glory**.

In the grand tapestry of our faith, the thread of sanctification is interwoven from beginning to end. From Peter's preaching in the porch of the Temple, through Paul's teachings to the churches and to Titus, the message remains consistent and clear. Christ's sacrifice was not just about redemption. It was, and still is, about transformation and sanctification, about making us a people peculiarly His own, passionate for good works, and holy without blemish.

May we continue to walk in the light of this truth, knowing that the divine purpose of our salvation is not merely redemption, but also sanctification. To be like Christ, to mirror His righteousness and holiness, is our ultimate goal. This, indeed, is the divine purpose of our salvation. It is an unending journey, a continuous process of being transformed into His image, from **Glory** to **Glory**, by the power of His Spirit within us.

A Journey from Sin to Salvation

How can we, who have renounced sin, continue living in its shadow? Do we not know that when we were baptized into Jesus Christ, we were immersed into His death? Thus, we are interred with Him through baptism into death, that just as Christ was resurrected from the dead by the Father's **Glory**, we too should embrace a life reborn.

This comes directly from the Holy Scripture, *Romans 6:2-4*, (KJV), which states, *"God forbid. How shall we, that are dead to sin, live any longer therein? Know ye not, that so many of us as were baptized into Jesus Christ were baptized into his death? Therefore we are buried with him by baptism into death: that like as Christ was raised up from the dead by the Glory of the Father, even so we also should walk in newness of life."*

Fellow Christians, can you accept the Bible's guidance on this matter? The same inquiries that rattled the Church in the Apostle Paul's time trouble us today.

Firstly, *"Shall we continue in sin so that grace may abound?"*

Secondly, *"Do we nullify the law through faith?"* Our responses should echo Paul's fervent declaration, *"God forbid"*; accompanied by his victorious proclamations that instead of nullifying it, *"we uphold the law";* and *"what the law couldn't do, being limited by human nature, God did. He sent His own Son in a body like the bodies we sinners have. And in that body, God declared an end to sin's control over us by giving his Son as a sacrifice for our sins"*.

Can we conceive for a moment that the holy God, who detests sin in the sinner, would tolerate it in the Christian? Do we dare think that His plan for salvation is designed in such a way as to absolve us from the guilt of sin without offering liberation from its grip? As the esteemed Dr. Chalmers accurately put it, "Sin is the scourge that must be eliminated from the divine household that God cherishes... It would indeed be an unusual scheme if sin, so hateful to God as to condemn all who committed it to death, is permitted to persist after being resurrected into life. Would it be possible that the unchangeable God has so abandoned His loathing for sin that humanity, devastated yet redeemed, can continue to indulge in what previously led to their downfall under the new covenant?"

In conclusion, living as Christians doesn't mean being saved only from the guilt of sin, but also experiencing deliverance from its grip. As we are reborn in Christ, we are called to leave our old selves behind, including the sins that once ensnared us. The power of Christ's sacrifice offers us freedom and a fresh start to live a new life aligned with God's righteous laws, walking not after the flesh, but in the Spirit.

Let us, therefore, earnestly strive to live lives that reflect this divine truth and freedom. Let our actions mirror our rebirth in Christ, as we continually seek to establish the law, casting off the shackles of sin, and walking in the light of the Spirit.

God's Unyielding Stand Against Sin

Doesn't the same God who cherished righteousness and detested sin six thousand years ago still feel the same today? His divine essence is unchanging, His attitude towards sin unwavering. I now breathe in the tender mercies emanating from Heaven and can walk with God in a state of peace and grace. But I ask myself, would I dare to reconcile the utterly incompatible notions of a God who approves and a sinner who persists? How could we, having been rescued from such an appalling disaster, continue in the behavior that originally plunged us into it?

The cross of Christ, with the same powerful and decisive blow that lifted the curse of sin from us, surely also sweeps away sin's power and allure over us. This is not only my sentiment but also a truth professed by many other devout individuals across generations, including our own. These men and women affirm that the redemption achieved for us by our Lord Jesus Christ on the cross at Calvary liberates us from both the power and guilt of sin. He is capable of saving to the utmost those who approach God through Him, as stated in *Hebrews 7:25 (KJV): "Wherefore he is able also to save them to the uttermost that come unto God by him, seeing he ever liveth to make intercession for them."*

An insightful seventeenth-century divine once stated, "There is nothing so contrary to God as sin, and God will not permit sin to eternally rule His masterpiece, man." When we contemplate the limitless power of God to obliterate that which opposes Him, who among us can believe that the devil must always stand victorious? It contradicts the essence of true faith for individuals to claim Christianity, yet also believe that Christ, the eternal Son of God to whom all power in heaven and earth has been given, according to *Matthew 28:18 (KJV): "And Jesus came and spake unto them, saying, All power is given unto me in heaven and in earth,"* would allow sin and the devil to dominate them.

Yet, the contention persists: no man, regardless of his might, can redeem himself. No man can exist devoid of sin. To this, I join you in affirming, "Amen." However, should anyone propose that even when God's power comes to our aid and seeks to rescue us from sin, that such deliverance cannot be accomplished, then this teaching we must reject, as I hope you also would.

Consider this: would it be acceptable if I suggested to you that God exercises His power to perform a certain act, but the devil obstructs Him? Surely not! For God is mightier than any opposition, His plan is unthwartable, His love for us unyielding. As expressed in *Isaiah 14:27 (KJV): "For the LORD of hosts hath purposed, and who shall disannul it? and his hand is stretched out, and who shall turn it back?"* Thus, we must stand steadfast in our faith, believing in God's unchanging love for righteousness and His fierce opposition against sin.

In conclusion, let us hold firmly to the truth of God's eternal power and commitment to righteousness. Let's affirm His hatred for sin, His willingness to redeem us, and His power to transform us. It's in His unwavering stance against sin that we find our redemption, our transformation, and ultimately our victory over sin and the devil. As followers of Christ, we must resist the notion that sin or the devil can have dominion over us. Instead, let's step forward in faith, fully assured of the redeeming power of Christ's cross and God's eternal love for righteousness.

God's Victory Over Sin

I've often heard a woeful assertion that's been echoed in the corners of our gatherings, whispered amidst the body of believers. Can it be that God is unable to act because the enemy despises His actions? Is it truly conceivable that one cannot be free from sin because the adversary has gained such a stronghold that even God cannot eject him? This is a sorrowful claim, indeed. Has this not been the discourse presented? It overtly professes that even if God utilizes His supreme power, it remains futile, as sin has been ingrained deeply in the human nature by the devil.

However, let's remember, isn't man the creation of God Himself? Can He not remake him, dispelling sin from his being? While it's true that sin is entrenched within man, it's not so deep-seated that it eludes the reach of our Savior, Christ Jesus. His depth of reach into the root of human nature is so profound that He has been granted the authority to demolish the devil's deeds. He is capable of reclaiming and converting man back into a vessel of righteousness and purity.

Unless we dismiss the truth, that, as stated in *Hebrews 7:25, "Wherefore he is able also to save them to the uttermost that come unto God by him, seeing he ever liveth to make intercession for them."* If we assert that it's impossible for God to liberate man from sin, we may as well forsake the Bible.

Consider this: we know how it is when our friends are in bondage, whether in distant lands or otherwise. We are willing to spend our wealth to ensure their freedom. But would we still part with our coins if they were to remain in their shackles? Wouldn't one feel swindled if they paid a handsome sum for a friend's liberation, only to find that they are still enchained? And how long must they endure this? As long as life persists.

Yes, this example pertains to physical captivity. Yet now, I'm speaking of our souls. For me, and for all of us, Christ must embody redemption. He must rescue us from our spiritual imprisonment.

In conclusion, let us not be swayed by disheartening doctrines suggesting God's power is impotent against the enemy's hold. Instead, let us remember the Bible's teachings and trust in the almighty God, our redeemer. His love and power are limitless, capable of freeing us from sin's shackles, restoring us to a state of righteousness and purity. So let us rest in this comforting assurance: God's power is absolute, and in Him, we are indeed free.

The Exceeding Greatness of His Power

Are there chains that bind me? Absolutely, undoubtedly. As the words of Christ echo, *"Verily, verily, I say unto you, Whosoever committeth sin is the servant of sin" (John 8:34, KJV),* I find that when I sin, I am nothing more than a slave, a captive yearning for freedom from this imprisonment. But how can I be redeemed from this captivity? I find myself impoverished; devoid of resources, and incapable of buying my own freedom. Who will provide the needed ransom for me?

There is indeed One who has come forth, One who has paid a steep price for my freedom. Such a revelation brings a sigh of relief; I find in it good news that provides hope for my liberation from captivity. But who is this benevolent savior? Could it be that He is known as a Redeemer? If so, then surely I can anticipate the benefits of my redemption, even as I hope for liberation from my current state of servitude.

However, some would argue that you must dwell in sin as long as you live. But can this really be true? Must this twisted heart and perverse will of mine remain with me for all my days? Is it possible for me to be a believer, yet lack faith powerful enough to inspire sanctification and holy living? Will I never conquer, never achieve victory over sin? Will it maintain its dominion over me for the entirety of my life? If this were true, then what manner of Redeemer would this make Him? And what benefit could I possibly glean from my redemption in this life?

The sentiments expressed above echo those found in the writings of Marshall, Romaine, and others, demonstrating that this doctrine is not a recent construct within the Church. Rather, it is a timeless truth that has sustained many of God's saints throughout the ages, filling their daily lives with songs of triumph. Today, it is resounding anew, bringing untold joy to those wearied and burdened souls among us. So, dear reader, I implore you not to disregard this truth until you have earnestly examined the

Scriptures to determine its veracity.

Appeal to God in prayer, asking Him to enlighten your understanding through His Spirit, so that you may grasp *"what is the exceeding greatness of His power to usward who believe, according to the working of His mighty power, Which he wrought in Christ, when he raised him from the dead, and set him at his own right hand in the heavenly places" (Ephesians 1:19-20, KJV).* When you begin to perceive the faintest hints of this formidable power, I urge you to entirely shift your focus from your personal frailties. Place your situation in His capable hands, trusting in Him to deliver you.

In conclusion, remember that the struggle against sin is not fought in our own strength, but in the redeeming power of Christ, our Redeemer. His sacrifice has paid our ransom, giving us hope for victory over sin and the promise of sanctification. Let us hold fast to this truth, for in it, we find our freedom from captivity.

The Divine Harmony of Creation and Fulfillment

When I think about the words of Psalms 8:6, they penetrate my heart deeply, echoing God's intent for mankind. As per the Bible, it states, *"Thou madest him to have dominion over the works of thy hands; thou hast put all things under his feet."* In this divine plan, our Creator has crafted us with a specific intention in mind, that is, to rule over all the works He has created.

The accomplishment of this divine purpose echoes powerfully in the Apostle Paul's triumphant proclamation in *2 Corinthians 2:14: "Now thanks be unto God, which always causeth us to triumph in Christ, and maketh manifest the savour of his knowledge by us in every place."* We must take heart and consider this: if a human craftsman built a machine intended for a specific task, and then it failed to meet that purpose, we'd label the craftsman as deceitful. Certainly then, we can't venture to believe it's impossible for God's created beings to fulfill their stated purpose, especially when the Scriptures offer such resounding affirmations that Christ has made it possible.

The only roadblock, it seems, is if the created being fails to operate in harmony with the Creator's plans. If this discordance can be removed, then God can work His divine will. Our Savior, Christ, was sent to bring about a reconciliation between God and humanity. This atonement makes it possible for God to work within us, enabling us to desire and carry out His good pleasure. Therefore, we can carry courage in our hearts; for the work Christ has undertaken, He is surely capable and willing to carry out to completion.

Let us then take our steps emboldened by the faith of our spiritual forefather, Abraham. Reflect on the words from *Romans 4:20-21, "He staggered not at the promise of God through unbelief; but was strong in faith, giving Glory to God; And being fully persuaded that, what he had promised, he was able also to perform."*

In conclusion, I invite you to embrace this harmonious

dance between creation and fulfillment, echoing through the centuries from our spiritual ancestors to the present day. Understand that our ultimate purpose is to rule over God's creation, made possible by the work of Christ, who restores our relationship with the Creator. With this realization, may we strive to align our wills with His divine plans, honoring our Creator's purpose and holding firm to the faith of our father Abraham, who believed unswervingly in God's promises and power.

CHAPTER THREE

THE LIFE DEFINED

A Journey into Abiding Rest and Victory

In the preceding chapter, I endeavored to elucidate the reality of what many term as the **"Higher Christian Life"**. But I am of the opinion that a more fitting description would be **"the life hid with Christ in God"**. Henceforth, I will operate under the assumption that the Scriptures do indeed present us, believers in our Lord Jesus Christ, with a vision of a life steeped in unceasing tranquility and triumph. A life which far surpasses the conventional realm of Christian experience. A life where the Bible introduces us to a Savior who rescues us from the tyrannical clutches of our sins, just as He does from their associated guilt.

The subsequent discourse seeks to understand the essence of this hidden life, and how it sets itself apart from every other Christian experience. To put it simply, it is about surrendering our worries and concerns to the Lord, instead of trying to address them ourselves.

Consider the ordinary Christian experience akin to a man who trudges along the road, weighed down by a hefty load. A benevolent wagon driver offers him a ride, which he gladly accepts. Yet, even while seated, he continues to groan under the weight of his load which he insists on carrying himself.

Perplexed, the kind driver asks, "Why do you not lay down your burden?" The man replies, "Oh! I believe it is almost too much to ask you to bear me, and I could not dream of burdening you with my load as well."

Similarly, many Christians who have entrusted their lives to the care and guidance of Jesus, still find themselves burdened. They traverse their spiritual journey carrying their heavy burdens, often weary and heavy-laden.

When I speak of burdens, I mean everything that disturbs us, whether spiritual or temporal. The most pressing of these burdens is, undoubtedly, ourselves. Our self is the most cumbersome burden we bear in life, and the most challenging to handle. Our daily existence, our emotional states, our personal weaknesses and temptations, our unique temperaments, and our internal matters of all kinds. These are the elements that confound and vex us more than any other external concerns, and these are the issues that often plunge us into bondage and darkness.

Yet, the Bible gives us a promise of freedom from these burdens in *Matthew 11:28-30 (KJV), "Come unto me, all ye that labour and are heavy laden, and I will give you rest. Take my yoke upon you, and learn of me; for I am meek and lowly in heart: and ye shall find rest unto your souls. For my yoke is easy, and my burden is light."*

The unveiled life, this journey into abiding rest and victory, is about laying down our burdens at the feet of our Savior, trusting in His care and guidance, and finding in Him the strength to overcome, to transform, and to rise above our own selves. This life may seem hidden, but it is open to all who choose to seek, to surrender, and to trust. In this divine journey, we will find that victory and rest are not merely elusive ideals, but tangible realities to be lived and experienced in our daily walk with Christ.

A Journey of Divine Burdens

In the quest of shedding burdens, the first and foremost one you must be willing to relinquish is your own self. It's crucial to surrender your inner experiences, your temptations, your temperaments, your states of mind, and your feelings, all into the capable hands of your God. Trust in the fact that He who created you, understands you, and is proficient in guiding you. Have faith in Him to do so.

As stated in *Proverbs 3:5-6 (KJV), "Trust in the LORD with all thine heart; and lean not unto thine own understanding. In all thy ways acknowledge him, and he shall direct thy paths."* Confide in Him by saying, "Here, Lord, I surrender myself to you. I have made countless attempts to shape myself into what I believe I should be, but each time, I have met with failure. Now, I entrust you with my transformation. Take absolute possession of me. Fulfill in me the good pleasure of your will. Mold and fashion me into a vessel as you deem fit. I place myself in your hands, believing that you will, in accordance with your promise, transform me into a vessel fit for your **Glory**, 'sanctified, and meet for the Master's use, and prepared unto every good work.'"

This is where you must remain, continually and unconditionally entrusting yourself to Him.

Subsequently, you must relinquish every other burden -- your health, your reputation, your spiritual duties, your homes, your children, your business, your dependents; in essence, everything that concerns you, whether internal or external.

Most Christians are quick to entrust the safekeeping of their eternal souls to the Lord, as they understand without a hint of doubt that they're incapable of safeguarding them independently. However, when it comes to their earthly life, they prefer to shoulder the responsibilities themselves, perhaps hesitating to burden the Lord with their worldly concerns.

A case in point is a Christian woman I knew, weighed down by an enormous temporal burden. This burden robbed her of sleep and appetite, threatening her health. One day, amidst her heavy struggles, she found a little tract titled "Hannah's Faith." Intrigued by the title, she began reading it, little knowing it would revolutionize her entire spiritual journey. The tract narrated the story of a woman named Hannah, who, despite a life marked by unusual sorrow, had navigated through it triumphantly.

A visitor, moved by Hannah's tale, remarked, "O Hannah,

I do not see how you could bear so much sorrow!" To which Hannah promptly replied, "I did not bear it. The Lord bore it for me." The visitor agreed, saying that Hannah ought to bring her troubles to the Lord. "Yes," agreed Hannah, "but we must do more than that; we must leave them there. Most people take their burdens to Him but they bring them away with them again, and are just as worried and unhappy as ever."

In conclusion, it's essential to not only lay our burdens at the feet of the Lord but also to leave them there, trusting fully in His divine guidance and care. By surrendering ourselves and our burdens entirely, we allow the Creator to shape us into vessels of honor, sanctified and equipped for His use. Our faith in Him ought to extend to every facet of our lives, entrusting Him with our earthly concerns just as readily as we entrust our eternal souls. For it is in surrendering and trusting that we find rest in Him, as stated in *Matthew 11:28 (KJV), "Come unto me, all ye that labour and are heavy laden………*

An Enduring Lesson on the Higher Christian Life

There are times when I pick up my troubles and worries, lay them before Him, and then walk away, allowing myself to forget them. If these concerns attempt to creep back into my consciousness, I return them to Him once again. This becomes a repeated act, until eventually, I lose sight of my worries, achieving a state of perfect tranquility. A dear friend of mine was deeply inspired by this approach and decided to implement it in her own life. While she couldn't change her life circumstances, she entrusted them to the Lord, giving Him the reins to steer her life. Whenever anxieties attempted to claw their way back, she would turn them over to Him once more. The result was profound; despite the constancy of her circumstances, her soul was preserved in perfect peace amidst the chaos. She felt as though she had discovered a sacred secret, and from then on, she vowed never to carry her burdens alone, nor to steer her life independently.

This sacred secret that she applied so efficiently to her outward affairs proved even more effective in addressing her inner struggles, which were admittedly far more complex and challenging to control. She surrendered herself completely to the Lord, handing over all that she was and possessed. Believing that He accepted what she offered, she put an end to her fretful worrying, and her life became filled with sunshine, fueled by the joy of belonging to Him. This, she realized, was the essence of the Higher Christian Life!

It was a simple secret that she discovered. It was merely the realization that it was possible to follow God's commandment as stated in *Philippians 4:6-7: "Be careful for nothing; but in every thing by prayer and supplication with thanksgiving let your requests be made known unto God. And the peace of God, which passeth all understanding, shall keep your hearts and minds through Christ Jesus."* Obeying this commandment would inevitably result in experiencing the peace of God that transcends all understanding.

While there are many other aspects to discuss about this life hidden with Christ in God, the essence of it all is captured here. The soul that comprehends this secret has obtained the key that opens the vast treasure-house of God. It is my sincerest hope that these words have kindled a desire in you for this blessed life. Don't you yearn to cast off your burdens? Aren't you longing to entrust your uncontrollable self into the hands of the One who is fully capable of guiding you? Are you not tired and weary? Doesn't this peace I speak of seem incredibly inviting to you?

Have you ever experienced the blissful feeling of relaxation that washes over you after an intense day, when you finally collapse into bed? The exquisite feeling of letting go of all tension, surrendering your body to the comfort of the bed in a moment of pure relaxation. The worries and labor of the day are shed away, and you no longer have to bear the weight of a throbbing head or aching back. You entrust yourself to the bed with absolute confidence, and it supports you effortlessly, without strain or conscious thought on your part.

find rest. But imagine if you doubted the strength or stability of your bed, and feared it collapsing beneath you at any moment. Could you have found rest then? Would you not have tensed every muscle in a futile effort to support yourself, thereby increasing your exhaustion? Wouldn't it have been more exhausting than not going to bed at all? Let this analogy illustrate what it means to rest in the Lord. Allow your souls to lie down upon His gracious will, as your bodies lie down on your beds each night.

In conclusion, let us take a step towards embracing this divine tranquility, the Higher Christian Life. It is a simple secret, yet profoundly transformative - the act of surrendering our burdens, worries, and the management of our lives to the Lord. It is an act of trust, a commitment to a life of obedience as we follow His commandment, allowing the peace of God, which surpasses all human understanding, to keep our hearts and minds through Christ Jesus.

Reflect on the feeling of resting completely, of fully letting go, just as you do when your body sinks into a comfortable bed after a long day. This rest, this divine tranquility, is what we can experience when we choose to rest in the Lord, to surrender ourselves fully and trust in His strength and stability. As we do so, we can cast off the futile strain of trying to support ourselves and let the Lord carry our burdens.

As we journey further on this path of the Higher Christian Life, we unlock the vast treasure-house of God. We begin to live a life of not just survival, but abundance; a life not marked by constant struggle and strain, but by peace and joy, a life of not managing, but of being divinely managed.

Therefore, let us embrace the simple yet profound secret of the Higher Christian Life. Let us hand over our troubles to Him, trust in His divine management, and rest in the tranquility that comes from a life lived in His will. In doing so, we allow the peace of God, which surpasses all understanding, to permeate our hearts and minds. Thus, our lives become all sunshine in the gladness of belonging to Him, and we truly experience the blessed rest of the Higher Christian Life.

So I ask you again, aren't you tired and weary? Don't you yearn to cast off your burdens? Are you ready to find rest in Him? If you are, then step forward and embrace the Higher Christian Life. For in this surrender, you will find the peace and tranquility that your soul truly longs for. Embrace the divine tranquility. Experience the Higher Christian Life.

The Child-Like Faith: An Echo of Divine Trust

I urge you to let go of your burdens and tensions, to surrender yourself wholly in the comfort of perfect peace, knowing with certainty that when He holds you, your safety is unquestionable. Your role is simply to rest, to be held; His role is to uphold you, and He is incapable of failing in this task. For a better understanding, consider an analogy Jesus Himself has extensively endorsed—the analogy of a child's life. In the book of *Matthew 18:2-3 (KJV),* we read, *"And Jesus called a little child unto him, and set him in the midst of them, and said, Verily I say unto you, Except ye be converted, and become as little children, ye shall not enter into the kingdom of heaven."*

So, what are the primary characteristics of a little child, and how does this child live? This child lives through faith, with their most distinguishing trait being a carefree spirit. Their existence is a continuous journey of trust, from the start of the year to its end. The child trusts their parents, their caretakers, and their teachers. They often trust those unworthy of trust, purely due to their innocent and trusting nature. In return, this trust is richly rewarded. The child does not provide anything for themselves, yet everything is supplied. They give no thought to the future, and make no plans, yet every step of their life is mapped out.

The child finds their way made ready for them, unfolding day by day, hour by hour. They move freely about their father's house, relishing all the good things it offers, without having spent a penny to earn them. Even when dangers like disease, famine, fire, or war threaten their city, the child remains unaffected under their father's tender care. They live in the moment, accepting their life without question as it is handed to them each day from their father's hands.

One time, I visited a grand house where a single adopted child lived. This child received all the love, tenderness, and care human hearts could offer and human means could provide. The child accepted their extraordinary life with unbounded joy, living each day with the absolute trust that their needs would be met, and that they would be loved and cared for, no matter what.

So, I encourage you to live like this child, in unadulterated faith and trust. Rest assured that you are in His hand, and He is unflinching in His mission to sustain you. Our Heavenly Father is more reliable and loving than any earthly parent. As we learn *in Matthew 7:11 (KJV), "If ye then, being evil, know how to give good gifts unto your children, how much more shall your Father which is in heaven give good things to them that ask him?"*

To conclude, life under the Father's tender care is marked by the child-like trust that releases all worries and burdens. This trusting, child-like faith enables us to live in the present, knowing that we are held safely in the hands of our Heavenly Father. Our role is to simply rest in His love; His role is to hold us securely. He never fails in this role. The life of faith, then, is a life of trust—a divine echo of a child's faith in their father's love.

"Childlike Faith: The Freedom of Divine Trust"

As I found myself caught in the idyllic scene of a child dashing about joyously, her spirit light and unfettered, it struck me as the perfect portrayal of our privileged status as children in the divine house of our Heavenly Father. In this spectacle of pure innocence, I perceived an echo, "If seeing this little one overwhelmed with worries about her needs - her nourishment, clothing, education, or future sustenance - would deeply sadden and distress the loving hearts surrounding her, how much more would our compassionate God and Father suffer to see His children burdened with such worry!"

This revelation enlightened me to the wisdom underlying our Lord's directive, so potent and clear: *"Take therefore no thought for the morrow: for the morrow shall take thought for the things of itself. Sufficient unto the day is the evil thereof" (Matthew 6:34, KJV).*

Who receives the most tender care in every household?

Isn't it the young ones, especially the most helpless - the baby? As one wise author observed, the baby "works not, neither does he spin; yet he is nurtured, clothed, cherished, and celebrated," no one is more so than he. Hence, the life of faith that I am exploring is tantamount to living as a child in our Father's house.

And with this revelation, every life weighed down by toil and care can be transformed into a blessed state of tranquility. Allow the guileless trust and absence of worry that you admire in your own children to guide you towards a similar relationship with God. Abandon yourselves to His providence and discover the true meaning of being **"careful for nothing."** As it is written, *"And the peace of God, which passeth all understanding, shall keep your hearts and minds through Christ Jesus" (Philippians 4:7, KJV).* Pay heed to the word "nothing" in this Scripture; it encompasses all potential sources of anxiety, both internal and external.

In the whirlpool of life, we often convince ourselves that worrying over certain things is our responsibility. Yet, in our quest to become true children of God, we must strive to embody the innocence and unquestioning faith of the child I observed. For in abandoning our needless worries and entrusting our lives to His care, we are granted a peace that surpasses all understanding, secured and fortified through our faith in Christ Jesus.

In the embrace of God's grace, like children, we must shed the weight of our worries, surrendering them to our Heavenly Father's loving care. In doing so, we grant ourselves the gift of liberation, relinquishing the burden of tomorrow's uncertainties. As Christ implored us, *"Which of you by taking thought can add one cubit unto his stature?" (Matthew 6:27, KJV).* Our worries and anxieties yield no fruitful results; rather, they inhibit our ability to fully trust in God's divine plan.

Consider the beauty of nature that surrounds us, each creature and plant provided for by our Heavenly Father's generous hand. As Jesus reminded us, *"Consider the lilies of the field, how they grow; they toil not, neither do they spin: And yet I say unto you, That even Solomon in all his Glory was not arrayed like one of these" (Matthew 6:28-29, KJV).* If God so meticulously takes care of the smallest flower, will He not much more care for us, His own children?

When we acknowledge the depth of God's love for us, recognizing His ever-present hand in our lives, we can abandon our habitual anxieties. As children of the Most High, our care is assured. God's provision is a promise, as is His love. This realization provides a transformative peace that transcends the bounds of human understanding, encasing our hearts and minds within a fortress of serenity.

Reflect upon the artless faith and worry-free existence of your own children, allow their demeanor to be a divine lesson. In surrendering yourself to His divine providence, you truly become a child of God, exemplifying the essence of faith. In doing so, we manifest the truth of the scripture: *"And we know that all things work together for good to them that love God, to them who are the called according to his purpose" (Romans 8:28, KJV).*

In conclusion, let us strive to adopt the childlike faith our Lord so esteems. Let us cast off the shackles of anxiety, embracing the freedom granted by complete trust in our Heavenly Father. After all, we are His children, loved, provided for, and cherished. In this realization, we find ourselves enveloped in a peace that exceeds all comprehension, a peace that acts as a bulwark protecting our hearts and minds, anchored in our unwavering faith in Christ Jesus. In this childlike trust, we truly embody the essence of faith and secure a life of blessedness and rest.

Lessons from Sparrows and Lilies

In moments of quiet reflection, a notion might cross my mind, affirming, "Indeed, it's noble to abandon all worry in broad strokes, and, without a doubt, anxiety is ill-suited in matters of spirituality. But aren't there certain affairs about which it would be sinful not to harbor anxiety? Surely, concerns for our children, our loved ones, our church activities, the cause of truth, or even our business affairs. To be without worry for these matters would reflect a distressing lack of proper sentiment."

In another thought, I might tell myself, "Yes, it's fitting to entrust our dear ones and all outward affairs to the Lord, but when it comes to our internal lives, our spiritual experiences, our temptations, our recurring sins, our spiritual growth, and such matters, oughtn't we to be anxious? For if we don't worry, won't these areas surely be overlooked?"

To these inclinations, and all akin to them, the answer lies in our key scripture - *"Be anxious for nothing"* *(Philippians 4:6, KJV).* The Gospel of *Matthew 6:25-34* provides a vivid illustration of this divine guidance. Our Lord guides us to observe the birds in the sky and the lilies in the field as emblems of the kind of existence He wishes us to experience. Just as the birds rejoice in their Creator's care, fed without worry, and as the lilies flourish under His warming light, we too must exist, free from anxiety and fear. Let the sparrows impart wisdom:

I am but a simple sparrow,
A bird of humble station,
My life might seem of little consequence,
Yet the dear Lord showers His compassion.
I possess no granary nor storehouse,
Neither do I sow nor reap;
God grants me a sparrow's portion,
But never a seed to keep.

Writing in the vein of Jesus, let's acknowledge the simplicity and depth of these lines. They inspire us to live a life of profound trust, surrendering our cares and anxieties to our Heavenly Father. Every worry about our children, our loved ones, the cause of truth, our business affairs, and our spiritual growth must be given over to the Lord. For just as He tends to the sparrows and adorns the lilies, He shall provide for us. Our duty, then, is to live in simple trust, free from anxiety, secure in His providence.

In conclusion, we must strive to embody the simplicity

of sparrows and the beauty of lilies. Just as they exist untroubled, basking in the Lord's providence, we too must adopt an attitude of divine trust, relinquishing all our anxieties unto Him. When we do this, we'll find that our lives, like the sparrows and lilies, will flourish under His tender care, and we'll sing a new song: *"In nothing be anxious."* Indeed, this is the profound simplicity of divine trust.

A Lesson in Divine Guidance and Trust

In my daily flight, I keenly observe that sparrows are plentiful. Their presence graces every corner of this vast globe. Yet, even in their multitude, our Heavenly Father is acutely aware of them. His attention is so meticulous, He knows the very moment one of them falls from the sky. As it is written in *Matthew 10:29 (KJV), "Are not two sparrows sold for a farthing? And one of them shall not fall on the ground without your Father."*

Despite their diminutive size, we are never left out of God's sight; we are never forsaken. Even though we may seem feeble to many, fear doesn't grip our hearts. For we trust in the unwavering promise of our Creator, the one who nurtures and cherishes every life He forms.

"If they fly through the thickest forest, and alight upon many a branch. Though they lack a map or compass, they never lose their way.*" Much like the psalmist declares in Psalm 119:105 (KJV), "Thy word is a lamp unto my feet, and a light unto my path."* Their confidence in navigation comes not from worldly tools, but from an innate trust in their Creator's guiding hand.

Sparrow: As twilight descends, I calmly tuck my wings, settling to rest wherever I find myself. In the tranquil certainty of the Father's ever-watchful eyes, I find my refuge. I understand no harm will befall me under His vigilant watch, as He promises in *Psalm 121:7-8 (KJV)*, *"The LORD shall preserve thee from all evil: he shall preserve thy soul. The LORD shall preserve thy going out and thy coming in from this time forth, and even for evermore."*

I am but a humble sparrow, an avian of modest stature. Nevertheless, I'm firm in the knowledge of my Father's love for me. Does this surprise you, that I, a mere bird, hold such faith? Do you, a child made in the Creator's image, carry a faith lesser than mine?

In conclusion, let the unwavering trust of the sparrow serve as a reminder of our Heavenly Father's relentless love and care. Let it be a call to each of us to trust in Him unreservedly, just as the sparrow does. Let the words of Matthew 6:26 (KJV) echo in our hearts, *"Behold the fowls of the air: for they sow not, neither do they reap, nor gather into barns; yet your heavenly Father feedeth them. Are ye not much better than they?"* Just as He cares for every sparrow, so too will He care for each of us. Remember, faith as tiny as ours, when placed in the Almighty, can move mountains.

Chapter FOUR
HOW TO ENTER IN

Embracing God's Gift by Consecration and Trust

I strove to decipher the essence of living a life of unwavering trust in God, guided by His holy scripture. I attempted to shed light on the nature of such a life. Now, it is crucial to explore how this life can be achieved and truly experienced. Before delving into the particulars, I must clarify that this blessed life should not be perceived as an achievement, but rather as a divine grant. It is not within our means to earn it, reach it by climbing, or gain it by conquest. Our role lies solely in asking for it and accepting it with gratitude. It is, indeed, the gift of God in Christ Jesus.

Reflect upon a gift, dear friends. Do we not merely accept it with gratitude, praising the generosity of the giver, rather than boast about our skill or wisdom in attaining it? For truly I say unto you, our salvation too, from its inception to its culmination, is such a gift. As it is written in *Romans 6:23 (KJV), "For the wages of sin is death; but the gift of God is eternal life through Jesus Christ our Lord."*

As receivers of God's love, we must be in an open and receptive state, completely understanding that this internal life of trust is a divine gift, beyond our efforts or deeds. This understanding simplifies our quest remarkably. The remaining question, then, is to whom does God present this gift, and how is it to be received?

In response, I say that He grants this blessing solely to those souls that are wholly consecrated to Him, and that it is received through faith. Consecration is the starting point. Not in any legalistic way, nor to earn or deserve the blessing, but to remove hindrances, making it possible for God to bestow it upon us.

Consider a lump of clay, dear friends. For it to be molded into a beautiful vessel, it must be entirely surrendered to the potter, and must remain passive in his hands. Similarly, for a soul to be molded into a vessel for God's **Glory**, *"sanctified, and meet for the master's use, and prepared unto every good work," as written in 2 Timothy 2:21 (KJV),* it must be wholly surrendered to Him, and remain passive in His hands.

In conclusion, the path to a life of unfettered faith is not an achievement but an acceptance of a divine gift. It requires complete consecration and faith in God's benevolence. Like clay in the potter's hands, we must surrender ourselves entirely to God, ready to be shaped according to His divine plan. It is through such surrender and trust that we realize the full depth of our interior life, experiencing God's love and grace in abundance. Let us, then, welcome His gift with open hearts, bask in His love, and live a life of unwavering trust in His divine purpose.

"Total Surrender: Requirement for Divine Healing"

A personal experience once drove home a profound truth for me, a truth that seemed so simple yet astonishingly deep. I found myself in a conversation with a doctor, a man responsible for the well-being of countless patients in a vast hospital. He found it challenging to grasp the concept of consecration and its importance.

In an attempt to illustrate the point, I proposed a scenario to him, "Imagine," I began, "that as you perform your rounds, tending to the myriad of patients in your care, you encounter one who pleads with you to take his condition under your personal attention. However, this same man withholds some of his symptoms, and further declines to adhere to all the treatments you recommend. He insists on picking and choosing which directions to follow, and in other matters, he prefers to rely on his own judgement. In such a situation, what would you do?" I queried.

"Do?" he responded, aghast, "I would promptly leave such a man to his own devices! After all," he added, his tone seething with frustration, "it would be utterly impossible for me to help him unless he completely surrenders his condition to my expertise, with no reservations, and pledges to follow my directives without question."

"Is it then vital," I pushed on, "for a doctor to be unquestioningly obeyed if there's any hope of the patient's recovery?"

"Implicit obedience!" he declared emphatically. "That," I continued, "is the essence of consecration. God must have our entire lives entrusted to Him, without any reservations. His guidance must be dutifully and fully obeyed."

His face lit up with comprehension. "I see it!" he exclaimed. "From this moment forward, God shall have His way with me."

For some, the term 'abandonment' might aptly convey this notion. However, no matter the term we employ, the intent is to fully yield our entire existence - our spirit, soul, and body - to God's supreme authority. We offer ourselves for Him to guide and mold as He deems fit.

This principle is mirrored in the words of Jesus, as recorded in *Luke 9:23*, *"And he said to them all, If any man will come after me, let him deny himself, and take up his cross daily, and follow me."* Here, Christ invites us to let go of our self-driven ambitions and desires, and instead, surrender to the divine direction.

Such a consecration is not just a one-time act, but a daily exercise of self-surrender, much like the patient's consistent obedience to the physician's directives. As reiterated in *Romans 12:1, KJV, "I beseech you therefore, brethren, by the mercies of God, that ye present your bodies a living sacrifice, holy, acceptable unto God, which is your reasonable service."*

In conclusion, the path to divine healing and spiritual

growth calls for a 'Total Surrender,' a complete consecration of our lives to God's command. When we yield entirely to His guidance and trust in His love and wisdom, we welcome His transformative power into our lives. We must remember that God, the supreme physician of our souls, asks for nothing less than our complete trust and obedience. Only then can His divine healing fully manifest in us.

"Embracing Divine Will: A Path to Inner Bliss"

Dear reader, the language of our souls must always exclaim, **"Thy will be done,"** irrespective of our circumstances. This means, we must relinquish our personal liberty of choice and embrace a life of unconditional obedience. To those unfamiliar with the divine, this may seem like a daunting task. Yet, for those of us who truly know God, we understand this as the most blissful and serene path in life.

God, our Father, loves us with an incomprehensible love. He knows exactly what is best for us. Therefore, His will is indeed the most blessed thing that could ever occur in our lives under any circumstance. It baffles me how Satan has managed to obscure this profound truth from the Church.

Indeed, it appears that God's own children often fear His will more than anything else in life. This fear clouds the perception of His beautifully loving will, which only brings kindness, mercy, and immeasurable blessings to our souls. If only I could unveil the unimaginable sweetness of God's will to all! Heaven is a place of infinite joy because God's will is perfectly carried out there, and we can partake in this joy in proportion to the completeness of His will being enacted in our lives.

God's love for us is boundless. The will of love always seeks to bless the loved ones. Many of us have experienced the act of loving others. We know that if we could have our way, our beloved ones would be inundated with blessings. Our hands would pour out all that is good, sweet, and delightful in life upon them, if only we possessed the power to fulfill our will for them. How much more, then, must this be the case with our God, who is the embodiment of love. If we could only glimpse, even for a moment, into the vast depths of His love, our hearts would instantly align with His will and treasure it as our most valuable possession.

Despite this, many Christians seem to harbor the notion that all their Heavenly Father desires is to render them miserable and strip away their blessings. This erroneous belief leads them to cling onto things with their own will, thinking they can prevent God from bringing about their perceived misery. A Christian lady, overwhelmed with such fears, once expressed her inability to utter the words, **"Thy will be done,"** and how she feared the implications of doing so.

This lady was a mother of a little boy, who was her heart's delight and also the heir to a considerable fortune. After sharing her concerns, her friend asked her a poignant question, "Imagine if your little Charley came running to you tomorrow and said, 'Mother, I've decided to let you guide me from now on. I will always obey you, and I want you to do what you think is best for me. I trust your love for me.' How would you react? Would you seize this chance to make Charley's life miserable? Would you strip him of all joys and fill his life with hardships? Would you give him commands that he cannot possibly fulfill?"

"Absolutely not!" exclaimed the mother, horrified at the thought. "I would embrace him, shower him with affection, and strive to fill his life with the sweetest and best things." Her friend then gently asked, "And don't you think God is more tender and loving than you are?" Realization dawned on her and she replied, "Ah, I see my mistake. I will no longer fear saying 'Thy will be done' to my Heavenly Father any more than I would want my Charley to fear saying it to me."

In conclusion, our Heavenly Father, in His infinite love and wisdom, only seeks the best for us for us, and His will is a testament to this boundless love. We, as His children, must strive to embrace His divine will, for therein lies our true happiness and inner peace. Just as a loving parent wouldn't desire any harm for their child, God doesn't intend suffering for us. His will is intended to guide us, protect us, and lead us to a life of profound joy and fulfillment.

"Thy will be done" should not be an utterance we fear but rather, a heartfelt plea that we make with trust and love, fully aware that our Father in Heaven seeks the best for us. We must remember the words of *Proverbs 3:5-6 "Trust in the LORD with all thine heart; and lean not* *unto thine own understanding. In all thy ways acknowledge him, and he shall direct thy paths."*

Just as the Christian lady realized her mistaken perception of God's will, it is my sincere prayer that we all grasp the unchanging love of our Heavenly Father. We must strive to mirror the faith of a child, who, with complete trust and innocence, allows their parent to guide their steps. Let us surrender our will to the Divine, trust in His love, and confidently echo, **"Thy will be done."**

The fear of divine will, which seems to be a common misapprehension, needs to be replaced with faith and a deep understanding of God's love. His will, cloaked in infinite wisdom, seeks to bless us and not to harm us. As His children, our duty lies in understanding, accepting, and following His divine will with a heart full of love and a spirit ready to obey.

In the scripture of *Matthew 6:10 (KJV),* Jesus Himself teaches us to pray, saying, *"Thy kingdom come, Thy will be done in earth, as it is in heaven."* These words speak volumes about the absolute trust and surrender that Jesus exhibited towards His Heavenly Father's will.

So, dear reader, may we, with hearts full of faith, take this leap of trust and echo the prayer of our Savior, **"Thy will be done."** For in the embrace of divine will, we are not losing but gaining - gaining a life of blessings, peace, and joy. By seeking His will in all aspects of our life, we are choosing a path filled with His love, mercy, and the promise of eternal life. May we all bask in the bliss of our Heavenly Father's will, for it is the most precious gift that we can ever receive.

Embracing God's Will and Living by Faith

I must tell you, dear friend, of something even more satisfying than health, companionship, wealth, fame, ease, or prosperity: it is the indescribably beautiful will of our God. His will illuminates the darkest moments with a divine aura and fills the gloomiest pathways with radiant sunshine. Those who have embraced His will as their kingdom are forever under His reign, and no misfortune can truly befall them.

Allow me to share with you this revelation, and remember, it is not a stern requirement but an extraordinary privilege that I present before you. To step into the life that is hidden with Christ in God, your first step must be one of complete dedication, a wholehearted surrender, a total consecration to God's will. Take this step gladly, gratefully, with fervent enthusiasm. Embrace what I call the 'privilege side of consecration'. I can assure you from my blessed journey that you will find this the most joyous path you've ever embarked upon.

The next step on this divine journey is faith. Faith is a vital element in accepting any gift. For although a friend may generously give us a gift, it does not truly become ours until we believe in it, until we claim it as ours. This concept holds particularly true for gifts that are mental or spiritual in nature. As written *"For by grace are ye saved through faith; and that not of yourselves: it is the gift of God: Not of works, lest any man should boast" (Ephesians 2:8-9).*

Most Christians understand this principle when it comes to the forgiveness of their sins. They acknowledge that, despite the preaching of the forgiveness of sins through Jesus, it only becomes their conscious possession when they believe and claim this forgiveness as their own. However, in living the Christian life, some tend to forget this principle. They wrongly think that having been saved by faith, they must now live by works and efforts, not realizing that faith continues to be integral in their walk with Christ.

The scripture clearly says, *"As ye have therefore received Christ Jesus the Lord, so walk ye in him" (Colossians 2:6 KJV).* You received Him by faith, and hence, you should walk in Him by faith alone. The faith that leads us into this hidden life is akin to the faith that ushered us from the kingdom of darkness into God's radiant kingdom, yet it grasps a different facet of our Christian journey.

At first, we believed that Jesus was our Savior, freeing us from the guilt of sin, and according to our faith, it was so. Now, we must believe that He is our Savior from the power of sin, and according to our faith, it will be so. Initially, we trusted Him for our justification; now, we must trust Him for our sanctification. We embraced Him as our Savior from future penalties of our sins; now, we must accept Him as our Savior in the present from the bondage of our sins.

Theologically and judicially, I understand that every believer receives everything immediately upon conversion. However, practically, nothing is ours until we claim it by faith. As the scripture states, *"Every place that the sole of your foot shall tread upon, that have I given unto you" (Joshua 1:3 KJV)*. God *"hath blessed us with all spiritual blessings in heavenly places in Christ" (Ephesians 1:3 KJV),* but until we step on these blessings with the foot of faith, they do not practically become ours.

Our faith must be grounded in the present. A faith that only looks forward to the future doesn't suffice. One may believe eternally that his sins will be forgiven in the future, yet he will never find true peace until he believes in the present forgiveness.

Let's turn to *Romans 5:1 (KJV): "Therefore being justified by faith, we have peace with God through our Lord Jesus Christ."* It is clear that it's through present, living faith that we enter this life hid with Christ in God.

But faith doesn't mean mere belief. It's more than just accepting certain truths. Faith is dynamic; it's active. Faith involves entrusting our entire selves into the hands of Jesus, believing He saves us not only from the guilt of sin but also from its power.

At first, we trusted Jesus as our Redeemer who lifted us from the pit of sin and guilt. But now, we should believe that He is our life, the one who seats us in heavenly places with Himself. As *Ephesians 2:6 (KJV) says,*

"And hath raised us up together, and made us sit together in heavenly places in Christ Jesus."

In conclusion, embarking on this path to the life hid with Christ in God requires both complete consecration and a living faith. When we fully surrender to God's will and live by present, active faith, we begin to experience the divine halo that gilds our darkest hours and shines brightly on our gloomiest paths. The life hidden with Christ in God becomes a joyous journey, a glorious privilege that surpasses all earthly treasures. So, let's take this step gladly, gratefully, and with fervent enthusiasm, as we walk faithfully with our Savior.

The Power of Abandonment and Absolute Faith

As I walk my journey of faith, I've learned that acknowledging and accepting, by faith, "My sins are now forgiven," is a necessary first step before embracing a renewed life in Christ. Similar to this, faith that anticipates a future release from the grip of sin is not enough to lead anyone into the divine life I have come to know. The enemy is pleased with such deferred faith because he knows it lacks the power to effect real change. However, he quakes and retreats when a believer dares to assert current freedom, considering themselves emancipated from his control.

To simplify: to enter this blessed inner life of peace and victory, there are two crucial steps to take. Firstly, total surrender, and secondly, unwavering faith. No matter the complexity of your personal journey, your struggles, your environment, or your relationships, these two steps, once taken resolutely and persisted in, will guide you to the serene pastures and calm waters of a more profound Christian life.

Remember the words of the Lord in *Jeremiah 29:11, "For I know the thoughts that I think toward you, saith the LORD, thoughts of peace, and not of evil, to give you an expected end" KJV*. Let this assurance inspire your faith and resolve.

Let's recapitulate these steps, to prevent any misunderstanding. You, as a child of God, yearn to please Him. You adore your precious Savior and are exhausted and disheartened by the sin that causes Him sorrow. You long to break free from its hold. Previous attempts have failed, and in your despair, you're wondering if the Lord is indeed capable and willing to liberate you. The words in *Psalm 34:17* of the KJV assure us: *"The righteous cry, and the LORD heareth, and delivereth them out of all their troubles."* Therefore, trust Him, commit your case to Him with total surrender, and believe in His promise.

Claim that, just as you believed He absolved you of sin's guilt because He promised to do so, He now sets you free from sin's power because He has assured you of that. Extend your faith to embrace a new aspect of Christ. You have trusted Him as your dying Savior; now trust Him as your living Savior.

As He came to save you from future punishment, He also came to rescue you from current bondage. As assuredly as He bore your sins, He has also come to live His life within you. You are as powerless in the one case as in the other. Christ, and only Christ, must do both for you, and your role in both cases is merely to entrust it to Him and then believe that He carries it out.

A fellow believer, now a shining example of this life of faith, shared in a moment of great darkness and confusion that she was unsure how to 'abandon herself and trust.' It seemed daunting, but with the guidance of God, she persevered and found her way into the light.

In conclusion, just as you were unable to rid yourself of your sins, you can't achieve righteousness by your own strength. Only through Christ can we find salvation and deliverance. The path may seem challenging, but remember the promise in ***Philippians 4:13 KJV, "I can do all things through Christ which strengtheneth me."*** Our task is to abandon ourselves to His will and have absolute faith in Him, knowing that He has promised to deliver us. These two steps, taken resolutely, will guide us toward the restful green pastures and still waters of a higher Christian life. May your journey be blessed and your Embrace these steps, wholeheartedly. To abandon oneself completely is to let go of personal control and surrender all to Christ. It means entrusting your struggles, fears, hopes, and dreams into His hands. To have absolute faith means to believe, without a shadow of doubt, that Christ has the power to fulfill His promises. It is to trust in His love, His mercy, and His guidance.

And while these steps may seem daunting, remember, you are not alone. Christ Himself said in ***Matthew 28:20***

KJV, "Lo, I am with you always, even unto the end of the world." His presence is a constant source of strength and encouragement.

Even though we live in an imperfect world, marked by trials and tribulations, our faith in Christ provides a safe harbor. Just as a ship navigates through the storm, guided by the lighthouse, we too can navigate the storms of life, guided by our faith in Christ.

Take these steps, walk this path, and immerse yourself in the love and grace of Christ. Allow His teachings to illuminate your path, His love to fill your heart, and His grace to guide your actions. Trust in Him as you make this journey, and you will surely experience the profound peace and victory that comes from a higher Christian life.

In conclusion, remember that you are a beloved child of God, longing to live a life that honors and glorifies Him. The steps to achieving this are clear - complete abandonment to God's will and absolute faith in His promises. Trust in Christ, your living Savior, and believe that He is working in your life right now, freeing you from sin's power and guiding you towards spiritual triumph.

May your faith remain steadfast, your heart full of love, and your spirit fortified as you take these steps and journey towards a deeper, more meaningful relationship with Christ. As Paul wrote in *Ephesians 3:17-19 KJV, "That Christ may dwell in your hearts by faith; that ye, being rooted and grounded in love, may be able to comprehend with all saints what is the breadth, and length, and depth, and height; and to know the love of Christ, which passeth knowledge, that ye might be filled with all the fulness of God."* With these words in your heart, step forward in faith and embrace the blessed life Christ offers to all His children.

Entrusting Ourselves to the Divine Keeper

There are moments when I ardently wish you would speak your heart's desires out loud, allowing me to witness your faith in action. "Will you show me?" you ask. "Will you offer your prayers aloud for me to understand?" With all humility and sincerity, I shall.

"Lord Jesus," I start, "I firmly believe that Thou art capable and willing to liberate me from the unrest, the worry, and the shackles that often accompany my Christian journey. I am convinced that Thou didst sacrifice Yourself not only for my future salvation, but for my present peace and freedom as well. I have faith that Thou art stronger than Satan and that Thou canst keep even me, in my deepest weakness, from falling into his deceptive traps or complying with his commands.

"And, Lord Jesus, I am entrusting myself into Thy care. My attempts at self-preservation have failed, and they have failed most grievously. I acknowledge my utter helplessness; and so, I now put my faith in Thee. Withholding nothing, I offer myself to Thee. Body, soul, and spirit, I present myself to Thee, a mere lump of clay, to be molded into whatever Thy love and Thy wisdom choose. Now, I belong to Thee. I am certain that Thou dost accept my humble offering; I believe that even at this moment, Thou hast taken possession of my frail, foolish heart, and have begun Thy divine work in me, enabling me to will and do of Thy good pleasure. I trust Thee utterly, and I trust Thee now!"

Does this declaration of faith inspire fear in you? Does it appear abrupt, akin to a blind leap into the unknown? Remember, dear friend, faith steps might seem to fall into emptiness, but always find a solid foundation beneath.

Consider the plight of a man descending a well by a rope. He discovers, to his horror, that he has reached the rope's end, still suspended about thirty feet above the well's bottom. He lacks the strength and skill to climb back up, yet releasing his hold meant certain doom. His strength failing, he decides to let go, bracing himself for the inevitable. And then, he falls... merely three feet!

Dear friend, to experience the solid foundation of God's grace and providence, you must surrender yourself entirely to Him. Only by releasing your tight grasp on self-sufficiency and plunging into His arms can you experience His divine support. Taking this leap of faith today might spare you months, even years, of struggle and fatigue.

In the ancient castles of England, there was a secure sanctuary known as the "keep." This was the most fortified part of the castle, a refuge for the weak and defenseless in times of peril. If you were a fragile, fearful woman seeking safety during a siege, would seeking shelter in this stronghold appear like a leap in the dark to you? Would you hesitate to do so?

Likewise, we should not hesitate to place our faith in the Divine Keeper, who never slumbers nor sleeps. As stated in *Psalm 121:7-8, (KJV), "The Lord shall preserve thee from all evil: he shall preserve thy soul. The Lord shall preserve thy going out and thy coming in from this time forth, and even for evermore."* Entrust your life to Him who promises perpetual protection and peace.

In conclusion, surrendering ourselves to our Divine Keeper should not be seen as a leap into darkness but rather as a leap of faith into the arms of the One who promises eternal preservation. Let us entrust ourselves completely to Him, finding our rest and refuge in His unfailing love and immeasurable strength.

This leap of faith is not about abandoning reason or ignoring our challenges. Rather, it's about recognizing our limitations and trusting in the superior strength and wisdom of our Lord Jesus Christ. His promise in *2 Corinthians 12:9, (KJV), rings true: "And he said unto me, My grace is sufficient for thee: for my strength is made perfect in weakness."* Therefore, let us rejoice in our weakness, for in it, His strength is made manifest.

In surrendering to God, we're not forfeiting our lives, but rather allowing Him to reshape and remold us according to His divine plan and purpose. As stated in *Isaiah 64:8, (KJV), "But now, O LORD, thou art our father; we are the clay, and thou our potter; and we all are the work of thy hand."*

Finally, we must remember that our faith is not a passive acceptance but an active trust, a decisive leap into the divine presence of God. We must continually choose to entrust our lives to Him, knowing that He is faithful and just. As Jesus says in *Matthew 11:28-30, (KJV), "Come unto me, all ye that labour and are heavy laden, and I will give you rest. Take my yoke upon you, and learn of me; for I am meek and lowly in heart: and ye shall find rest unto your souls. For my yoke is easy, and my burden is light."*

By embracing this truth, we find our burdens lifted and our souls at peace. The leap of faith may seem daunting, but remember, it's not a leap into the abyss, but into the loving arms of our Lord and Savior, Jesus Christ. So, dear friend, take that leap of faith, surrender yourself to Him, and discover the profound peace and joy that come from entrusting your life to your Divine Keeper.

In the depths of surrender, we find the heights of God's love and mercy. By giving ourselves wholly to our Lord Jesus, we allow His divine love to permeate our being, transform our hearts, and guide our steps according to His purpose. The Apostle Paul expressed this transformative surrender in *Galatians 2:20, (KJV), "I am crucified with Christ: nevertheless I live; yet not I, but Christ liveth in me: and the life which I now live in the flesh I live by the faith of the Son of God, who loved me, and gave himself for me."*

Indeed, the power of surrender is profound. It is not a surrender to defeat, but a surrender to victory—a victory won not by our might, but by the love of our Lord Jesus Christ. As stated in *1 John 4:4, (KJV), "Ye are of God, little children, and have overcome them: because greater is he that is in you, than he that is in the world."*

Yet, this surrender is not a one-time act. It is a continual process, a daily commitment to choose faith over fear, trust over doubt. We must renew our surrender each day, entrusting our lives to our Divine Keeper anew. As written in *Lamentations 3:22-23, (KJV), "It is of the LORD'S mercies that we are not consumed, because his compassions fail not. They are new every morning: great is thy faithfulness."*

In conclusion, my dear friend, the leap of faith might seem terrifying, but it is the path to true freedom and peace. In surrendering our lives to our Divine Keeper, we find ourselves cradled in His eternal love, guided by His infinite wisdom, and fortified by His everlasting strength. May we have the courage to take this leap, to embrace the 'seeming void,' only to discover that beneath us is not emptiness but the solid rock of God's unchanging faithfulness. In His arms, we are kept safe, secure, and eternally loved!

CHAPTER FIVE

DIFFICULTIES CONCERNING CONSECRATION

The Divine Pathway of Consecration and Trust

I want to communicate something crucial to my fellow believers, a message of immense importance that must not escape our understanding. We must be acutely aware of the wiles of our adversary, who ceaselessly labors to hinder our spiritual journey towards the fullness of God's righteousness. His activities become particularly intense when he perceives a believer's awakening, a profound hunger and thirst for righteousness, and an aspiration to embrace the abundant richness found in our Lord Jesus Christ.

One such formidable challenge, a stumbling block often hurled in the believer's path, pertains to consecration. The pilgrim of holiness is instructed to consecrate oneself, and so they undertake this endeavor. However, they quickly encounter a quandary. They have performed the act of consecration as they understand it, yet they don't perceive any change in themselves. The anticipated transformation seems absent. In a state of bewilderment and despair, they question, **"How can I discern when I**

am truly consecrated?"

The primary temptation, persistent and pervasive, that greets such a soul in this predicament, centers on the realm of feelings. A believer is inclined to remain unconvinced of their consecration unless they can tangibly feel it. They find it difficult to trust that God has accepted their dedication because they don't experience an emotional validation of it. Commonly, they prioritize feeling over faith. However, the divine order unequivocally places faith before feeling in all circumstances. Trying to reverse this sequence is akin to swimming against the current.

The Word of God reminds us in *2 Corinthians 5:7, "For we walk by faith, not by sight."* We must put our trust in Him, not in our fleeting feelings. To overcome this temptation concerning consecration, we must stand with God and prioritize faith over feeling. Surrender yourself entirely to the Lord, guided by the illumination you currently possess. Ask the Holy Spirit to reveal anything in your heart or life that opposes God's will. If anything comes to light, immediately surrender it to God, declaring wholeheartedly, **"Thy will be done."**

If nothing is revealed, you must maintain faith that there is nothing hindering your relationship with God and infer that you have offered all to Him. You must then trust that He has accepted your consecration. Resist the temptation to wait for an emotional confirmation that you have surrendered yourself or that God has accepted you. Instead, let your faith guide you, believe, and consider it done.

In conclusion, remember that the journey of holiness and consecration isn't rooted in our feelings, but in unwavering faith. As ***Romans 1:17*** beautifully affirms, ***"For therein is the righteousness of God revealed from faith to faith: as it is written, The just shall live by faith."*** Faith first, feelings follow. Let this divine order guide you in your path of consecration and holiness, thereby leading you closer to the embrace of our Lord Jesus Christ.

"An Act of Faith: Consecration as an Eternal Gift"

When I bestowed an estate upon a dear friend of mine, I did so without the expectation of tangibly handing it over. Much like our faith in our Lord Jesus Christ, the transaction was mental - an act of unwavering trust. An estate cannot be lifted, transferred, and placed into the palms of another; it must be given and received in faith, as it is written in ***Hebrews 11:1 (KJV), "Now faith is the substance of things hoped for, the evidence of things not seen."***

Imagine this scenario - you provide an estate to a friend one day and the next, uncertainty plagues you. You begin to question whether you had truly given the gift, whether your friend had genuinely received it as his own. To quell your doubts, you renew your gift the next day. Despite this, on the third day, a similar uncertainty lingers, prompting you to renew the gift once again, and again on the fourth day. This cycle repeats for days, months, even years.

What thoughts would your friend harbor in such circumstances? He might question the sincerity of your initial intention. You, on the other hand, would be in a state of constant confusion, uncertain if the estate is still yours, rightfully his, or lost somewhere in between.

Doesn't this bear a striking resemblance to our consecration to God? You may have often found yourself pledging your life to Him, day in and day out, only to walk away questioning if you had truly given yourself over, if He had truly accepted you. This may have led you, after many tormenting doubts and fears, to conclude that your attempts at consecration were unsuccessful. My dear brethren, be aware that this type of confusion can persist indefinitely, unless you wield the sword of faith to sever it.

One must reach the point of considering the act of consecration as an accomplished, immovable fact. You must leave it in God's hands, and only then can you anticipate a change in your feelings. As it is beautifully stated in *Proverbs 3:5-6 (KJV), "Trust in the LORD with all thine heart; and lean not unto thine own understanding. In all thy ways acknowledge him, and he shall direct thy paths."*

This holds true according to the law of offerings to the Lord. Once given to Him, any gift becomes holy, set apart from all other things, to be used exclusively for His purpose, as it is written in *Leviticus 27:28 (KJV), "Notwithstanding no devoted thing, that a man shall devote unto the LORD of all that he hath, both of man and beast, and of the field of his possession, shall be sold or redeemed: every devoted thing is most holy unto the LORD."*

In conclusion, the act of giving to the Lord, of consecrating oneself, is an act of faith and trust. It's not to be mired in uncertainty, but rather affirmed with confidence in His acceptance and grace. As we devote ourselves to Him, we become most holy, set apart for His divine purpose. Thus, let us cast off our doubts and affirm our faith, knowing that we belong to Him and His glorious Kingdom.

Consecrating Ourselves to the Lord

Every day, I witness a significant verse in the Bible. It says, *"Notwithstanding, no devoted thing that a man shall devote unto the Lord of all that he hath, both of man and beast, and of the field of his possession, shall be sold or redeemed: every devoted thing is most holy unto the Lord" (Leviticus 27:28, KJV).* It means that once a person gives something to the Lord, it is recognized as belonging to the Lord by everyone in Israel. It can't be taken back or sold. This offering could be made hesitantly or half-heartedly. But, once given, it belongs solely to God. It's not the intention of the giver that makes it holy but the holiness of the receiver.

Now, you might ask, what if a person started questioning his intentions after giving his gift? What if he was worried that he didn't do it right or wasn't entirely honest in his actions? I believe that the priest would remind him, "Whether you gave your offering with right intentions or not, it's in God's hands now. Every dedicated thing is most holy to Him. It's too late to reconsider now." Any person daring to reclaim their offering would shock the whole community of Israel.

Nevertheless, I've noticed that some Christians, who condemn such sacrilege actions by Jews, commit similar acts themselves. They offer themselves to the Lord in a solemn consecration and then take back what they've offered due to a lack of faith. The fact that God isn't physically visible makes it challenging for them to perceive their commitment as real.

Let's say, if you could visibly see God while making your act of consecration, you'd feel it to be more real. You'd know that you have made a promise to God and breaking it wouldn't even cross your mind. We need to understand that God's presence is an absolute fact. Every word we speak in prayer is directly addressed to Him. We should be mindful of this when we engage in prayer or any acts of devotion.

Some might interject here, "Well, if only God would confirm that He accepts me when I offer myself, I wouldn't have any doubts." The thing is, God usually doesn't say this unless we prove our loyalty by believing in His words first. As stated in *Deuteronomy 26:17-19 (KJV), "Thou hast avouched the Lord this day to be thy God, and to walk in His ways, and to keep His statutes, and His commandments, and His judgments, and to hearken unto His voice; and the Lord hath avouched thee this day to be His peculiar people, as He hath promised thee, and that thou shouldst keep all His commandments. "*

God wouldn't ask us to present ourselves as living sacrifices if He didn't intend to accept us. It's incomprehensible that an honorable person, let alone a loving God, would request a gift they don't wish to accept. Therefore, we must believe with utmost confidence that when we surrender ourselves to God, He accepts us, and from that moment on, we belong to Him. A real transaction has taken place, and we must honor it.

In conclusion, the act of dedicating oneself to God is a profound commitment that should not be taken lightly. Once made, this pledge is irreversible and demands the utmost sincerity and faith. It's a sacred bond, one that is 'most holy unto the Lord'. The Almighty does not need our offerings, but He cherishes our love, loyalty, and commitment. When we honor our oath to Him, we are expressing our faith, which is the most precious gift we can give to God.

To be sure, maintaining such a commitment is no simple task. We may sometimes feel doubts creeping in, testing our faith. However, it's essential to remind ourselves of the truth: every word spoken in prayer, every act of consecration is heard and seen by God. There's no question of our offerings being unseen or unheard. It's not about if we can physically see God; it's about the faith we place in Him.

Perhaps you're one of the people who has said, "If He

would only speak to me and say that He took me when I gave myself to Him, I would have no trouble then in believing it." However, remember that the Lord usually speaks to those who have first demonstrated their faith by believing in His words. As it says in *John 20:29 (KJV)*, *"Jesus saith unto him, Thomas, because thou hast seen me, thou hast believed: blessed are they that have not seen, and yet have believed."*

Remember the words from *Deuteronomy 26:17-19*, where it's stated, *"Thou hast avouched the Lord this day to be thy God, and to walk in His ways and to keep His statutes, and His commandments, and His judgments, and to hearken unto His voice; and the Lord hath avouched thee this day to be His peculiar people, as He hath promised thee, and that thou shouldst keep all His commandments."* These words reassure us of His promise.

The moment we give our hearts to God, He accepts us. There's no hesitation, no second thoughts. We have committed ourselves to Him, and He has received us. That's a real, honest transaction, one that demands honor and respect.

In conclusion, we must learn to trust in the Lord and our relationship with Him. Despite our inability to physically see Him, we should understand that He is always present. Every word we say, every prayer we utter, and every act of devotion is before Him. It's our faith in God that makes these acts of consecration real and binding. So, let's stand firm in our faith, honoring our sacred oath of dedicating ourselves to God, knowing that He has received us the moment we gave ourselves to Him. In this way, we honor not only our commitments but also the unwavering faith we hold in our hearts.

Walking in His Commandments

My dear ones, when we proclaim with conviction that the Lord is our God and promise to tread His paths, to observe His edicts, He acknowledges us as His own and affirms our pledge to uphold His commandments. At that instant, He claims us. This, throughout all ages, has been His principle of engagement, and remains as such. The book of Leviticus asserts, *"Every devoted thing is most holy unto the Lord" (Leviticus 27:28, KJV).* To my understanding, this is so evident that it scarcely allows for any dispute.

However, if your heart still harbors uncertainty or faces hurdles, I implore you to heed a declaration from the New Testament that provides another perspective on the matter, but clarifies it equally, if not more, definitively. This proclamation resides in *1 John 5:14-15, KJV, "And this is the confidence that we have in Him, that, if we ask any thing according to His will, He heareth us: And if we know that He hear us, whatsoever we ask, we know that we have the petitions that we desired of Him."*

Does it align with His will that you should be wholly consecrated to Him? There exists only a singular answer to this, as He has commanded it. Isn't it also in line with His will that He should operate within you to will and execute His good pleasure? This question, too, possesses only one possible response, for He has expressed it to be His intention. Consequently, you must acknowledge these things as according to His will, thus by the Lord's own word, you are compelled to know that He hears you. And knowing this, you are obligated to proceed further and understand that you possess the petitions you have sought from Him. I emphasize, you possess, not will possess or may possess, but possess in the here and now.

This is how we, by faith, **"obtain promises."** This is how we gain "access by faith" into the grace bestowed upon us in our Lord Jesus Christ. It is in this manner and no other that we come to realize our hearts are "purified by faith," and become equipped to live by faith, stand by faith, and walk by faith.

With a desire to simplify and actualize this topic to a point that it leaves no room for further confusion, I will once again iterate the necessary actions of your soul that can alleviate any difficulty you may be encountering about consecration. I assume that you have entrusted your sins to Lord Jesus for forgiveness and understand a fraction of what it means to be a part of God's family, to become an heir of God through faith in Christ. Now, within your soul, you sense a yearning to be molded in the image of your Lord. For this to be achieved, you acknowledge there must be a complete surrender of your being to Him, so He may work His will within you. Despite your repeated attempts to do so, your efforts have seemed unsuccessful thus far.

However, remember, the Lord hears us when we seek

according to His will, and it is within His promise that we already possess the petitions we have put forth to Him. It is the act of faith, the pure belief in His word that grants us access to His grace, purifies our hearts, and empowers us to live, stand, and walk by faith. Therefore, let us entrust ourselves entirely to Him, for He has avouched us to be His, and we shall endeavor to uphold His commandments.

Embracing divine ownership, walking in His commandments, and being completely consecrated to Him is not just our obligation, but also our path to fulfillment and peace. In our attempts to surrender, we may find ourselves falling short. Yet, our dear Lord is patient and gracious. His will is to cultivate His goodness within us. Therefore, our efforts, no matter how imperfect, are not in vain.

Indeed, the scripture says in *Philippians 2:13, KJV, "For it is God which worketh in you both to will and to do of His good pleasure."* This promise, my dear ones, should offer us comfort and courage. Even when we stumble in our path, our Lord is there, working within us, guiding our will, and leading us towards His good pleasure.

It is vital that we understand the importance of consecration, of surrendering to His will completely. This means giving up our worldly desires, our self-centered thoughts, and our own plans, to embrace His divine will. It is a journey, not a single act, a journey that requires constant effort, constant faith, and constant surrender to His will.

As it says in ***Proverbs 3:5-6, KJV, "Trust in the LORD with all thine heart; and lean not unto thine own understanding. In all thy ways acknowledge him, and he shall direct thy paths."*** Trust in the Lord, acknowledge Him in all you do, and He will guide your path. Your efforts to consecrate yourself to Him, to live, stand, and walk by faith, are not in vain. They are seen and acknowledged by our Lord.

In conclusion, my dear ones, the path of consecration, of surrendering to His will, may seem challenging and, at times, overwhelming. However, remember His promises. He hears us, He is working within us, and we possess the petitions we have sought from Him. Therefore, let us courageously and faithfully continue on this path, guided by His word and His promises, knowing that we are His, and He is ours. Amen.

Journey into the Embrace of Divine Will

I long to guide you at this crucial juncture, and my guidance is straightforward and sincere. Embrace the sacred mission to return once again to the Lord, giving your whole self-up to His divine will. Make your surrender as complete as your understanding allows. Ask Him to illuminate, through His Spirit, any concealed resistance within your heart. If He unveils no such rebellion, trust in His revelation, and rest assured that your surrender is indeed complete.

Henceforth, consider this as a firm truth: You have entrusted yourself to the Lord, relinquishing any claim to yourself. Never shall you entertain any suggestion otherwise. If the doubt arises, questioning the extent of your surrender, dispel it decisively with the affirmation of your dedication. There is no room for debate on this matter. Cast away any conflicting thought immediately and resolutely. You pledged your surrender then, you uphold it now, and thus it is done.

Your emotions may rally against this surrender, yet it is your will that must prevail. It is your intent, not your feelings towards that intent, that the Lord sees, and hence, it is your intent that must be your primary concern. Having made your surrender, one never to be doubted or withdrawn, the next step is to trust that God accepts what you have given. Consider it as His possession now - not at some distant point in the future but at this very moment. Believe that He has begun His divine work in you, stirring both the will and the action for His good pleasure. This is where you must find peace.

There remains no further task for you, for now, you belong to the Lord completely. You are now under His care, His management, and His guidance. According to His word, He will work in you, molding you to be pleasing in His sight, all through Jesus Christ. *"Being confident of this very thing, that he which hath begun a good work in you will perform it until the day of Jesus Christ" (Philippians 1:6 KJV).*

Your faith must remain unwavering. If you allow yourself to question your surrender or God's acceptance of it, your wavering faith will yield a wavering experience, hindering His divine work. But as long as you trust, He continues His work. The fruit of His divine labor is always transformation, morphing you into the image of Christ, from **Glory** to **Glory**, by His mighty Spirit. *"But we all, with open face beholding as in a glass the Glory of the Lord, are changed into the same image from Glory to Glory, even as by the Spirit of the Lord" (2 Corinthians 3:18 KJV).*

At this moment, do you surrender yourself wholly to Him? You respond affirmatively, "Yes."

In conclusion, our journey into the embrace of Divine Will is a sacred surrender - a lifelong commitment where we entrust ourselves completely to God's care and guidance. As we walk this path, we find that He begins a divine work within us, shaping us to be pleasing in His sight. By holding steadfast in our surrender and faith, we allow Him to transform us into the image of Christ. In this surrender, we find our true purpose and achieve a deeper sense of peace and fulfillment.

Yielding Ourselves to God's Will

My dear fellow believer, let us commence this spiritual journey with the understanding that we are His chosen ones, that He has extended His grace to us and is working in us to fulfill His divine pleasure. Reiterate this to yourself consistently; it becomes a source of profound comfort to verbalize your faith, repeating to yourself and to God, "Lord, I am Yours; I wholly submit myself to You, and I trust that You have embraced me. I entrust myself to You. Fulfill Your good will in me, and I will remain tranquil in Your hands, placing my faith in You."

Make this a conscious, daily act of your will and revisit it multiple times a day, reaffirming it as your perpetual attitude before Him. Acknowledge it within yourself. Declare it to God. Proclaim it to your companions. Constantly assert that the Lord is your God and communicate your intent to follow His path and uphold His laws. As you do so, you will experience that He has claimed you as His distinctive people, and you will commit to keeping His commands, thereby becoming *"a holy people unto the Lord, as He hath spoken" (Deuteronomy 26:19, KJV).*

To guide you on this path, here are a few elementary yet essential principles. Incorporate these into your daily moments of devotion, letting them define the stance and state of your soul until enlightenment dawns on this matter.

I. Articulate your faith in Jesus Christ as your Savior and affirm your belief that He has reconciled you with God, in alignment with *"And all things are of God, who hath reconciled us to himself by Jesus Christ" (2 Corinthians 5:18, KJV)* and *"To wit, that God was in Christ, reconciling the world unto himself" (2 Corinthians 5:19, KJV).*

II. Explicitly acknowledge God as your Father and recognize yourself as His redeemed and pardoned child, following *"For in Christ Jesus neither circumcision availeth any thing, nor uncircumcision; but faith which worketh by love" (Galatians 5:6, KJV)*.

III. Explicitly surrender yourself to the Lord—body, soul, and spirit—and commit to obeying Him in every aspect where His will is revealed, mirroring *"Rejoicing in hope; patient in tribulation; continuing instant in prayer" (Romans 12:12, KJV)*.

IV. Maintain faith, despite any contrary appearances, that God takes ownership of what you relinquish to Him, and that He will persistently work in you to fulfill His good pleasure, unless you deliberately resist His grace, as shown in *"Wherefore come out from among them, and be ye separate, saith the Lord, and touch not the unclean thing; and I will receive you" (2 Corinthians 6:17, KJV)*, *"And will be a Father unto you, and ye shall be my sons and daughters, saith the Lord Almighty" (2 Corinthians 6:18, KJV)*, and *"For it is God which worketh in you both to will and to do of his good pleasure" (Philippians 2:13, KJV)*.

V. Disregard your feelings as a gauge of your relationship with God, focusing instead on the state of your will and faith. Consider all these actions you're now taking as irrefutable, even when the adversary attempts to convince you otherwise, based on *"Let us draw near with a true heart in full assurance of faith" (Hebrews 10:22, KJV)*, and *"Let us hold fast the profession of our faith without wavering; (for he is faithful that promised)" (Hebrews 10:23, KJV)*.

VI. Never, under any circumstances, yield to doubt or despondency. Bear in mind that all discouragement is a tool of the adversary, and vehemently resist it, in accordance with *"Let not your heart be troubled: ye believe in God, believe also in me" (John 14:1, KJV)*, and *"Peace I leave with you, my peace I give unto you: not as the world giveth, give I unto you. Let not your heart be troubled, neither let it be afraid" (John 14:27, KJV)*.

VII. Cultivate the habit of verbalizing your faith in explicit terms. Repeat often, *"I am wholly the Lord's, and He is presently working in me to fulfill His good pleasure,"* following *"Make you perfect in every good work to do his will, working in you that which is wellpleasing in his sight, through Jesus Christ; to whom be Glory for ever and ever. Amen" (Hebrews 13:21, KJV)*.

To conclude, this spiritual journey is a process of self-surrender and trust in God's divine plan for us. Remember to reassure yourself of God's love and your faith in Him. Our relationship with God should not be determined by our fleeting emotions, but rather, it is to be established on the solidity of our faith and His unwavering promises. As we become proficient in practicing these principles, we find ourselves more deeply rooted in our faith, our will aligned with God's, and our lives progressively reflecting His grace and **Glory**. Indeed, we become a holy people unto the Lord, as He has spoken.

Chapter SIX

DIFFICULTIES CONCERNING FAITH

Pathway from the Wilderness to the Promised Land

Dear children of God, I'd like to share a journey with you. It's not a physical journey, but one of the soul. It's a progression from the wilderness of our Christian experience to the land of milk and honey, a place symbolizing a rich and abundant spiritual life.

Once we consecrate ourselves to God, we take the next step of this journey, and that step is faith. It is true that our enemy, the deceiver, is quite crafty in making this step seem more difficult than it is. He puts obstacles in our path and makes us feel as if we are walking through a dense fog.

Imagine a fellow believer who has just realized the fullness of Jesus Christ and yearns to make that fullness a part of himself. But every spiritual guide he turns to tells him that this fullness can only be obtained through faith. To him, faith seems like a tangled mystery, making his path to this spiritual bounty even more obscure and daunting.

He recognizes, like many of us do, that faith is an

essential part of our Christian walk. But he's in a predicament because he feels that he lacks faith. He doesn't understand what faith truly is or how to gain it. This confusion plunges him into darkness and on the brink of despair.

But my dear brothers and sisters, let me tell you that such trouble arises because of a misunderstanding of what faith truly is. The scripture in *Hebrews 11:1* tells us, *"Now faith is the substance of things hoped for, the evidence of things not seen."* Faith, in its true essence, is simpler and more straightforward than you may have thought, and it is indeed within your reach.

Perhaps you've imagined faith to be an entity, a religious exercise or an inner virtue of the heart. You may perceive it as something you could hold, something you could celebrate and use as a token of God's favor or a currency to purchase His gifts. You have prayed for this faith, waiting for this tangible entity to materialize, and when it didn't, you concluded that you have no faith.

However, faith, in its truest form, isn't tangible at all. It's not an object to be held but a trust to be held onto. As the scripture in *Romans 10:17* tells us, *"So then faith cometh by hearing, and hearing by the word of God."* Faith, in essence, is trust in the word of God and a firm belief in His promises.

In conclusion, embarking on the journey of faith may seem daunting at first. We may stumble, feel lost, or even despair. But we must remember that faith is simpler and more accessible than we often perceive. It is a firm trust and unwavering belief in God's promises. So, let's cast off our misconceptions and step forward in faith, for it is through faith that we can taste the spiritual fullness of the Promised Land.

"The Simplicity of Faith: Trusting in God's Word"

I am here to speak to you about the sheer simplicity of faith, a concept as basic and as necessary as sight. Just as we use our sight to perceive the world, faith is our inner sight, helping us understand and trust in the divine.

You would not close your eyes to determine if you have sight, would you? In the same manner, there is no need to delve deep within yourself to find your faith. It exists when you believe in something, just as sight exists when you see something. The act of seeing confirms the presence of sight; likewise, the act of believing confirms the existence of faith.

However, the crucial factor isn't merely the act of believing, it is the substance of what you believe in. If you believe in truth, your faith paves the way to salvation; if you believe in falsehood, it leads you astray. The faith you exercise in both situations is identical, yet the subjects of your faith are starkly different. This fundamental difference determines your spiritual fate. It isn't your faith itself that saves you, but rather, the fact that your faith connects you to the Savior who offers salvation.

The book of Ephesians affirms this, *Ephesians 2:8-9,*

"For by grace are ye saved through faith; and that not of yourselves: it is the gift of God: Not of works, lest any man should boast." Hence, your faith serves as a link, a bridge connecting you to the Savior.

Therefore, it's essential to comprehend the innate simplicity of faith. It is nothing more or less than believing in God when He promises to act on our behalf and then trusting Him to fulfill His promises. It is as simple as it is profound, and such simplicity often makes it challenging to explain.

In the Gospel of Matthew, Jesus spoke of this very simplicity in *Matthew 18:3, "And said, Verily I say unto you, Except ye be converted, and become as little children, ye shall not enter into the kingdom of heaven."*

Faith is akin to entrusting an important task to someone else. We place the responsibility in their hands, feeling no need to complete the task ourselves because we trust in their competence. We've all delegated critical tasks to others at some point, finding peace in our trust due to our confidence in their abilities. Consider how mothers trust their cherished infants to the care of nurses, free from any trace of worry.

In conclusion, the essence of faith lies in its simplicity. It is not a complicated or intricate concept but a straightforward act of belief and trust in God's words and promises. Remember that the power of faith isn't in the act of believing itself, but in the divine truth in which we place our belief. Just as we trust others with important tasks based on our confidence in them, let us have faith in God, trusting Him to fulfill His promises as stated in the Scriptures. Our faith is our link to salvation, a bridge leading us to our Savior. Trust in Him, believe in His word, and find peace in His promises.

"Trusting in God: A Lesson in Faith"

I often marvel at how trust plays a crucial role in our daily lives. From the moment we wake, we entrust our wellbeing to countless individuals without a trace of anxiety. The cooks who prepare our meals, the drivers who navigate our journeys, railway conductors, and various hired help all hold our safety in their hands. Even the slightest lapse in their vigilance could result in sorrow or catastrophe. And yet, we yield to this trust as part of our daily routine, hardly thinking it remarkable. You, dear reader, practice this trust, this faith in your fellow humans, every day.

Consider this: your very existence in this world and the order of your daily life depends on your ability to trust others. You don't contemplate the possibility of distrusting them. However, with a heavy heart, I observe that many of you readily express your inability to trust your God in the same manner. What if we were to apply this spiritual distrust to our worldly affairs? The results, I believe, would be startling.

Let us imagine a day fueled by such distrust. As you sit

down for breakfast, doubt takes hold. You cannot eat, for without faith, you fear the cook may have tainted the coffee or that the meat from the butcher could be spoiled. Hence, you leave the table empty and unsatisfied.

Traveling to your workplace or other daily destinations, you decline to board the railway train. You say, "I can't trust the engineer, conductor, the craftsmen of the carriages, or the managers of the road," all because faith eludes you. Consequently, you're left to walk everywhere, resulting in exhaustion and inability to reach far-off destinations, which the train could've taken you to easily.

When friends share news or your agent presents accounts, you'd respond with regret, claiming an inability to believe them due to a lack of faith. Reading a newspaper would be futile, for without faith, you'd doubt every statement, every place, and every individual mentioned. "I cannot believe in the existence of the queen, for I've never seen her, nor Ireland, for I've never been there," you'd say, claiming faithlessness as the reason for your disbelief. Imagine living a day in such a way.

Consider how catastrophic this lack of faith would be to your daily life, and how absurd it would seem to others. Think about the disappointment and insult your friends would feel, and how quickly your servants would abandon their duties, refusing to serve you another day. If such a lack of faith in fellow humans would be deemed dreadful and foolish, then consider how much more grievous it is when you express the same disbelief towards God.

In the Book of *Psalms,* Chapter *9,* Verse *10,* (KJV), it is said, *"And they that know thy name will put their trust in thee: for thou, LORD, hast not forsaken them that seek thee."* The scripture reminds us to put our trust in the Lord, as He will never abandon those who seek Him. If we can place such faith in our fellow humans, how can we not place the same, if not more, trust in our Heavenly Father?

In conclusion, we must reflect on the manner in which we exercise our faith, both in our worldly relationships and in our relationship with God. Just as we trust in the diligence and integrity of those around us to navigate our daily lives, so too should we trust in the love, grace, and protection of our God. Let us strive to mirror the faith we display in our fellow humans in our faith towards our Heavenly Father. Trust in Him should be our default, not our struggle.

"The Act of Faith: Trusting in the Divine Witness"

"I stand before you today as a humble child of God, reflecting upon the nature of faith and trust. Why is it, I ask, that you readily accept the testimony of men yet hesitate to accept the divine testimony of God? How can you trust the accounts of men, who are prone to failings, yet find it difficult to embrace the unerring message of God?

You entrust your dearest earthly affairs to your fellow

creatures, who are frail and fallible, without an ounce of fear. Yet, you hesitate to place your spiritual affairs in the hands of our blessed Savior, who offered His life for the salvation of us all. He is, as the Book of Hebrews declares, *"able to save them to the uttermost that come unto God by him, seeing he ever liveth to make intercession for them" (Hebrews 7:25,).*

I beseech you, dear believer, whose very title implies faith, to reconsider your stance. The plea of having no faith isn't acceptable, for it implies having no faith in God, not in oneself. If you feel this lack of faith, I urge you to articulate it fully. Admit that you say, **"I have no faith in God, I cannot believe God";** this truth may become so dreadful that it compels you to seek faith.

You may respond, 'I cannot believe without the Holy Spirit.' Indeed, but is your lack of faith due to the Holy Spirit's failure to fulfil His role? If that's your claim, then you bear no fault, and exhortations to believe are futile. Yet, dear ones, this is a grave misconception. By asserting a lack of faith, you aren't merely 'making God a liar', but you're expressing a lack of trust in the Holy Spirit.

The Holy Spirit is ever ready to assist us in our weaknesses. We do not have to await Him; instead, He patiently awaits us. I have unwavering faith in the blessed Holy Spirit and His readiness to guide us, and I boldly affirm to each one of you that you are capable of believing, here and now. If you do not, the Spirit is not at fault, you are.

So, place your will on the side of belief. As *Mark 9:23* in the Bible beautifully articulates, *"Jesus said unto him, 'If thou canst believe, all things are possible to him that believeth.'"*

In conclusion, dear believer, your faith and trust in God and His divine witness are paramount. They serve as your spiritual compass, guiding you through the trials of life. So, let us silence our doubts and surrender ourselves to His divine love and wisdom, for He is always ready to help us in our journey towards spiritual growth. Remember, dear ones, all things are indeed possible to those who believe.

Unwavering Faith in Our Heavenly Friend

In my words, I urge you to proclaim, "Lord, I have faith, I truly do," and affirm it unceasingly. Make a resolute choice to have faith, standing tall against every whisper of doubt that seeks to undermine your belief. From the depths of your own disbelief, hurl yourself fearlessly onto the words and promises of God, entrusting yourself fully to the protective and redeeming power of the Lord Jesus.

Consider this, if you have ever placed a cherished matter into the hands of an earthly friend, I beseech you, entrust your very self, along with all your spiritual concerns, into the hands of your Heavenly Friend. From this point on, never, ever permit yourself to question His trustworthiness.

Remember this crucial lesson: there are two elements that are even more incongruent than oil and water—trust and worry. Would you consider it trust if you handed over a responsibility to a friend, only to spend your nights and days consumed by anxious thoughts about whether the task would be completed correctly? The answer is no.

In the same vein, can you say you trust when you've given the salvation and protection of your soul to the Lord, yet find yourself spending countless hours wrestling with worries and doubts? When a believer truly trusts, he relinquishes his worries about that which he has entrusted. But when he worries, it is a clear sign that he doesn't fully trust.

This truth reveals a startling reality: in the Church of Christ, genuine trust is often found lacking. It's no surprise, then, that our Lord asked a poignant question in *Luke 18:8: "I tell you that he will avenge them speedily. Nevertheless, when the Son of man cometh, shall he find faith on the earth?"* When He returns, He may indeed find an abundance of activity, considerable earnestness, and many devoted hearts; but will He find faith, the one attribute He values above all else?

This question holds deep significance, and I urge every Christian heart to reflect on it earnestly. However, let our past lives, marked by shared doubt, suffice. Let us all, who know our blessed Lord and His immeasurable faithfulness, endorse His truthfulness with our complete and unreserved trust in Him.

In conclusion, let us strive to answer the Lord's question positively. Let Him find faith on earth when He returns by showing complete trust in His care and not worrying about the matters we've entrusted to Him. Trust in the Lord with all your heart and let His words guide you, for His faithfulness is eternal and true. Let our lives be an example of unwavering faith in our Heavenly Friend, inspiring others to do the same.

" Walking Faithfully in God's Light"

In my early days as a follower of Christ, an appeal from a collection of vintage sermons moved me deeply. It called to all those who loved our Savior Jesus to display to the world His deservingness of trust, reflected in the firmness of their own faith in Him. As I recall, my soul yearned with an intense desire that I might tread paths so obscured, where a complete surrender of trust would be my blessed and glorious honor. As written in *Joshua 3:4, "Ye have not passed this way heretofore,"* it may indeed be so. However, today it is your joyful privilege to demonstrate, as never before, your loyal faith in the Lord by embarking on a journey of faith in Him. This journey lived moment by moment, will be rooted in absolute, childlike trust in Him.

Remember, you have trusted Him with a few things, and He has not disappointed you. Now, trust Him with everything. The Lord can exceed all that you could ever ask or imagine. This is not according to your power or capacity, but His mighty power, as it is written in *Ephesians 3:20: "Now unto him that is able to do exceeding abundantly above all that we ask or think, according to the power that worketh in us".*

Consider how easily you entrust the Lord with the management of the universe and all creation. Surely, your personal circumstances cannot be more complex or challenging than these! It is unworthy to harbor doubts. Stand firmly in the power and reliability of your God and observe how swiftly difficulties dissipate before an unwavering resolve to believe. Trust in the dark, trust in the light, trust at night, trust in the morning. You will discover that faith that begins with a mighty effort will gradually transform into the easy and natural disposition of the soul. *"For with God all things are possible" as written in Mark 10:27,* and *"all things are possible to him that believeth" (Mark 9:23).*

Remember, in the past, faith has *"subdued kingdoms, wrought righteousness, obtained promises, stopped the mouths of lions, quenched the violence of fire, escaped the edge of the sword, out of weakness were made strong, waxed valiant in fight, turned to flight the armies of the aliens" (Hebrews 11:33-34).* Faith can indeed perform such feats again. Our Lord Jesus says to us in *Matthew 17:20, "If ye have faith as a grain of mustard seed, ye shall say unto this mountain, Remove hence to yonder place; and it shall remove; and nothing shall be impossible unto you."*

If you are a child of God, you must have at least as much faith as a grain of mustard seed. Thus, you cannot claim that you cannot trust because you have no faith. Assert instead, "I can trust my Lord, and I will trust Him, and not all the powers of earth or hell shall be able to make me doubt my wonderful, glorious, faithful Redeemer!"

The emancipation of our slaves is a powerful example of how faith operates. Like these freed individuals, we too must receive our spiritual freedom by faith. They gained their freedom when the government declared their emancipation. Technically, they were free as soon as the Proclamation was signed. However, they didn't truly experience their freedom until they heard the good news and believed in it. The fact must come first, then the belief in the fact, and the feeling follows. This is the divine order. It is, I. The fact. II. The faith. III. The feeling. However humanity often tends to reverse this order, insisting on: I. The feeling. II. The faith. III. The fact.

In this divine order, we can see how faith in God's proclamations and promises allows us to experience His blessings in our lives. First, God declares the fact - our salvation, freedom, and redemption through Christ. It's up to us to have faith in this truth. This faith, this trust in His word, brings the feeling of peace, joy, and security that comes with being a child of God.

It's crucial to realize that our feelings do not dictate facts, nor should they drive our faith. Trust in God should not hinge on whether we 'feel' saved, or 'feel' like trusting Him. Instead, our faith should be based on the certainty of God's character and His promises, as revealed in the scriptures.

This is why we must stand firm in our faith, even in times

of difficulty or doubt. As we steadfastly trust God in every situation, our faith becomes second nature, a habit that strengthens us and lights our path. In darkness or light, morning or night, we continue to trust, for faith is our shield and strength. With it, as history has shown, all things are possible.

We are reminded in *Romans 10:17, "So then faith cometh by hearing, and hearing by the word of God."* This is the way of faith. Trust in God, believe in His promises, and allow your feelings to follow in alignment with this faith. This is the divine order, the way of wisdom, and the pathway to a peaceful and prosperous spiritual journey.

In conclusion, trusting the Lord is not merely an abstract concept but a transformative, life-affirming decision that impacts every facet of our existence. Faith, like a grain of mustard seed, might seem small and insignificant. Yet, it holds the power to move mountains. Remember, our faith is not in ourselves or our feelings. Instead, it is in God, our wonderful, glorious, faithful Redeemer. By maintaining faith, we demonstrate our unwavering belief in His word and promises. In doing so, we strengthen not only our relationship with Him but also become testimonies of His enduring love and grace. Let us strive to uphold this faith, for in doing so, we find the true meaning and purpose of our lives.

A Journey from Bondage to Freedom

Long ago, if the enslaved people had simply accepted

what their masters told them about their freedom and didn't believe in it until they felt it for themselves, they could have remained in slavery for much longer. Let me share a story I once heard. It happened in a small Southern town, somewhat hidden away, where a Northern lady discovered something startling, a few years after the Civil War had ended. She found that there were still slaves who hadn't grasped their freedom.

When she told them that the North had granted them their liberty, an older lady, a former slave, eagerly asked her, "Miss, are we truly free?" "Yes, of course, you are," the lady replied. The older woman couldn't hold back her excitement and repeated her question, "Are you certain, miss?" The Northern lady confirmed, "Yes, I'm sure. Did you not know?"

The woman explained, "We heard whispers that we were free, but when we asked our master, he denied it. So, we were scared to leave. We heard again about our freedom, went to the colonel, but he suggested we stay with the old master. Our hearts were a rollercoaster of hope and doubt. But now, if you're certain we're free, could you explain it to us?"

Seeing the desperate need for understanding, the lady kindly explained everything to her: the war, the Northern army, Abraham Lincoln, the Emancipation Proclamation, and their current freedom. The older woman listened with a heart full of anticipation. She heard the wonderful news and she believed it. After the lady finished telling her story, the older woman stood tall, walking out with confidence, declaring, "I'm free! I won't stay with the old master anymore!" She finally grasped her freedom, and she did so through faith. Her freedom was declared long ago by the government, but it hadn't mattered until she believed it. This life-changing news hadn't helped her before because she hadn't placed her "faith" in the person who shared it.

But, just as the Book of Hebrews says, *"Now faith is the substance of things hoped for, the evidence of things not seen" (Hebrews 11:1, KJV).* Now, she believed, and in believing, she had the courage to consider herself free. Not because of any change in her circumstances or feelings, but because she trusted the word of another, a messenger who came bearing the liberating news of her freedom.

The lesson? God has told us many times through His word that we are spiritually free. He insists we consider ourselves free. So, place your faith in His declaration and affirm its truth. Tell yourself, your friends, and whisper in the quiet of your soul to God, that you are free. Don't listen to the deceiving claims of your old master, saying that you're still enslaved. Don't let anything discourage you, neither your internal emotions nor external circumstances. Stay firm in your faith, despite any opposition, and I assure you, based on our Lord's authority, that *as Matthew 9:29 (KJV) says, "...According to your faith be it unto you."*

Out of all the ways we can worship God, none is as pleasing to Him as complete trust in Him. It glorifies Him the most. So, remember, during the tough times, even when you *"are in heaviness through manifold temptations,"* as *1 Peter 1:6-7 (KJV)* says, these trials of faith, more precious than gold, will be found "unto praise and honour and **Glory** at the appearing of Jesus Christ."

In conclusion, faith is a powerful tool that unlocks doors and shatters chains. Just as the woman in the story claimed her physical freedom through faith, we too can embrace our spiritual freedom, made possible by the sacrifice of Jesus Christ. The journey to freedom may be fraught with doubt and trials, but it is our steadfast belief in the word of God that will lead us to liberation.

Always remember, you are free. Stand firm in your faith and do not be swayed by contrary voices. Even in the face of challenges and adversities, hold on to your belief, and let it guide you towards the path of freedom. Take heart in the words of the Apostle Paul in *Romans 8:31 (KJV), "What shall we then say to these things? If God be for us, who can be against us?"* Let these words be a source of strength and courage as you journey from bondage to the joyous freedom in Christ.

Indeed, our faith is tried and tested, much like gold in the fire. Yet, it's through this process that it becomes more precious and valuable. It's through these trials that our faith grows, and with it, our relationship with God. Let's celebrate this freedom granted to us, not just by acknowledging it but by living it out daily in our lives. Remember, you are free, and your faith is the key to this freedom. Embrace it, live it, and share it. After all, the most potent freedom is the one we claim and live by faith...

CHAPTER SEVEN
DIFFICULTIES CONCERNING THE WILL
Embracing the Divine Reality Beyond Emotion

As a devoted child of God, I took the leap of faith, completely surrendering myself and placing my absolute trust in Christ. I dared to venture into the realm of divine grace, tasting the sweetness of a life concealed with Christ in God. Along this sacred journey, I encountered a perplexing obstacle that left me bewildered.

My initial sense of tranquility and peace began to ebb, and in some moments, seemed as though they never truly graced me. I started to perceive a strange unreality in my experiences. There were times when my newfound faith felt skin-deep, resonating only in words but not seeping into the core of my being. I worried that my surrender wasn't a heartfelt offering, and consequently, it wouldn't find favor with God.

I hesitated to profess that I belong entirely to the Lord, fearing it might be an untruth. But the yearning for this complete surrender was so profound, I found myself unable to deny its existence. This predicament was genuine, and it dampened my spirits. However, upon gaining a deeper understanding of the principles of my new life in Christ and learning how to live it fully, this apparent impasse became a stepping stone for spiritual growth.

I had initially assumed that my hidden life with Christ in God was to be primarily experienced in the realm of emotions. As a result, I gave undue attention to my emotional state, letting it decide my inner tranquility or turmoil. But I soon discovered the crux of the matter: This divine life wasn't about dwelling in emotions, but about anchoring the will in God's plan. The ebb and flow of emotions no longer held sway over my divine reality as long as my will remained steadfast, centered in God's will.

Allow me to elaborate, drawing upon the wisdom of Fenelon, who once stated, "Pure religion resides in the will alone." This notion of anchoring the will, not emotions, in God is fundamental in understanding and living our new life in Christ.

This journey is mirrored in the words of Jesus Christ Himself, as recorded in *John 14:1 (KJV), "Let not your heart be troubled: ye believe in God, believe also in me."* This scripture underscores that belief, stemming from the will, is the anchor of our spiritual journey, not transient emotions.

In conclusion, we, as children of God, must learn to navigate through the perceived unreality, understanding that our journey isn't to be dictated by fleeting emotions, but by our will steadfastly abiding in God's. With a clear understanding of this principle, we can joyfully declare, following Paul's words in *Galatians 2:20 (KJV), "I am crucified with Christ: nevertheless I live; yet not I, but Christ liveth in me: and the life which I now live in the flesh I live by the faith of the Son of God, who loved me, and gave himself for me."* In this divine surrender of our will, we find our true home within Christ, everlastingly secure and supremely blessed.

The Sovereign Will: An Unseen Power Within Us

In the profound tapestry of our being, the will stands as the sovereign, the guiding force within our nature. As I understand it, by 'will,' I am not referring to a mere wish or even a specific intent, but rather the choice, the determinative power, the monarch of our inner kingdom, to which every aspect of our being pledges allegiance. This will is our core essence, the 'Ego,' the distinct 'I' we perceive as our self.

Sometimes, we may erroneously assume that our emotions wield the scepter in our human nature. However, through the lens of practical experience, I believe each one of us discerns an underlying entity residing deeper than our emotions and wishes. This entity is an independent self that ultimately decides and governs all. Yes, our emotions are part and parcel of us, experienced and savored, yet they are not our entire selves.

If God is to make us His dwelling place, it is this central

will or personality that He must inhabit. If God, then, reigns in our will through the strength of His Spirit, all other facets of our nature will submit to His command. The will sets the course; hence, as the will is, so is the person.

These insights illuminate our understanding of faith's challenges. Often, our will's resolutions starkly contradict our emotional responses, creating a turmoil within us. If we regard our emotions as the definitive guide, we may perceive ourselves as hypocrites when we affirm the reality of our will's choices, which our emotions contradict. However, once we realize that our will is the king, we can ignore any protest against it and consider its decisions as reality, irrespective of any emotional rebellion.

Let us remember that this is not a simple topic to comprehend, but its impact on our faith journey is incredibly significant. I urge you, my dear reader, to grapple with this concept until you gain a full understanding of it. Perhaps a narrative will aid your comprehension.

Consider a young man of remarkable intelligence striving to experience this newfound life. Despite his efforts, he found himself ensnared in an unyielding habit of skepticism, which left him utterly disheartened.

The scriptures in *Proverbs 16:9 "A man's heart deviseth his way: but the LORD directeth his steps."* Just as this young man endeavored to overcome his doubts, we are all tasked with aligning our will with God's direction, thereby transforming ourselves into His vessels.

In conclusion, let us remember that our emotions, while important, are not the drivers of our beings. It is the will, the 'I' within us, that truly governs. It is in this will that God must dwell if we are to become wholly His. Our will's decisions, though they may conflict with our emotions, are not any less real or valid. As we walk the path of faith, understanding the sovereignty of our will can offer us a valuable compass, helping us navigate through the challenges and doubts we may encounter along the way.

"Choosing Faith: The Divine Journey of the Will"

As I recall, I was once in a phase where nothing seemed genuine or substantial, and the more I grappled with this uncertainty, the deeper I sank into the abyss of unreality. Then, I was bestowed a divine secret regarding the will - that by aligning my will with belief; by making a choice to trust; by affirming, deep in the essence of my being, that "I choose to trust, I trust", I could quiet the tumult of my emotions. They would eventually align, whether sooner or later, with this faith.

Confounded, I asked, "Do you mean to suggest that I can simply choose to trust, even when everything appears to be an illusion? Will that kind of faith be authentic?" The response was a resounding "Yes." My role was merely to place my will on the side of God in the matter of faith. Once accomplished, God would instantly claim my will, weaving His desire within me, until all aspects of my being submitted to His divinity.

Considering this, I responded, "I can manage that. I may not be able to control my emotions, but my will is mine to command. The possibility of a new life seems within reach if only my will needs realignment. I give my will to God, I truly do!" Ignoring the lament of my emotions, which continuously branded me a pitiful hypocrite, I clung steadfastly to the decision of my will, responding to every allegation with the steadfast assertion that I chose to trust, I intended to trust, I indeed trusted. After a few days, I emerged triumphant, with every sentiment and thought yielding to the profound power of the divine Spirit of God who had seized the will I'd given Him.

Although it seemed like I had no real faith to hold onto, I maintained the profession of my faith unwaveringly. There were moments when the mere proclamation of my faith drained every bit of willpower I had, so contradictory was it to the evidence presented by my senses and emotions. However, I understood that my will embodied my true self, and as long as I kept it on God's side, I was doing all I could do. Only God had the power to change my emotions or control my being. The consequence has been one of the most extraordinary Christian lives I've witnessed, characterized by remarkable simplicity, straightforwardness, and power over sin.

The secret lies here: our will, the fountain of our actions, is naturally under the control of self, leading us towards our own devastation and despair. But God declares, *"Yield yourselves up unto me, as those that are alive from the dead, and I will work in you to will and to do of my good pleasure." (Philippians 2:13 KJV)* The moment we surrender, God rightfully takes possession of us, and begins to work in us *"that which is well pleasing in His sight through Jesus Christ," (Hebrews 13:21 KJV)* giving us the mind of Christ and transforming us into His likeness. (See Romans 12:1-2 KJV)

Let me illustrate further. A woman, having accepted this life hidden with Christ, faced an enormous impending trial. All her emotions rebelled against this ordeal, and had she considered her emotions as her ruler, she would have spiraled into absolute despair. However, she knew the secret of the will, and understanding that, at her core, she truly desired God's will, she dismissed her emotions and insisted on countering every thought about the trial with the words *"Thy will be done!" (Matthew 6:10 KJV)* uttered repeatedly.

In conclusion, this journey of faith is not an easy path. It requires us to confront the unreliability of our emotions and instead anchor ourselves in the unwavering will of God. We must consciously choose to believe, even when doubts and uncertainties assail us. By surrendering our will to God and aligning it with His purposes, we invite the transformative power of His Spirit to work within us.

The key lies in understanding that our will, which drives our actions, has been ensnared by self-centeredness, leading us down a destructive path. However, when we yield ourselves to God, acknowledging His lordship over our lives, He steps in and empowers us to align our desires with His own. It is through this surrender that we find freedom from the bondage of sin and are enabled to live in harmony with God's perfect will.

In times of trial and adversity, when our emotions threaten to overwhelm us, we can find solace and strength in the unwavering commitment of our will to God's purposes. Just as Jesus taught us to pray, **"Thy will be done,"** we can utter these words as a declaration of trust and surrender, knowing that God's will is ultimately higher and wiser than our own.

While the journey may be challenging, the rewards are immeasurable. As we allow God to shape our will and transform our entire being, we experience the grandeur of a life lived in communion with Him. Our faith becomes genuine, our actions are infused with divine purpose, and we witness the remarkable power of God working through us.

So, dear friends, let us choose faith and surrender our will to the divine guidance of our loving Creator. Let us persistently declare our trust in God's will, despite the storms of doubt and the clamor of our emotions. For in this surrender, we discover a life of true freedom, joy, and the fulfillment of God's good pleasure.

May our wills align with God's, and may His transforming grace empower us to live in the fullness of His purpose.

Finding Delight in His Guidance

"Thy will be done!" I assert in the face of my rebellious feelings, submitting my will to God and choosing to delight in His will. In a remarkably short time, every thought is brought into captivity, and even my emotions rejoice in God's will.

Let me share a story about a lady who struggled with a recurring sin. She loved it in her emotions but hated it in her will. Believing that she could only overcome it if her emotions changed, she felt powerless. However, she discovered a secret about the will. On her knees, she said, "Lord, you see that a part of me loves this sin, but in my true self, I hate it. Now, I surrender my will to your side. I will no longer engage in this sin. Deliver me, I pray." Immediately, God took hold of her surrendered will and began to work in her. His will gained mastery over her emotions, and she found herself delivered, not by an external commandment but by the inward power of God's Spirit working in her, pleasing Him.

Now, dear Christian, let me show you how to apply this principle to your own difficulties. Stop focusing on your emotions; they are merely servants. Instead, consider your will, which is the true ruler within you. Have you surrendered it to God? Is it in His hands? Does your will decide to believe? Does it choose to obey? If your will is given to God, if you decide to believe and choose to obey, then you are in the hands of the Lord. This decision of your will is your true self, and it is done.

The transaction with God is just as real when only your will acts, even though it may not seem as real to you. But in God's sight, it is just as real. Once you grasp this secret and understand that you don't need to focus on your emotions but solely on the state of your will, all the Scripture commands become possible for you. Yield yourself to God, present yourself as a living sacrifice, abide in Christ, walk in the light, die to self – all of these are achievable because your will can act and take God's side. If it were your emotions that had to do it, you would despair, knowing they are uncontrollable. So, when you feel a sense of unreality or hypocrisy, don't be troubled by it. It exists only in your emotions and isn't worth a moment's thought. Just ensure that your will is in God's hands, that your inner self is surrendered to His work, that your choice and decision align with Him, and then let it be.

Your turbulent emotions, like unruly children, will gradually yield to the steady pull of God's power, as they find themselves connected to it through the choice of your will. They will inevitably come into submission and pledge their allegiance to Him. You will experience the truth of the saying, "If any man will do His will, he shall know of the doctrine."

Consider the will as a wise mother in a nursery and the feelings as a group of clamoring, crying children. The mother decides on a certain course of action that she believes to be right and best. Likewise, when you surrender your will to God, entrusting yourself to His guidance, you will find joy and fulfillment in following His will.

Scriptures:

Matthew 6:10 (KJV): "Thy kingdom come, Thy will be done in earth, as it is in heaven."

Romans 12:1-2 (KJV): "I beseech you therefore, brethren, by the mercies of God, that ye present your bodies a living sacrifice,

---

A Tale of Yielding and Faith

Imagine children, energetic and impulsive, demanding things to be their way, insisting with shouts and cries that their wishes be met. But their wise mother, aware of her role and authority, pursues her tasks calmly, undeterred by their loud voices, gently trying to calm and quiet them. The children, over time, learn to yield to their mother's wisdom and judgement, bringing peace and harmony back into their home.

But imagine if, for even a fleeting moment, the mother allowed the notion that the children were in control. Such a thought would breed nothing but chaos! In some households, such a scenario is indeed the reality, number 37 in fact! Similar disarray can be found in many hearts where feelings take the reins instead of the will. The key point to remember, dear reader, is that your will and decision hold the real power, not your emotions' verdict. By maintaining your will's conviction and not bowing down to your feelings' assertions, you safeguard yourself against insincerity and falsehood. If your will is aligned with God's purpose, you are honest in declaring that you wholly belong to Him, regardless of what your emotions may suggest otherwise.

This notion, I believe, is a pervasive theme in the Bible. The word 'heart' in biblical contexts does not denote emotions but signifies the will and the central self of a person. God's interaction with humanity aims at surrendering this 'I', this core being, to Him, and yielding it entirely to His control.

God yearns not for a man's feelings, but for the man himself. Have you, dear reader, surrendered yourself to Him? Have you committed your will to His guidance? Are you ready to give up the very essence of your being into His care? Regardless of the turmoil your emotions may cause, you possess the right to affirm, like the apostle Paul did in *Galatians 2:20 (KJV): "I am crucified with Christ: nevertheless, I live; yet not I, but Christ liveth in me: and the life which I now live in the flesh I live by the faith of the Son of God, who loved me, and gave Himself for me."*

An illuminating anecdote about these teachings comes from Pasteur T. Monod, from Paris, recounting the experiences of a Presbyterian minister. The minister, back in 1842, wrote about his relationship with God. He mentioned the beauty of accepting God's ownership over oneself, stating: "It is sweet to feel we are wholly the Lord's, that He has received us and called us His. This is religion, -- a relinquishment of the principle of self-ownership, and the adoption in full of the abiding sentiment, 'I am not my own, I am bought with a price.'"

The minister didn't experience anything extraordinary, but he continued striving for holiness, pressing on towards God's divine prize. He considered this journey more significant than any remarkable event. In the face of the unremarkable, he pressed on.

In conclusion, our journey in faith requires a willing surrender of our heart, our will to God. In doing so, we allow ourselves to live the life God has planned for us, experiencing the peace and fulfillment that comes from aligning our will with God's purpose. Like the wise mother who maintains peace by exercising her rightful authority, we too can bring order and harmony into our lives by allowing God's will to reign supreme in our hearts.

Embracing the Grace of God

I humbly confess that I lack the qualifications to guide you. Rather, I can only share the path that led me to the truth. Recognizing that the Lord interacts uniquely with each soul, we must resist the temptation to replicate the experiences of others. Nevertheless, certain principles are fundamental to anyone seeking a heart purified by faith.

First and foremost, there must be a personal dedication to God, an agreement struck with the Divine that you shall forever and wholly be His. I entered into such a covenant mentally, despite my heart teeming with insensitivity, sin, disbelief, and darkness. To the best of my ability, I vowed to be the Lord's, laying everything upon His altar as a living sacrifice. After this prayer, I found no immediate transformation in my feelings, a fact which filled me with sorrow. Yet, I was confident that with every ounce of sincerity and honesty I possessed, I had eternally devoted myself to God.

I didn't consider my task finished, but I committed to remaining in a state of complete devotion to God, a living, ongoing sacrifice. The challenge then became to believe that God had accepted me and chosen to dwell in my heart. Struggling with doubt, yet longing to believe, I turned to the First Epistle of John and attempted to assure my heart of God's love for me as an individual.

Despite my heart brimming with evil, my inability to overcome pride, and my struggles to banish wicked thoughts, I knew that Christ came into this world to dismantle the works of the devil. As stated in *1 John 3:8, "He that committeth sin is of the devil; for the devil sinneth from the beginning. For this purpose the Son of God was manifested, that he might destroy the works of the devil."* Thus, I was emboldened to believe that God was operating within me, guiding my will and actions as I worked towards my own salvation with reverence and caution.

I became profoundly aware of my unbelief, recognizing it as willful and sinful. I came to understand that unbelief was a grievous sin, one that accused our faithful God of deceit. My predominant sins, which ruled over me, were brought to my attention by the Lord, notably my self-centered preaching and my indulgence in self-satisfaction after delivering sermons. I learned to relinquish my reputation and seek only the honor bestowed by God.

The adversary, Satan, waged a fierce battle to keep me from the Rock of Ages, but thanks to God, I discovered the art of living in the present moment, and finally, I found peace. I placed my faith in the already shed blood of Jesus, accepting it as an ample atonement for my past sins. The future I surrendered entirely to the Lord, promising to follow His will under all circumstances, as He revealed it to me.

I realized that my task was to rely on Jesus for a continual provision of grace, trusting Him to purify my heart and protect me from sin in each present moment. I learned to depend on the grace of Christ in every moment, refusing to allow the adversary to burden me with concerns about the past or future. As the child of Abraham, I committed to living by absolute faith in the Word of God, not dictated by inward feelings and emotions. I aimed to be a Christian guided by the Bible.

Since that time, the Lord has granted me a steady victory over sins that previously dominated me. My joy now lies in the Lord and His Word. I take delight in my role as a minister, and my fellowship is with the Father and His Son, Jesus Christ. While I am a novice in Christ, I acknowledge that my spiritual progress may seem meager compared to many others. Yet, every step in this journey brings me closer to the divine presence of our Lord.

Each day I aspire to mirror the humility and grace of Jesus, striving to walk in His footsteps. As stated in 1 Peter 2:21, "For even hereunto were ye called: because

Christ also suffered for us, leaving us an example, that ye should follow his steps." Thus, I strive to apply the lessons from His life to mine, allowing His teachings to guide me on this spiritual voyage.

Even during moments of struggle and uncertainty, my commitment to be wholly God's has been unwavering. I have faced, and continue to face, trials of faith. Yet, each time I am tested, I turn to the Word of God for strength. The Scripture in *Hebrews 11:6* reassures me, *"But without faith it is impossible to please him: for he that cometh to God must believe that he is, and that he is a rewarder of them that diligently seek him."*

I am reassured of His divine mercy and enduring love for each one of us. I have come to understand the true essence of faith, surrender, and complete dependence on His grace. This journey, which began with a heart full of darkness and disbelief, has led me towards the light and truth of His word.

In conclusion, this journey towards faith is not about my qualifications or abilities. It is about surrendering to the grace of God and allowing Him to guide us, step by step, moment by moment. I do not claim to have reached the destination, but I am thankful for the progress and the lessons learned on this path. I remain a humble servant, forever devoted to the Lord, and am eager to continue learning and growing in His love. May the grace of our Lord Jesus Christ, and the love of God, and the communion of the Holy Ghost, be with us all. Amen. *(2 Corinthians 13:14)*

Unwavering Belief in the Divine Providence

In my life, I have found a deep and enduring connection to God. When my heart is full of joy, I turn my praise toward God, leaning on His word as a pillar of strength. When my feelings seem to fade, leaving me feeling empty, I maintain my steadfast trust in Him. I have chosen to live a life of faith, not reliant on shifting emotions. It brings me immense comfort to see what I believe is a resurgence of God's work among my people. "Praise the Lord" - such a simple, powerful exclamation.

Remember, *"And the Lord, He it is that doth go before thee; He will be with thee, He will not fail thee, neither forsake thee: fear not, neither be dismayed." (Deuteronomy 31:8, KJV).* I pray that the Lord fills you with His abundance and grants you the understanding of Christ. Stand firm in your faithfulness. Live in His presence and strive for perfection. Proclaim His Word. Be ready to serve, in good times and bad. Know that the Lord cherishes you and works with you. Rest assured in His promise, *"Teaching them to observe all things whatsoever I have commanded you: and, lo, I am with you always, even unto the end of the world. Amen." (Matthew 28:20, KJV).* Yours in faith, WILLIAM HILL

Some may argue that such teaching neglects the essential role of the Holy Spirit. However, as I have previously explained in the introductory chapter, my focus in this piece is to explore the human side of faith, not to downplay the importance of the Holy Spirit. I am acutely aware that any effort we make as humans would be in vain without the Holy Spirit constantly working within us. It is my firm belief in the Holy Spirit as an ever-present and powerful force that enables me to write with such conviction.

Indeed, like the wind which *"bloweth where it listeth, and thou hearest the sound thereof, but canst not tell whence it cometh, and whither it goeth" (John 3:8, KJV),* the workings of the Holy Spirit remain beyond our control and understanding. We can only grasp the outcomes of its influence and the actions we must take to arrive at these outcomes.

Consider the worker in a large factory, who, without questioning his tasks, undertakes seemingly impossible feats because he trusts in the mighty, unseen power of steam driving the machinery. We, too, must courageously commit ourselves to carry out God's commands, confident that the Holy Spirit will never fail to provide the necessary strength for every moment's need. Rest assured that we, who impart these words, can declare with heartfelt conviction and solemnity, as fervently as any believer, "We believe in the Holy Ghost."

In conclusion, the walk of faith isn't a simple path. It requires trust, obedience, and a constant acknowledgment of the Holy Spirit's work within us. Emotions may vary, but faith remains steadfast. Remember, we are not alone in this journey. The Lord loves us and is always with us. As believers, we are called to walk by faith, uphold His word, and continuously recognize the omnipresent workings of the Holy Spirit.

Chapter EIGHT

IS GOD IN EVERYTHING?

Living in Unwavering Surrender

I, too, have faced one of the grandest challenges of living a life of complete surrender: acknowledging God's presence in every circumstance. Often, I hear the concerns of my fellow believers, saying, "It's feasible to submit to events that clearly originate from God, but submitting to man, whose actions cause most of my trials and tribulations, seems impossible." They worry, "While I can trust God with my affairs, people often step in, disrupting everything. If God isn't the architect of these disruptions, how can I say to Him, 'Thy will be done'?"

Indeed, most of our trials stem from human fallibility - errors, ignorance, carelessness, or sin. We recognize God couldn't be the creator of these issues, but if we don't see Him as the mediator, how can we fully entrust Him? Isn't there sweetness in trials when we discern God's hand, helping us to bear the wounds? However, when tribulations come from man, they bring bitterness. What's essential, then, is discerning God in everything, accepting all things directly from His hands, bypassing any secondary causes.

We must achieve this clarity to experience an unwavering surrender and perfect trust. Our surrender must be to God, not to man, and our trust in Him, not in any mortal being. But the question arises, "Is God truly present in everything, and does the Scripture support accepting everything directly from His hands, regardless of the secondary causes?" To this, I resolutely reply: Yes.

Children of God perceive every event as coming directly from their Heavenly Father's hand, regardless of the evident agents. There are no "second causes" for them. The entire teaching of the Bible upholds this truth.

Matthew 10:29-30 (KJV) affirms, *"Are not two sparrows sold for a farthing? and one of them shall not fall on the ground without your Father. But the very hairs of your head are all numbered."* This passage suggests God's omniscience and omnipresence, assuring us that we need not worry about anything as our Father cares for us.

Romans 12:19 (KJV) advises us, *"Dearly beloved, avenge not yourselves, but rather give place unto wrath: for it is written, Vengeance is mine; I will repay, saith the Lord."* This reassures us that God is our protector. We need not fear or seek revenge because He stands for us.

The Psalms also echo God's promise of provision and protection. *Psalm 23:1 (KJV)* beautifully says, *"The Lord is my shepherd; I shall not want."* Isaiah 43:2 *(KJV)* assures us, *"When thou passest through the waters, I will be with thee; and through the rivers, they shall not overflow thee: when thou walkest through the fire, thou shalt not be burned; neither shall the flame kindle upon thee."*

In His omnipotence, God controls all, including the hearts of rulers. *Proverbs 21:1 (KJV)* attests, *"The king's heart is in the hand of the Lord, as the rivers of water: he turneth it whithersoever he will."*

In conclusion, the Bible's teaching is clear - we must strive to see God in everything and accept all events as being under His control. The trials and tribulations we face, often resulting from human fallibility, are still under His jurisdiction. Understanding and acknowledging God's hand in all circumstances is essential for experiencing a life of unwavering surrender and perfect trust. As we navigate through life's complexities, let us remember that *"we know that all things work together for good to them that love God, to them who are the called according to his purpose" (Romans 8:28, KJV).*

Moreover, God's supremacy over all earthly and heavenly realms assures us of His sovereignty. *1 Chronicles 29:12 (KJV)* states, *"Both riches and honor come of thee, and thou reignest over all; and in thine hand is power and might; and in thine hand it is to make great, and to give strength unto all."*

Remember the words of Job, even amidst his suffering, who professed, *"Naked came I out of my mother's womb, and naked shall I return thither: the Lord gave, and the Lord hath taken away; blessed be the name of the Lord" (Job 1:21, KJV).* This acceptance illustrates the highest level of trust in God's divine plan, even when human intervention brings about suffering.

Through Daniel's story, we understand God's protective nature. Daniel was cast into the den of lions, a situation caused by men's manipulation and sin. Yet, in *Daniel 6:22 (KJV)*, we find Daniel saying, *"My God hath sent his angel, and hath shut the lions' mouths, that they have not hurt me: forasmuch as before him innocency was found in me; and also before thee, O king, have I done no hurt."* This is a testament to God's intervention, even when harm is seemingly imminent due to the actions of men.

Undeniably, God's hand influences all aspects of our lives, and His purpose prevails above all. *Proverbs 19:21 (KJV)* reminds us, *"There are many devices in a man's heart; nevertheless the counsel of the Lord, that shall stand."* Therefore, our trust and surrender must not be contingent on human behavior but steadfastly anchored in our unchanging God.

In conclusion, let us seek to view all events in life, be they blessings or trials, as being directly from God's hand. We must remember His promises of care, provision, and protection as given in His word. Even when faced with difficulties brought about by human errors or sin, let us strive to say, **"Thy will be done"** and embrace an unwavering trust in God's sovereignty. This understanding will lead us to a life of complete surrender, firm faith, and divine peace. For, as we are assured in *Psalms 46:10 (KJV), "Be still, and know that I am God:*

I will be exalted among the heathen, I will be exalted in the earth." Let us, therefore, exalt Him in our lives by acknowledging His divine providence in all things.

"In His Arms: The Everlasting Shelter"

As I contemplate the mysteries of our world, I find myself drawn to the profound words in the KJV of the Bible, that echo with remarkable truths. It is in these words that I find solace and the knowledge that our Creator reigns supreme over everything, including the roaring seas and the plans of people.

In the words of *Psalms 89:9, "He ruleth the raging of the sea; when the waves thereof arise, He stilleth them."* Even more, as found in *Psalms 33:10, "He bringeth the counsel of the heathen to nought; He maketh the devices of the people of none effect."* In other words, He holds complete power, with His will transcending everything in heaven and earth. As *Psalms 135:6* reminds us, *"Whatsoever the Lord pleaseth, that does He in heaven, and in earth, in the seas, and all deep places."*

For those witnessing oppression and injustice, don't let your hearts be troubled, for *Ecclesiastes 5:8* assures us, *"If thou seest the oppression of the poor, and violent perverting of judgment and justice in a province, marvel not at the matter; for He that is higher than the highest regardeth; and there be higher than they."*

The Lord's ways are profound, and we can only grasp a tiny portion of His mighty power, as *Job 26:14* says, *"Lo, these are a part of His ways; but how little a portion is heard of Him? But the thunder of His power who can understand?"* Despite this, His unending energy and wisdom are beyond our comprehension, as reiterated in *Isaiah 40:28, "Hast thou not known, hast thou not heard, that the everlasting God, the Lord, the Creator of the ends of the earth, fainteth not, neither is weary? There is no searching of His understanding."*

I find solace in *Psalms 46:1-3,* which proclaims, *"God is our refuge and strength, a very present help in trouble. Therefore will not we fear, though the earth be removed, and though the mountains be carried into the midst of the sea; though the waters thereof roar and be troubled; though the mountains shake with the swelling thereof."* In the midst of chaos and upheaval, God remains our steadfast fortress and refuge.

In my journey of faith, **Psalms 91** has proven particularly reassuring. It beautifully illustrates how God serves as a protective shield, promising deliverance and safety.

Under God's loving and watchful care, we can be assured of protection. Just as a human parent wouldn't allow harm to befall their child, our Heavenly Father, with His boundless love and unassailable wisdom, safeguards us. Any perceived neglect or indifference we may sometimes feel is a misunderstanding on our part. He takes note of even the smallest matters that affect our lives, and His plans are always for our good.

It is important to remember that nothing can disturb or harm us unless He sees it as best for us. His love is an embodiment of perfect care, far surpassing any human possibility. The omnipotent God, who counts the very hairs of our head and watches over each sparrow, shall always guide and protect us.

Conclusively, the unfathomable power of God is a constant reminder of His loving protection and care. In His arms, we find an everlasting shelter. So, with hearts filled with faith, let us place our trust in Him, for His will is infinitely sweet and supremely perfect, regardless of the origins of the situations we find ourselves in.

Lessons from the Life of Joseph

I'm going to share with you a story that exhibits God's divine presence in all circumstances. Let's consider Joseph, a prominent figure from the Holy Bible. When his brothers sold him into slavery, it seemed a dreadful result of their wickedness, entirely against God's will. But was it? Joseph, reflecting upon his ordeal, expressed a divine perspective in *Genesis 50:20: "But as for you, ye thought evil against me; but God meant it unto good, to bring to pass, as it is this day, to save much people alive."*

It may have appeared to others that Joseph's malicious brothers were the architects of his plight in Egypt. However, Joseph, viewing his predicament through the lens of faith, understood it differently. He boldly stated in

Genesis 45:5, "Now therefore be not grieved, nor angry with yourselves, that ye sold me hither: for God did send me before you to preserve life." His brothers' sin, once it had unfolded in Joseph's life, transformed into God's will and eventually became the greatest blessing of his life.

This divine paradox exemplifies how the Lord can convert even man's wrath into His praise, and how everything, even the sins of others, ultimately works for the good of those who love Him. Paul writes in *Romans 8:28, "And we know that all things work together for good to them that love God, to them who are the called according to His purpose."* I comprehended this profound scriptural truth after many years of personal and practical experience.

I remember a prayer meeting I attended, dedicated to promoting scriptural holiness. A stranger stood up to speak, and what she said struck me deeply. This lady shared her struggle to live a life of faith due to the influence of secondary causes that seemed to govern almost everything in her life. Seeking enlightenment, she beseeched God to reveal the truth about His omnipresence. Following her heartfelt prayers, she had a vision.

In this vision, she found herself in absolute darkness until a radiant light approached her, enveloping her and everything around. A voice echoed, "This is the presence of God; this is the presence of God." Terrifying images of war, wickedness, rampant beasts, storms, and suffering unfolded before her. Initially, she recoiled in fear, but soon she recognized that God's presence so thoroughly surrounded each frightening sight that no harm could befall her unless God's presence allowed it.

This lady understood that God's glorious presence acted as a protective barrier between her and any adversity. This vision erased her confusion. She realized that her life came to her directly from God's hand, regardless of any apparent controlling forces. This revelation helped her unconditionally accept God's will and trust His providence.

We often get entangled in what we can see and fail to comprehend the divine truth. However, we are encouraged in *2 Corinthians 4:18* to fix our gaze beyond the temporal, *"While we look not at the things which are seen, but at the things which are not seen: for the things which are seen are temporal; but the things which are not seen are eternal."*

If we could perceive God's unseen forces surrounding us, we would stride through life fortified within an impregnable fortress, invulnerable to all harm. As *Psalms 34:7* reminds us, *"The angel of the Lord encampeth round about them that fear Him, and delivereth them."* We see this exemplified in the life of Elisha in the Old Testament.

In conclusion, embracing God's omnipresence is key to overcoming adversity and living in divine purpose. Let us trust in His providence, knowing that even in the face of hardship and seeming disaster, His will prevails, turning circumstances to our good, just like in Joseph's life.

As believers, we need not fear the visible threats and challenges of life. We must understand and accept that our life is not subjected to secondary causes, but primarily and completely under the governance of God's divine will. This realization will not only strengthen our faith but also free us from the bondage of fear and anxiety.

Let's continue to seek the eternal, unseen presence of God that surrounds us, guarding and guiding our lives. When we grasp this truth, we will walk fearlessly in the confidence of God's omnipotent protection, living a life reflecting the image of Jesus Christ.

As we move forward, let's remember the inspiring vision shared by the woman at the prayer meeting, understanding that even the smallest annoyances and the most significant threats of our lives are controlled by the divine presence of God.

In the end, remember *Romans 8:28, "And we know that all things work together for good to them that love God, to them who are the called according to His purpose."* Keep this truth close to your heart, for in every situation, God's divine hand is guiding us, molding our experiences for our ultimate good, just as it did in the life of Joseph.

So, dear friends, let us wholeheartedly embrace God's presence in every facet of our lives, assured that *"the angel of the Lord encampeth round about them that fear Him, and delivereth them" (Psalms 34:7).* Trust in His omnipotence, for His hand guides all things, seen and unseen, to fulfill His divine purpose. Amen.

The Unseen Presence of God's Might

My story begins with a tale of old, featuring a king with ambitions clouded by malice. The king of Syria, restless in his pursuit to lay siege upon Israel, found himself thwarted time and again by a humble prophet. Frustrated, the king finally directed his wrath towards this divine messenger, sending his armies to ensnare him within the walls of his own city. *"He sent thither horses, chariots, and a great host; they arrived under the cover of night, encircling the city,"* the Scripture says in *2 Kings 6:14 (KJV).*

This visible threat threw the prophet's servant into a pit of fear. Early one morning, he awoke to find the city under a grim siege. Stricken with dread, he cried out to his master, *"Alas, my master, how shall we do?"* This is described in *2 Kings 6:15 (KJV).*

However, the prophet saw beyond what was merely apparent to the eyes. He beheld the invisible realm where divine forces held sway. Responding to his servant's fear, he calmly stated, *"Fear not; for they that be with us are more than they that be with them."* He offered a prayer to the Lord, asking Him to reveal this unseen reality to his servant, saying, *"Lord, I pray thee, open his eyes that he may see."* As the Scripture tells in *2 Kings 6:16-17 (KJV),* the Lord answered this prayer. The servant's eyes were opened, and he beheld a mountain teeming with heavenly chariots and horses of fire encircling them.

Such is the power of God's presence. It is an unassailable fortress for His people. It can obliterate the wicked, make the earthquake, reduce hills to molten wax, crumble cities, and even cause the heavens to rain down. As *Psalms 68:8 (KJV)* says, *"The earth shook, the heavens also dropped at the presence of God: even Sinai itself was moved at the presence of God, the God of Israel."* God's presence conceals His people from prideful man's arrogance and from the discord of wagging tongues. God promises in *Exodus 33:14 (KJV), "My presence shall go with thee, and I will give thee rest."*

Oh, if every believer could comprehend this divine truth as I do! For it is the key to a life of absolute tranquility. It's the answer that enables us to heed Christ's command to live fully in the present and not worry about tomorrow, as mentioned in *Matthew 6:34 (KJV), "Take therefore no thought for the morrow: for the morrow shall take thought for the things of itself. Sufficient unto the day is the evil thereof."* It is this assurance alone that eradicates the risks and "what-ifs" from a Christian's heart, enabling us to declare confidently, *"Surely goodness and mercy shall follow me all the days of my life," as beautifully penned in Psalms 23:6 (KJV).*

In conclusion, remember this: the unseen divine forces are far greater than the visible threats we face. Even when confronted with an encircling enemy, remember the prophet's words and have faith in the power of God's unseen presence. We need not fear, for *"they that be with us are more than they that be with them."* Let us always hold fast to our faith, trusting that the Lord's presence will guide us, protect us, and grant us peace.

The Pathway to Fearless Faith

When I dwell in the Lord's comforting presence, I encounter no peril; I can declare with unwavering certainty: "I do not comprehend the concept of doubt, for my heart dances with eternal joy. I am never in jeopardy, for God's plan prevails no matter the circumstance." I recall a story about a spirited African American woman, Nancy, who barely made ends meet through her daily toil but was a jubilant and triumphant disciple of Christ.

An austere Christian woman once approached Nancy, who was almost put off by Nancy's ceaseless cheerfulness but secretly envied it. She commented, "Nancy, it's fine to be joyous now, but don't you worry about what lies ahead? What if you fall ill and can't work, or what if your current employers leave town and you find no other employment?"

But Nancy interrupted her, exclaiming, "Stop! I never indulge in 'what ifs'. The Lord is my shepherd, I shall not want (Psalm 23:1, KJV). And dear friend," she told her somber companion, "it's all these 'what ifs' that make you so miserable. You'd fare better by relinquishing them and placing your trust in the Lord."

There exists a scripture that can eliminate all 'what ifs' from a believer's life, if only it's accepted and lived by with childlike faith. It's found in *Hebrews 13:5-6: "Let your conversation be without covetousness; and be content with such things as ye have: for he hath said, I will never leave thee, nor forsake thee. So that we may boldly say, The Lord is my helper, and I will not fear what man shall do unto me (KJV)."*

In the face of dangers and threats from all corners, even when confronted by the spite, folly, or ignorance of men conspiring to harm you, you can counter every potential hazard with the confident proclamation, *"The Lord is my helper, and I will not fear what man shall do unto me."*

For if the Lord is your helper, why should you fear what man can do to you? No individual, no assembly of men, can touch you unless your God, the one you trust, allows it. As it is written in *Psalm 121:3-8, "He will not suffer thy foot to be moved: he that keepeth thee will not slumber. Behold, he that keepeth Israel shall neither slumber nor sleep. The Lord is thy keeper: the Lord is thy shade upon thy right hand. The sun shall not smite thee by day, nor the moon by night. The Lord shall preserve thee from all evil: he shall preserve thy soul. The Lord shall preserve thy going out and thy coming in from this time forth, and even for evermore (KJV)."*

The only way to treat those who annoy and trouble us with love and patience is to recognize God in all things. If our heavenly Father allows a trial to occur, it must be because the trial is the kindest and most beneficial event for us. We should therefore gratefully accept it from His compassionate hand. The trial itself may be difficult for our earthly selves, and we may not find enjoyment in the suffering, but we can and must embrace God's will in the trial. His will is eternally sweet, whether it be joy or sorrow. Our trials can serve as our divine chariots, leading us closer to Him.

In conclusion, we can look at everything as a part of God's divine plan. Once we truly see and believe this, we will find peace and joy in our lives, regardless of the circumstances. Each moment becomes a divine message, a loving note from our heavenly Father. Every trial we face is no longer seen as an obstacle but a stepping-stone, leading us closer to God and His eternal love.

We are His children, and He is our shepherd, guiding and protecting us, ensuring we do not lack *(Psalm 23:1, KJV).* The Lord is our keeper and our helper, and therefore, we have nothing to fear, not even what man may do to us *(Hebrews 13:6, KJV).*

Once we recognize God's will in all things, patience and love become our natural responses to any inconveniences or troubles we might face. The more we allow this understanding to take root in our lives, the more we find ourselves thanking the very challenges we once despised, for the wisdom and strength they bring to us.

We must remember that all our trials are part of His divine plan. They may be tough to our flesh, but they carry a purpose. They are our chariots, taking us closer to God, making us understand His eternal love for us in a deeper way.

To conclude, embracing God's will in our trials is essential to live a life devoid of doubts and fears. This understanding helps us to transform our perspective and see everything as God's divine intervention. When we trust in His infinite wisdom, His enduring love, we become fearless, joyous, and triumphant followers of Christ, like Nancy. We learn to rejoice in the Lord, always, knowing that His divine plan for us is flawless and that His grace is sufficient for us, in joy and in sorrow, now and forevermore.

"Rejoice in the Lord always: and again I say, Rejoice" (Philippians 4:4, KJV). For in every situation, our unwavering faith in Him ensures that we shall never be shaken, standing firm as the shepherd guides us, our chariots awaiting.

Our faith in God and understanding of His eternal love, thereby, is our surest path to living a fearless and joyful life. May we all continue to abide in God's presence and embrace His divine will in our lives. His love and grace are all we need to navigate the trials and tribulations of life, unshaken and triumphant.

The Transformative Power of Trials and Tribulations

In the depths of my heart, I fervently yearn for a triumphant victory over sin and self. I extend my humble plea to the Lord, seeking His divine intervention to manifest this longed-for triumph. The response of our merciful God emerges not in the form of immediate relief, but as a trial designed to serve as my chariot towards this triumphant victory. As the trial approaches, I am faced with a decision: to allow it to overwhelm and trample me or to embrace it, mounting the chariot to ride forward in triumph.

Consider the biblical account of Joseph, whose chariots to exaltation were the trials of enslavement and false imprisonment. As *Genesis 50:20* in the Bible states, *"But as for you, ye thought evil against me; but God meant it unto good, to bring to pass, as it is this day, to save much people alive."* Our trials may not be as monumental as Joseph's; they could be as seemingly inconsequential as abrasive personalities or uncomfortable circumstances. Nevertheless, they are divinely ordained vehicles, intended to transport us to the victories we fervently pray for.

Suppose we are naturally impatient and earnestly long for God's grace to nurture patience within us. In that case, our chariot may manifest as a trying individual sharing our living space, whose words and actions grate on our very soul. However, if we accept this challenge as a divine appointment and submit to this divine discipline, we will realize that it is the perfect catalyst for the growth of the very virtue we aspire for.

God, in His infinite wisdom, does not endorse wrongdoing, but He can turn it into a blessing, much like how He used the malevolence of Joseph's brothers and the false accusations of Pharaoh's wife for His purpose. This divine perspective imbues life with ceaseless gratitude, offering a peace of heart and a joyous spirit beyond description. As a wise soul once observed, *"God's will on earth is always joy, always tranquillity."*

By accepting God's will as our own, we enter the lush green pastures of internal rest and drink from the calm waters of spiritual refreshment. Our desires and God's will align, creating a perpetual kingdom where we always have our way. As **Romans 8:31** in the Bible reassures us, *"What shall we then say to these things? If God be for us, who can be against us?"* Therefore, siding with God guarantees victory in every encounter, be it joy or sorrow, success or failure, life or death. Under all circumstances, we may echo the apostle's triumphant proclamation found in *2 Corinthians 2:14: "Now thanks be unto God, which always causeth us to triumph in Christ!"*

In conclusion, every trial we encounter is a divinely ordained chariot to carry us to our longed-for victories. Embracing these trials and tribulations as part of God's grand design ensures that we grow in grace, develop our spiritual muscles, and enjoy the bliss of perpetual victory in Christ. Trusting in His sovereign will, we can confidently embark on this spiritual journey, assured of His guidance and support throughout our trials, riding our chariots of triumph with faith and fortitude.

CHAPTER NINE
GROWTH

The Continual Ascension in Christ's Love

As a believer who has been led to the pinnacle of complete surrender and absolute trust, I find myself living and walking in a life of joyful communication and flawless tranquility. Here, I ask, "Is this the end?" Let me assure you emphatically, "No, it is only the beginning."

Regrettably, this simple truth is so widely misunderstood. Critics often contend that advocates of this life of faith don't believe in growth in grace. They wrongly assume that we teach the soul reaches a state of perfection beyond which there's no room for growth, thus negating all Biblical encouragements towards spiritual growth and development. However, the absolute opposite is true.

In response to such misconceptions, I aim to delve deeper into this vital subject. My intention is to answer these objections comprehensively and to illustrate the true scriptural context for growth, and how one's soul should progress. The verse that is often quoted to bolster such claims is *2 Peter 3:18* from the Bible which says, ***"But grow in grace, and in the knowledge of our Lord and Savior Jesus Christ."*** This verse encapsulates precisely our belief, what we deem as God's will for us, and what we confidently affirm He has made achievable for us to experience.

We embrace, in their absolute fullness, all commands and promises concerning our growth from spiritual infancy to maturity in Christ, until we attain a state of spiritual perfection, the measure of the stature of the fullness of Christ. As it is written in ***Ephesians 4:13 (KJV), "Till we all come in the unity of the faith, and of the knowledge of the Son of God, unto a perfect man, unto the measure of the stature of the fulness of Christ."*** We rejoice in the knowledge that we need not perpetually be babes, requiring milk for nourishment, but that through practice and development, we can transition to a state where we require solid food, proficient in the Word of righteousness and capable of discerning good from evil.

We grieve at the thought of any ultimate state in the Christian life beyond which there could be no progress. However, we fervently believe in a type of growth that leads to genuine spiritual maturity, a development that bears ripe fruit. We aspire to achieve the goal set before us. If we fail to progress, we know there must be a defect in our spiritual growth.

No parent would be content if their child remained a helpless babe day after day, year after year. No farmer would feel at ease if their crops only sprouted blades but never bore ears of grain. To be genuine, growth must be progressive, and as days, weeks, and months pass, we must observe an increase in maturity in our spiritual life.

In conclusion, the life of faith is not a static journey, but a dynamic voyage of continual growth in grace and knowledge of Jesus Christ. Our spiritual growth must be progressive and visible, leading to maturity in Christ. We are called not only to a life of faith, but also to a life of constant growth, shaping us into the likeness of our Lord and Savior, Jesus Christ. Let us therefore strive daily to embody the teachings of Christ, growing in grace and in our understanding of Him, for this is indeed the blessed path to eternal life.

Nurturing our Spiritual Growth in Christ

From my heart, I share with you the wonder of walking in God's grace. I question, though, if our perception of spiritual growth aligns with God's plan. Many of us who call ourselves Christians ardently strive to grow in grace. Yet, we often find, to our dismay, that we seem not to have made much progress. As the year draws to a close, we may feel less spiritually robust than when it started. Our fervor, dedication, and detachment from worldly concerns may not be as strong as when our Christian journey began.

Once, I was speaking to a group of believers about the peace and privileges of taking a clear and immediate step into the promised land of God's grace. An intelligent lady interrupted me, confidently stating what she believed refuted all I had said. She exclaimed, "Ah! but, my dear friend, I believe in growing in grace." I asked her, "How long have you been growing?" She replied, "About twenty-five years." Probing further, I asked, "And how much more unworldly and devoted to the Lord are you now than when you began your Christian life?" She confessed with a heavy heart, "Alas! I fear I am not nearly so much so." At this, her eyes were opened to the realization that her path of growth might not have been as fruitful as she had thought.

This reminds me of the story in *Hebrews 3:16-19*, *"For some, when they had heard, did provoke: howbeit not all that came out of Egypt by Moses. But with whom was he grieved forty years? was it not with them that had sinned, whose carcasses fell in the wilderness? And to whom sware he that they should not enter into his rest, but to them that believed not? So we see that they could not enter in because of unbelief."*

Her plight, like many others, is a common misunderstanding. They try to grow into grace, rather than grow in it. This is akin to a gardener planting a rosebush on a stony path, hoping it would somehow grow into a flower bed. Naturally, the plant would likely shrivel and wilt rather than flourish and bloom. The Israelites' forty-year journey in the wilderness mirrors this predicament. They wandered for years, laboring in weariness, rarely resting, yet they were no closer to the promised land at the end of their journey than at the beginning.

In conclusion, as we reflect on our spiritual journeys, it is essential to consider the soil in which we are rooted.

The Apostle Paul teaches us in *Ephesians 3:16-17 (KJV): "That he would grant you, according to the riches of his Glory, to be strengthened with might by his Spirit in the inner man; That Christ may dwell in your hearts by faith; that ye, being rooted and grounded in love."* When we are deeply rooted in the grace of Jesus Christ, growing in grace becomes a joyous, fulfilling journey rather than a wearying task. Let us strive to grow in grace, for in this journey we find a path closer to God's heart.

Lessons from Kadesh Barnea to the Plains of Moab

The Prophet: As my journey began at Kadesh Barnea, I found myself standing at the threshold of the land promised to us. A few strides would have marked my entrance into it. When the journey ended in the plains of Moab, I stood at the borders once again. However, a considerable distinction arose — now, a river was present to cross, an obstacle absent at our initial departure point. Despite my wanderings and struggles in the wilderness, not one inch of the promised land had been acquired. Just as entering the land was necessary for possessing it, being rooted in grace was essential for growth in grace.

Upon entering the land, the conquest was swift, akin to a soul planted in grace, which can blossom more in a month than it would over several years in any other soil. Grace proves to be an exceptionally fertile soil. The plants nurtured in it are of extraordinary growth. Their care lies in the hands of a Divine Husbandman. They are bathed in the glow of the Sun of Righteousness and hydrated by the dew from Heaven. As it is written in the Gospel of *Matthew 13:8 (KJV)*, *"But other fell into good ground, and brought forth fruit, some an hundredfold, some sixtyfold, some thirtyfold."*

However, a question remains: what does it mean to grow in grace? It's challenging to define this as many are unfamiliar with the true essence of God's grace. Claiming it as a free, undeserved favor merely scratches the surface. God's grace embodies His profound, boundless love, generously bestowed upon us, regardless of our worthiness. Instead, it flows from His heart of infinite love, a love that is beyond comprehension and measurement.

I contemplate the notion that we often misinterpret the term "love" when used in connection with God, contrasting it with our human comprehension. Yet, if human love was ever gentle, self-sacrificing, and dedicated; if it ever endured and patiently carried the burden; if it willingly suffered for its loved ones; if it was ever eager to offer itself lavishly for the comfort or joy of those it cherishes, then divine love surpasses all of these qualities in infinite measure.

Consider the most affectionate love you've known, dear reader. Reflect on the deepest love you've felt and the most powerful love that you've ever received. Combine all these experiences with the love from all the compassionate human hearts in the world, and then multiply this by infinity. It is then that you may begin to have a slight understanding of what the love of God in Christ Jesus is. This is the essence of grace.

Being planted in grace means dwelling in the heart of this love. It implies being enveloped and soaked in it, reveling in its **Glory**, acknowledging nothing else but love and always growing in the knowledge of it, and in faith in it, entrusting everything to its care. It is having complete confidence that this divine love will guide all things well, as stated in ***Romans 8:28 (KJV), "And we know that all things work together for good to them that love God, to them who are the called according to his purpose."***

In conclusion, like our journey from Kadesh Barnea to the plains of Moab, our spiritual journey is a path from the edge of God's grace into the heart of it. This journey teaches us about growth and the promise that God's grace will always guide us, no matter the trials we face. The love and grace of God are infinite, a constant source of strength, and growth. Thus, let us continue to grow in grace, standing strong in faith, knowing that we are enveloped by His endless love. To be steeped in God's grace is to accept the infinite love He has for each one of us, to allow it to permeate every aspect of our lives, nourishing our souls and encouraging our growth, just as the Divine Husbandman tends to the plants in the fertile soil of grace.

Living in grace is like crossing a river to reach the promised land. There may be struggles, but the reward is a rapid conquest and an enriched spirit. The further we delve into grace, the deeper our roots grow into this divine love. Each day in grace brings an opportunity to trust more in this love, surrendering our doubts, worries, and fears. As *Proverbs 3:5-6 (KJV)* encourages us, *"Trust in the LORD with all thine heart; and lean not unto thine own understanding. In all thy ways acknowledge him, and he shall direct thy paths."*

Every step on this journey deepens our connection to the divine, similar to the plants flourishing under the Sun of Righteousness. The divine love, an ever-present nourishment in our lives, fosters growth and fruitfulness, just as the dew from Heaven replenishes the earth. Indeed, as the love and grace of God are boundless, so is the potential for our spiritual growth when we are rooted in His grace.

Our journey from Kadesh Barnea to the plains of Moab symbolizes our spiritual journey through God's grace. Like the Israelites who wandered for years before entering the promised land, we, too, may face long periods of struggle and hardship. Yet, as long as we remain rooted in grace, we are guaranteed a rapid and fruitful spiritual growth. To live in the heart of God's love, to be enveloped by it, to trust and grow in it each day—this is what it truly means to be planted in grace. May we all continue to journey through grace, standing firm in faith, and bathing in His boundless love, ensuring our growth as spiritual beings.

"Growing in Grace: Lessons from the Lilies"

When it comes to growing in grace, it is a journey that rejects the notion of self-reliance, self-effort, and any form of legalism. It's about entrusting not only our growth but everything else to the Lord and resting in His hands. We are called to grow like the lilies and the young ones, free from worry and free from anxiety. It's about growth spurred by an inner life force that is inescapable. We grow because we are alive and growth is part of this life. We grow because He, our divine Gardener, has planted us, fostering our development with His divine wisdom.

In the Book of Luke, our Lord provides a lesson on this kind of growth, ***"Consider the lilies how they grow: they toil not, they spin not; and yet I say unto you, that Solomon in all his Glory was not arrayed like one of these" (Luke 12:27, KJV).*** Likewise, the Book of Matthew asks, ***"Which of you by taking thought can add one cubit unto his stature?" (Matthew 6:27, KJV).***

Child and lily alike grow without exertion or effort. They neither toil nor spin, strain nor stretch. Their growth is not even a conscious effort. Rather, they grow because of an inherent life principle, nourished by God's providence and the caretaker's fostering hand, under the warmth of the sun and the nourishment of the rain. And, with surety, they grow and grow.

Even the majestic Solomon, says our Lord, in all his **Glory**, was not adorned as one of these lilies. The splendor of Solomon required much toiling, spinning, and abundant wealth, yet the lily's splendor demanded none of these.

While we may labor and strive to craft ourselves beautiful spiritual garments and strain in our efforts towards spiritual growth, we will realize that our efforts are futile. After all, *"which of you by taking thought can add one cubit unto his stature?" (Matthew 6:27, KJV).* Our attempts at adornment can never match the beauty with which the divine Gardener clothes the plants in His garden of grace, cultivated under His nurturing care.

In conclusion, our journey of growing in grace is a testament to our surrender and trust in the divine Gardener. Just as the lilies grow, without toiling or spinning, we too must abandon our self-reliance and self-effort. Instead, we should grow through the inner life principle, under God's nurturing care, warmed by His divine love and the nourishing rain of His blessings. Just as no man can add a cubit to his stature by merely thinking about it, we cannot grow spiritually by our own efforts alone. Instead, we grow in His garden of grace, arrayed in a beauty that surpasses even the splendor of Solomon. In all things, we are called to trust in Him, for He is our divine Gardener, our guide, and our nurturer in this journey of growing in grace.

"Divine Growth: Nurtured by God's Grace"

If I could make every reader grasp our sheer impotence in this subject of growth, I am assured that many would feel an immediate lifting of burdens from their lives. Picture a child obsessed with the notion that growth is wholly dependent on his own effort. Suppose he conjured up a contraption of ropes and pulleys to stretch himself to the desired height. He could, undoubtedly, expend his days and years in exhausting strain, but in the end, the immutable truth remains: *"Which of you by taking thought can add one cubit unto his stature?" (Matthew 6:27, KJV).* His years of toil would be wasted, possibly even detrimental to his desired growth.

Now, consider a lily straining to clothe itself in splendid colors and elegant lines, stretching its leaves and stems to grow, and attempting to manipulate the clouds and sunshine to ensure its needs are properly met. Yet, I believe these illustrations accurately reflect the futile efforts of many Christians who, aware they should grow and yearning for growth, strive to attain it through labor, spinning, stretching, and straining. They live a life of relentless self-effort that is tiresome to even think about.

Grow, my dear friends, but grow, I implore you, in God's way - the only effective way. Be rooted in grace and allow the Divine Husbandman to cultivate you in His own way and by His own means. Place yourselves in the radiant sunshine of His presence, let the dew of heaven descend upon you, and behold the result. Leaves, flowers, and fruit will surely sprout in their due season, for your Divine Husbandman is adept, and His harvest never falls short.

Ensure that nothing obstructs the warming light of the Sun of Righteousness or the descending dew from Heaven. Even a thin covering can hinder the heat or moisture, causing the plant to wither, and the smallest barrier between your soul and Christ can cause you to dwindle and fade, much like a plant in a cellar or under a bushel. Keep the sky clear. Open every aspect of your being to receive the blessed influences our Divine

Husbandman may exert upon you. Bask in the warmth of His love. Absorb the waters of His benevolence. Keep your face upturned to Him. Look, and your soul shall live.

You need not strive to grow; rather, focus all your efforts on remaining firmly connected to the Vine. The Divine Husbandman, who tends to the vine, will likewise care for its branches, pruning and cleansing, watering and tending them so they grow, bear fruit, and their fruit will last. Like the lily, they will find themselves adorned in attire so magnificent that even Solomon's attire will pale in comparison. What if you find yourselves planted in seemingly barren soil at this moment?

In conclusion, remember that it is not through our individual efforts that we truly grow, but through the divine nurturing of our Heavenly Father. Trust in His ways and His timing, and you will find that growth, grace, and **Glory** flourish beyond expectation, even in the most challenging of circumstances. For He is our skilled and unfailing Divine Husbandman, guiding our growth in His perfect love.

Embracing Trust and Grace

When I imagine myself in the tender care of the Divine Gardener, I envision a barren landscape turning vibrant with life, blooming like a rose amid the desert. He creates springs and fountains in the sandy expanses, fulfilling His promise. As stated in *Jeremiah 17:8 "For he shall be as a tree planted by the waters, and that spreadeth out her roots by the river, and shall not see when heat cometh, but her leaf shall be green; and shall not be careful in the year of drought, neither shall cease from yielding fruit."* Such is the extraordinary power of our Divine Gardener. He can take any soil, no matter its condition, and turn it into fertile ground for growth the moment we yield ourselves to His care.

He doesn't need to move us to a new field; right where we are, amid our current circumstances, He makes His blessings shine upon us. He turns our greatest obstacles into the most powerful tools for growth. The elements—storms, sunshine, winds, and rain—are at His command and He uses them to ensure our swift and sturdy growth.

I encourage you, then, to let go of your struggle to grow and simply allow yourself to bloom under His care. Trust in Him completely and unconditionally. No hardship, no stunting of your growth in the past, no seeming dryness of your spirit, no deformation in your past development, can interfere with the perfect work He will achieve, provided you surrender fully to His guiding hands.

His promise to His children who have strayed is filled with grace: *"I will heal their backsliding, I will love them freely: for mine anger is turned away from him. I will be as the dew unto Israel: he shall grow as the lily, and cast forth his roots as Lebanon. His branches shall spread, and his beauty shall be as the olive tree, and his smell as Lebanon" (Hosea 14:4-6, KJV).*

When Jesus said, *"Consider the lilies, how they grow;*

they toil not, neither do they spin" (Luke 12:27, KJV), He described a life and growth far different from our usual Christian experience. It's a life of peace, a growth without struggle, and it results in a glorious transformation. Those who embrace this way of life, growing as the lilies do, will experience the fulfillment of the mystical saying, *"He feedeth among the lilies" (Song of Solomon 2:16, KJV).*

The lilies, simply by being in the presence of the sun, grow and transform. *Likewise, those who gaze upon the Glory of the Lord change into His image, going from Glory to Glory, as led by His spirit (2 Corinthians 3:18, KJV).* These faithful ones trust in the promise of Jesus in *John 15:5, KJV: "I am the vine, ye are the branches: He that abideth in me, and I in him, the same bringeth forth much fruit."*

As we conclude, remember, those who truly flourish in the Lord's care focus not on their growth but on remaining in Him. They keep their eyes on Jesus, entrusting their cultivation, growth, training, and pruning to their divine Gardener. To grow like a lily in the Lord's garden is to let go, trust, and abide in Him. As a result, His magnificent work is made manifest within us, transforming us from mere seeds into glorious flowering plants that bear abundant fruit.

Lessons from the Life of Christ

I do not strain nor struggle to dress myself in spiritual garments but place my trust and faith entirely in the hands of the Lord, allowing Him to adorn me as He sees fit. Self-reliance and self-sufficiency no longer bind me. My concern for self has ceased, entrusted into the hands of the One far greater. Self holds no significance, and it is Christ alone who has become my all in all. Such surrender leads to a divine outcome: even Solomon, in all his splendid **Glory**, cannot compare to the radiant array of those surrendering to Christ.

Scripture teaches us this in *Matthew 6:28-29 "And why take ye thought for raiment? Consider the lilies of the field, how they grow; they toil not, neither do they spin: And yet I say unto you, That even Solomon in all his Glory was not arrayed like one of these."*

We must apply this truth in a practical manner. Growing is not a product of effort, but the manifestation of an inward life force, a principle of growth. Attempting to stimulate growth in a dead oak through stretching and pulling would prove futile. Conversely, a live oak grows effortlessly, driven by the life within. This clarifies the essential aspect of growth: you must have the life force that enables growth within you. That life force is the divine life of the indwelling Holy Ghost, a life that is hid with Christ in God. Be filled with this, beloved believer, and, even if you are not aware of it, you must grow, for growth will be inevitable.

My advice is this: focus not on the growth itself, but on ensuring that you possess the life force that encourages growth. **Abide in the Vine. Allow the life from Him to surge through your spiritual veins. Do not obstruct His powerful life-giving force, allowing it to**

accomplish His good will in you. Surrender yourself entirely to His loving authority. Entrust your spiritual growth to Him as you have entrusted all your other concerns. Allow Him to govern it as He deems appropriate. Do not worry about it, nor allow it to occupy your thoughts. Trust Him completely and at all times. Accept each moment's circumstance as it arrives from His loving hands, recognizing it as the necessary sunlight or dew for your growth at that precise moment. Echo a constant "Yes" to your Father's will.

In the past, like many, you may have tried to be both the flower and the gardener, both the vineyard and the vine-dresser. You may have shouldered burdens and responsibilities that are rightfully the Divine Gardener's, those which He alone can bear. From this point forward, agree to occupy your rightful position and to be solely what you are meant to be. Remember, if you are the garden, not the gardener, if you are the vine, not the vinedresser, then it is vital for your appropriate growth and well-being that you maintain your position as the garden or the vine, and do not attempt to assume the position or responsibilities of the gardener or the vine-dresser.

In conclusion, spiritual growth comes from surrendering yourself fully to the Lord, allowing His divine life to flow within you. Trust Him, abide in Him, and be content to let Him work His will in your life. With this mindset, you will flourish, not by your own efforts, but by the divine power of the living God working within you. Let Christ be your all in all, and you will find yourself arrayed in a spiritual **Glory** that surpasses even that of

Solomon.

Cultivating a Soul with Grace

In the grand scheme of God's work, we must refrain from choosing our ground, from marking our territory. We shouldn't sow our seeds, nor toil, nor trim, nor guard our own vineyards. Instead, we should find comfort in the care and arrangements orchestrated by the Divine Husbandman. Let Him select the type of plants and fruits He deems best to nurture, and gladly accept a humble potato growing as much as a blooming rose, if that aligns with His will. Embrace the simple, everyday virtues as eagerly as the lofty fervors.

Accept the seasons He dispatches, the sunlight and rain He bestows, the rate of your growth, whether fast or slow. Above all, be content with His divine workings, no matter how puzzling they might seem to our limited understanding. There's an immense tranquility in this surrender.

Just as the violet finds peace nestled in its small nook, receiving its daily provision without a worry, so should we rest in the present that God grants us. Embrace our daily lot without apprehension, trusting in His grand plan of creation and redemption.

Consider this verse from *Matthew 6:34 (KJV): "Take therefore no thought for the morrow: for the morrow shall take thought for the things of itself. Sufficient unto the day is the evil thereof."* These words remind us to focus on today and trust in God's plan.

The wind that sweeps through can never obliterate the tree God plants. Whether it blows east or west, the tender leaves find little rest. But whichever direction it takes is for the best. The tree planted by God drives deeper roots, grows taller still, extends wider branches, for God's benevolence fulfills all its needs.

There is no frost with the power to damage the tree under God's protection. Its roots stay warm beneath the soft snow. And when spring arrives, it awakens, with each bud blooming. The tree shielded by God flourishes day and night until its fruit, delightful to taste and pleasing to the eye, is ready for harvest.

No storm holds power to devastate the tree under God's watchful eye. No thunderbolt, pelting rain, flash of lightning, or hurricane can damage it. After these forces have spent their energy, the tree stands unscathed. The tree known by God stands strong through every tempest, and from its inception to its last day, it continues to grow more beautiful.

When God sows a tiny seed in the tranquil garden of the soul, it will soon sprout and become known to all, for He commands it to flourish. This seed, sown by God, shoots up day and night; through life, through death, it grows eternally.

In conclusion, we must understand that our growth and cultivation, just like that of the tree and the seed, lie in

God's hands. He plants, shields, knows, and sows in His own divine way, for His love and wisdom exceed our understanding. By accepting this, we can find true peace and contentment, knowing that we are a part of His great creative and redemptive plan. Our growth, whether it resembles a humble potato or a glorious rose, is part of His divine will, and all we need to do is trust in Him.

Chapter TEN

DIVINE SERVICE TO GOD

The Transformative Journey of Service

In my journey as a follower of Christ, I've noticed a profound shift in my experience, particularly in my service. This transformation becomes evident as I grow deeper into a life hidden with Christ in God. Often, in our initial encounters with Christian life, there's a certain element of bondage associated with service. We tend to serve purely out of duty, which can sometimes feel like a cross we must bear. Things that once sparked joy and delight may start to feel like wearisome tasks. We do them faithfully, of course, but often with a hidden reluctance or even an overt longing not to do them at all.

As the Apostle Paul so aptly puts it in *Romans 7:15*

(KJV), "For that which I do I allow not: for what I would, that do I not; but what I hate, that do I." Indeed, instead of expressing the "May I" of love, we may find ourselves questioning, "Must I" out of obligation. The yoke of service, once light, may start to rub harshly, turning the once light burden into a cumbersome load.

A fellow believer once confided in me, sharing her transformation in faith. "When I was first converted," she revealed, "my heart was so overflowing with joy and love that I leaped at every opportunity to serve my Lord. As time passed, however, my fervor cooled and my eagerness turned into weariness. The tasks I once embraced with joy gradually morphed into burdens I would rather shirk. My commitment to various lines of service became a millstone around my neck, making each duty increasingly distasteful and onerous."

She went on to explain how the expectations others placed upon her—visiting the sick, attending prayer meetings, always being ready for Christian work—felt as though they were smothering her. She started to resent the Christian life she had enthusiastically embraced, now forced into a treadmill of daily Christian work that seemed to eclipse all else. She yearned for the simplicity of manual labor, envying those who scrubbed floors or labored over wash-tubs.

Can you identify with this, dear reader? Have you ever faced your Christian duties with a sense of dread, rebounding back into your genuine interests the moment the work is finished? We might feel guilty for such feelings, knowing they seem to conflict with our calling, yet often, we see no alternative.

In another instance, you may love your work in theory, but the reality brings a heavy load of cares, responsibilities, doubts, and fears about your capacity or fitness for the task. In *Matthew 11:28-30 (KJV)*, Jesus addresses this feeling, saying, *"Come unto me, all ye that labour and are heavy laden, and I will give you rest. Take my yoke upon you, and learn of me; for I am meek and lowly in heart: and ye shall find rest unto your souls. For my yoke is easy, and my burden is light."* But often, despite these comforting words, we approach our service burdened and weary even before we begin.

In Christ, however, we find the capacity to transform our perspective. If we turn to Him with our burdens and concerns, His grace enables us to find joy and freedom in our service once more. With our hearts aligned with Christ, we no longer approach service out of obligation or duty, but rather out of love and desire to serve Him. As Paul beautifully expressed in *Galatians 2:20 (KJV)*, *"I am crucified with Christ: nevertheless I live; yet not I, but Christ liveth in me: and the life which I now live in the flesh I live by the faith of the Son of God, who loved me, and gave himself for me."* In this light, service transforms from a burdensome duty into a fulfilling expression of our faith and love for Christ.

In *1 John 4:19 (KJV)*, the scripture enlightens us: *"We love him, because he first loved us."* Thus, when our service springs from love, we no longer ask, "Must I?" out of obligation, but "May I?" with sincere delight. The

175

yoke of service becomes not a source of discomfort, but a cherished connection to our Savior. Even when we encounter difficulties and challenges in our service, we can endure with joy, for we know that our labor in the Lord is not in vain *(1 Corinthians 15:58, KJV)*.

Moreover, when we serve with love, the worries and fears that once burdened us dissolve. For the scripture in *Philippians 4:6-7 (KJV)* reassures us, *"Be careful for nothing; but in everything by prayer and supplication with thanksgiving let your requests be made known unto God. And the peace of God, which passeth all understanding, shall keep your hearts and minds through Christ Jesus."*

Conclusively, the transformative journey of Christian service, from duty-bound to love-driven, mirrors our spiritual growth in Christ. This transformation does not dismiss the reality of hardship or struggles in service, but instead brings a new perspective. It offers a refreshing lens to view these challenges as opportunities for growth, not as burdens. When we allow ourselves to be guided by Christ's love, our service becomes a joyful offering, a testament to our faith and love for our Savior, Jesus Christ. In the grand scheme of God's plan, the "Must I" of obligation transforms into the "May I" of love, and service in Christ's embrace becomes a profound joy, rather than a burdensome duty.

Embracing Faith and the Love of God's Will

I find myself, as many do, often vexed with the outcome

of my endeavors, should they not turn out precisely as I desire. This ceaseless self-distraught serves only as an enduring burden. However, in the light of faith, I have found deliverance from these shackles.

As my soul yields its will into the hands of the Lord, I discover a new-found delight in service. The Lord, in His grace, begins to guide my desires according to His good pleasure. In doing His work, I find joy, for it aligns with the newfound purpose He has planted within me.

Consider the delight of accomplishing a task that resonates with your heart, no matter how challenging it may be or how much physical fatigue it entails. When a man's will aligns with a task, the hurdles along the path become mere trifles. Such a man would trek to the farthest corners of the Earth in the pursuit of worldly riches or to fulfill worldly ambitions.

Think of mothers who rejoice despite the hardships and separations their sons must face in the name of their country's service, perceiving it as an honor. Strangely though, these same individuals might perceive a similar sacrifice in Christ's service as a daunting cross to bear. It's all a matter of perspective, and our perception often defines if a task is a burden or a blessing.

It grieves me when Christians bemoan their service to Christ, which some others would gladly undertake for worldly gains. In our spiritual journey, we should yearn to do God's will as ardently as others strive to fulfill their own desires. This is the essence of the Gospel, the promise of God, and His intent for us.

In the book of Hebrews (8:6-13), God describes a new covenant, unlike the old one made on Sinai. It is not a law imposed externally but written within, guiding us through love. God promises, *"I will put my laws into their mind, and write them in their hearts" (Hebrews 8:10, KJV).* This promise implies that we shall cherish His law, for what is written on our hearts is inevitably loved.

This internal transformation, this divine working within us aligns our will with God's. We find ourselves desiring to follow His divine commands, not out of duty, but because our renewed hearts want to. This profound alignment between God's will and our desires is the most effective way to live a life of faith.

In conclusion, as we surrender ourselves entirely into the hands of the Lord, we discover a newfound delight in doing His will. This deep, soulful satisfaction, unfettered by the worldly perception of success and failure, is the secret to a life of faith, guided by God's will written in our hearts. This indeed is the path to a blessed and joyful life.

"The Power of Surrender: Embracing Divine Will"

I have often wondered, in my interactions with my own children, "If only I could reach into their hearts and shape their desires, aligning them with my own, wouldn't that make guiding them an effortless task?" There have been countless instances where I found, when dealing with individuals of stubborn disposition, it was not prudent to impose my desires upon them, but instead, to subtly lead them towards discovering these desires within themselves. Only then does the opposition cease. We, being naturally defiant, are prone to rebel against externally imposed rules, yet we enthusiastically accept the same rules when they seem to arise from within us.

In the Bible, God's intentions for us are clear. His plan isn't about enforcing external rules upon us. Rather, he aims to govern from within, to direct our will and guide our actions, rendering obedience a delight and service a liberating joy. The Psalmist captures this feeling exquisitely, saying, *"I delight to do thy will, O my God: yea, thy law is within my heart." (Psalm 40:8, KJV)*

What you need to do, dear fellow believer, if you feel shackled, is to yield your will entirely to the Lord, entrusting Him with absolute control. Utter a heartfelt "Yes, Lord, YES!" to every divine instruction and trust Him to work within you, conforming your desires and affections to His divine will, which is beautiful, compassionate, and supremely appealing.

I've witnessed this process repeatedly, even in situations that seemed utterly hopeless. For instance, I once encountered a woman who had spent years vehemently resisting something she knew to be right simply because she abhorred it. In a moment of despondency, devoid of any comforting emotion, she handed her will regarding that matter over to the Lord, repeating the words, "Thy will be done; thy will be done!" Miraculously, within an hour, she began to see the once-despised issue as something precious and desirable.

God indeed works wonders within those who unreservedly surrender their will to Him. He transforms challenges into triumphs, bitterness into sweetness. God doesn't replace the difficult with the easy, rather He miraculously turns the difficult itself into something easy. This is the essence of salvation. It's a divine experience. I urge you, especially if you're a believer struggling with the weariness of daily Christian living, to try this. See if your divine Master won't transform the life you currently view as burdensome into a joyous freedom!

If you love God's will in principle, but find executing it strenuous and taxing, there is deliverance in the wonderful life of faith. In this life, burdens are lifted, and anxieties are dissolved.

Let's remember Jesus' words in *Matthew 11:28-30 (KJV), "Come unto me, all ye that labour and are heavy laden, and I will give you rest. Take my yoke upon you, and learn of me; for I am meek and lowly in heart: and ye shall find rest unto your souls. For my yoke is easy, and my burden is light."*

In conclusion, surrendering our will to God isn't about losing control, but gaining a divine partnership that leads us toward peace and fulfillment. Our Lord seeks to work within us, transforming our struggles into victories and making our service a joyful and liberating experience.

The Power of Surrender and Trust in Our Lord

As I stand in this earthly existence, my heart overflows with gratitude, for I am anchored in the unchanging truth that the Lord is our mighty burden-bearer. He graciously invites us to cast every ounce of our cares upon Him, reminding us in the sweetest whispers that we are not meant to carry them alone. He tells us, in essence, *"Be careful for nothing; but in everything by prayer and supplication with thanksgiving let your requests be made known unto God." (Philippians 4:6, KJV).*

He reassures us not to worry, not even about our service unto Him. Above all, our service must be entrusted to Him, for we recognize our utter helplessness in this grand task. Our strength is insubstantial, our capabilities limited. But remember, it is not about us - it's about Him. It's not our fitness for the task, but His infinite might and wisdom that matters.

As the Master Craftsman, the Lord has the prerogative to use any tool He deems fit for His work. We, the humble instruments, are not in a position to decide our suitability for His tasks. He knows; and if He elects to use us, we must trust that we are indeed fit for purpose. Ironically, our primary fitness lies in our absolute weakness. For it is in our helplessness that His strength finds perfect expression, fulfilling the divine promise, *"My grace is sufficient for thee: for my strength is made perfect in weakness." (2 Corinthians 12:9, KJV)*

Let me illustrate this truth. During a visit to an institution for intellectually challenged children, I observed them performing exercises with dumb-bells. These children, endowed with physical strength but lacking the ability to effectively utilize it, displayed uncoordinated movements. Yet, a little girl stood out with her perfect movements. Her secret wasn't superior strength or skill, rather it was her total lack of strength. Unable to perform the exercises on her own, the master stood behind her, guiding her movements. She yielded herself completely to him, making his strength her own.

In her surrender, she mirrored our Christian journey. By yielding herself fully to the master, she provided him the space to demonstrate his expertise, making the movements harmonious and accurate. Her role was not to execute, but to allow herself to be an instrument in the hands of the master. She was a testament to the Apostle Paul's words, *"Most gladly therefore will I rather glory in my infirmities, that the power of Christ may rest upon me." (2 Corinthians 12:9, KJV)*

Such is the beauty of our walk with Christ. When we acknowledge our weakness and surrender ourselves to Him, His mighty power works through us. It is not about our capacity or skill, but His perfect strength and unending grace. Our utter weakness becomes our most significant strength.

Moreover, when the work is His, the responsibility is also His, and that leaves no room for us to worry. Our part is to yield and trust in His promise, *"Come unto me, all ye that labour and are heavy laden, and I will give you rest." (Matthew 11:28, KJV)*

In conclusion, let us bask in the comfort of His embrace, glory in our weaknesses, and give Him room to use us for His divine purpose. We need only to surrender and believe that His strength is made perfect in our weakness, and He will indeed make all things beautiful in His time.

Guided Steps in Service of the Divine

I find myself consumed by a profound understanding: everything, every nuanced detail, every conceivable entity, is known to Him - our Lord and Savior. In His omniscience, He is equipped to manage all matters with divine perfection. Here, I ask myself, and you, dear reader, why not entrust everything to Him? Why not embrace the innocent faith of a child, accepting His guiding hand as we journey through life?

Permit me to share with you a remarkable observation. The most effective workers I have had the privilege to encounter are those unburdened by worldly care or anxiety about their tasks. Instead, they surrender their work to their loving Master, seeking His guidance in every moment, and placing unwavering trust in His promise to provide the necessary wisdom and strength at the needed time. Observing them, one might question if they are perhaps too carefree, especially considering the significance of their duties. Yet, once you learn God's secret of absolute trust, and observe the beauty and power of a life submitted to His will, you would cease to judge. Rather, you'd be taken by wonder, pondering how any of God's servants could dare shoulder burdens or responsibilities that only He can carry with ease.

The life of trust I describe liberates us from other bonds of service as well. It reveals to us that we are not tasked with all the work in the world. The Lord's commands cease being general and transform into personal and individual directives. The Master doesn't outline a vague plan of action, expecting us to navigate through it with our limited wisdom and skill. Instead, He guides us meticulously, providing specific guidance for each distinct moment. His blessed Spirit, dwelling within us, reminds us of the necessary commands at the right time, ensuring that we do not have to worry about the future but simply follow each instruction as it is revealed, tracing the path where our Lord leads us.

Reflect upon this passage from the King James Bible, *Psalms 37:23, "The steps of a good man are ordered by the Lord: and he delighteth in his way."* It is not only his way that is directed by the Lord, but each individual step within that way. Many of our Christian brothers and sisters make the mistake of expecting to receive God's commands as a comprehensive list. They may believe that if the Lord guided them to share a spiritual tract with one person in a train, for instance, they are then compelled to do the same for everyone, burdening themselves with an impossible command.

I recall a young Christian who, having been guided by the Lord to share a message with a soul during a walk, took this as a permanent directive. She believed that she must now share the gospel with everyone she encountered. Naturally, such a task was beyond her capabilities, leading her into a state of unbearable bondage. She feared even stepping outside her door, living in a shadow of perpetual self-condemnation.

In conclusion, it is essential that we trust in the Lord's guidance, understanding that His directives are not only for the grand path of life but also for each individual step. We must remember that He equips us with the wisdom and strength needed for every moment. As we trust in Him and follow His lead, we are freed from burdens too heavy for us to bear, living a life that truly delights in His way. After all, in the words of Jesus in Matthew 11:30, KJV, "For my yoke is easy, and my burden is light."

A Journey Towards Faith-Filled Service

One day, feeling overwhelmed by my mission, I shared my struggles with a trusted friend, a well-versed disciple of God. My friend gently corrected my mistaken belief that I needed to shoulder every task. He compared it to a well-run household where each servant performs a unique function. Just as it would be chaos for each servant to attempt all tasks, so it was with us, the servants of the Lord. We were not meant to do everything.

He encouraged me to entrust my work to the Lord, to look to Him for guidance about the specific people I should serve. He assured me that just as a shepherd never sends his sheep out without leading the way, so too does our Lord prepare the way for His servants.

Taking this advice to heart, I entrusted my mission to God. In response, He led me down a joyful path of daily guidance. I was able to serve my Master without the burden of worry because He pointed out the way. It felt like connecting machinery to a steam engine. The machinery, on its own, is powerless; but once connected to the steam engine, it operates effortlessly because of the immense power behind it.

In the same manner, a Christian life becomes easy and natural when it aligns with the divine power within. Many Christians struggle because their wills aren't fully synchronized with God's will. They're like machinery that isn't fully connected to the engine. But when we completely connect with God, we allow the law of the Spirit of life in Christ Jesus to work within us. As stated in *Romans 8:2, "For the law of the Spirit of life in Christ Jesus hath made me free from the law of sin and death."* Then, we truly experience the glorious liberty of the children of God, leading lives devoid of friction.

Another form of service-related bondage, from which faith liberates us, concerns self-reflection after Christian work. These reflections can be of two types. Sometimes, we may take pride in our success and become self-important. Other times, we may be so disappointed by our failure that we plunge into despair. Either of these reactions is sure to happen and can bring trouble. But as we learn to trust more deeply in the Lord, we can commit ourselves and our work to Him. Then, regardless of success or failure, we will find peace in knowing that all is in His capable hands.

In conclusion, the journey towards faith-filled service is about surrendering ourselves to the Lord's divine guidance. Like machinery connected to a powerful steam engine, when we are aligned with God's will, we can perform our Christian duties effortlessly. Regardless of the outcome, we can find solace in knowing that we are serving under the Lord's watchful eyes. As stated in *Proverbs 3:5-6, "Trust in the LORD with all thine heart; and lean not unto thine own understanding. In all thy ways acknowledge him, and he shall direct thy paths."* This is the path to a truly peaceful, faith-filled service.

Trust, Service, and Finding Peace in Christ's

One day, many moons ago, I found a sentence in an old book that struck me like a bolt of lightning. It said, "Never wallow, at the end of a task, in any acts of self-contemplation, whether they be of self-celebration or of self-despair. Once they're done, leave your deeds in the past, placing them in God's hands." This humble sentence has been an immeasurable treasure in my life.

Whenever I find myself on the brink of falling into the trap of self-examination, whether positive or negative, I avert my gaze immediately. I simply refuse to mull over my deeds, entrusting them to the Lord to rectify any missteps and to bless them as He wills. To put it succinctly, what we require for fruitful and joyous service is just to lay our work in the Lord's hands, and let it remain there.

Avoid taking your troubles to Him in prayer, only to say, "Lord, guide me; Lord, provide me wisdom; Lord, arrange for me," and then rise from your prayers only to shoulder the load once more, attempting to steer your own course. Leave it all with the Lord. Remember this: what you entrust to Him, you must not fret over. Trust and worry are like oil and water – they simply do not mix. If your work weighs heavy on your shoulders, it is because you're not entrusting it to Him. But if you truly entrust it to Him, you'll discover that His yoke is easy, and His burden is light, just as *Matthew 11:30* promises, *"For my yoke is easy, and my burden is light."*

At this point, you may wonder if such teachings would turn us into mere puppets. To this, I say, "No." Rather, it would simply transform us into servants. As servants, we are not expected to plan, organize, make decisions, or provide the required resources. All we're expected to do is obey, as *Ephesians 6:6* states, *"Not with eyeservice, as menpleasers; but as the servants of Christ, doing the will of God from the heart."*

The Master is responsible for the rest. As servants, we are not accountable for the outcomes. The Master alone knows the results He desires, and thus, He alone can appraise them. Understanding His thoughts and plans will naturally inform our service, but we can't fully comprehend them nor transfer His responsibilities onto our shoulders.

Our perspective is limited, and our knowledge, while growing, still falls short. We can do very little more than align our will with our Divine Master's, trusting Him without fully understanding, and leaving all the results with Him. What appears as failure to our earthly eyes may often be glorious success in the unseen, spiritual realm. As such, if we allow ourselves to fret and lament, we risk weeping when we should be singing and rejoicing.

In conclusion, the true essence of our service to the Lord lies not in self-reflection or self-congratulation but in the pure act of obedience and trust. By entrusting our work to Him, we invite His guidance, blessing, and peace into our lives. So, let us serve joyously, trust wholeheartedly, and leave all worries to Him, for He cares for us *(1 Peter 5:7, "Casting all your care upon him; for he careth for you").* And let us remember, we are not mere puppets in His divine plan, but faithful servants walking in Christ's path.

A Lesson in Divine Ownership and Trust

Oh, dear brethren, it is of utmost importance to wholly resist the urge to dwell upon oneself; to shun the inclination to analyze one's self for good or ill. We must remember always that we are not our own. We are not for us to worry about, to dissect, or to manage. We are but instruments in the Lord's hands, His property, His business. And our Lord, in His infinite wisdom and care, never fails to attend to His business, and so, He will attend to us.

There is an illustration that comes to my mind, about a slave who was aboard a ship amidst a violent tempest. He whistled joyously while everyone else was swallowed by fear. When asked if he did not fear drowning, he replied with a toothy grin, "Well, missus, s'pose I is. I don't b'long to myself, and it will only be massa's loss any how."

This tale serves as a mirror for us, dear reader. An embodiment of this spirit could liberate us from our self-imposed suffering and quandaries in service to the Lord.

Consider what our Almighty God might accomplish with a band of servants so surrendered to His use and care. Verily, one such servant could drive away a thousand enemies, and two could send ten thousand fleeing. This is not an exaggeration, for our God promises in the Holy Scripture, *"One man of you shall chase a thousand: for the LORD your God, he it is that fighteth for you, as he hath promised you" (Joshua 23:10, KJV).* With God's divine intervention, nothing would be impossible for them, as is stated in the Bible, *"with God all things are possible" (Matthew 19:26, KJV).*

The Lord can offer help, whether the numbers are many or few, for it is nothing with the Lord *"to help, whether with many or with them that have no power" (2 Chronicles 14:11, KJV).* This underscores the immense might and mercy of our God, who does not discriminate based on numbers or strength.

Oh, how my heart yearns for the Lord to quickly raise such an army of dedicated servants! I implore you, dear reader, to enlist yourself in this divine battalion today. Submit yourself unto God as one revived from death, and let each of your members be dedicated to Him as instruments of righteousness.

In the words of Apostle Paul, *"Neither yield ye your members as instruments of unrighteousness unto sin: but yield yourselves unto God, as those that are alive from the dead, and your members as instruments of righteousness unto God" (Romans 6:13, KJV).*

Offer yourself willingly to be used by Him, just as He wills. Let us echo the psalmist's prayer, *"Create in me a clean heart, O God; and renew a right spirit within me" (Psalm 51:10, KJV).* Let us yield ourselves and trust in the divine plan of God, for we are His, and He will always attend to His own.

When we understand that we are God's chosen, when we embrace our position not as our own proprietors but as God's servants, the burdens of our hearts will be lifted. Indeed, there is immense peace in knowing that our worth is not measured by our self-perception or worldly standards, but by our inherent value as God's creation.

To illuminate this further, let's return to the tale of the slave on the tempest-tossed ship. While those around him were paralyzed by fear, he remained at ease, for he knew he was not his own. His life was in the hands of his master. He was simply a steward of a life that belonged to another. We too must remember that our lives are not our own; they are the Lord's. As it is written in the Bible, *"For ye are bought with a price: therefore glorify God in your body, and in your spirit, which are God's"* *(1 Corinthians 6:20, KJV).*

Beloved reader, when we surrender ourselves, when we wholly submit to the Lord, we are freed from the shackles of self. Our strength, our peace, our joy, are no longer dependent on ourselves or on the world, but on the infinite power and grace of the Lord.

Once again, the power of unity and faith is highlighted in the Book of Deuteronomy: *"How should one chase a thousand, and two put ten thousand to flight, except their Rock had sold them, and the LORD had shut them up?" (Deuteronomy 32:30, KJV).* Indeed, with God on our side, nothing is unattainable.

My prayer is that our Heavenly Father might amass such a band of devoted followers, trusting in Him, serving Him, caring not for themselves but for the glory of His name. As we yield ourselves to God, as we offer ourselves as instruments of righteousness for His divine work, imagine the marvelous deeds He might perform through us!

Our heavenly Father assures us in His holy word, *"For I know the plans I have for you, declares the LORD, plans for welfare and not for evil, to give you a future and a hope" (Jeremiah 29:11, KJV).* Yield yourself unto Him, dear reader, and let Him guide you towards a future filled with hope and prosperity.

In conclusion, let us remember that we are God's, bought at a price. Our purpose is to glorify Him in body and spirit, to yield ourselves as instruments of righteousness. Let's abandon our own interests, needs, and worries, and instead fully trust in God's divine plan for us. We belong to Him, and He will always take care of His own. Let's pray together, dear reader, for the strength to serve Him unreservedly, and let's rejoice in the marvelous things He is sure to do through us. Amen.

CHAPTER ELEVEN

DIFFICULTIES CONCERNING GUIDANCE

Today, I invite you to embark on a new journey - a life of faith. Like clay in the hands of a master potter, you've offered your entire self to the Lord, trusting Him to shape and mold you into a vessel of honor. Your deepest yearning now is to yield entirely to His touch, to follow His lead wherever He may guide you. You're putting your trust in Him, believing that He will stir up in you the desire and the energy to do what pleases Him. But, you're facing a huge challenge - identifying the voice of the Good Shepherd amidst the multitude of voices surrounding you. You're uncertain about what His will is for your life.

Perhaps, there are paths that appear to be God's call for you, but your friends strongly disagree. These friends, though they've been in the Christian faith longer and seemingly more advanced, might cause you to hesitate when your opinions differ. Their disapproval over your perceived callings makes you uneasy, yet you can't dismiss these persistent impressions. This situation throws you into a whirlpool of doubt and confusion.

Rest assured, there's a solution for the fully surrendered soul, someone who has given up all their will to God. It's important to remember that if there's a shred of resistance in any aspect, understanding God's intentions becomes difficult. So, your first step is to ensure your readiness to obey the Lord in every way. Once you're certain that your only desire is to know and follow God's will, you shouldn't doubt His willingness to reveal His plans and guide you in the right direction.

Consider these profound promises from the Scriptures. In *John 10:3-4 (KJV)*, it says, *"He calleth his own sheep by name, and leadeth them out. And when he putteth forth his own sheep, he goeth before them, and the sheep follow him: for they know his voice."* And in *John 14:26 (KJV)*, we read, *"But the Comforter, which is the Holy Ghost, whom the Father will send in my name, he shall teach you all things, and bring all things to your remembrance, whatsoever I have said unto you."* Further, *James 1:5-6 (KJV)* declares, *"If any of you lack wisdom, let him ask of God, that giveth to all men liberally, and upbraideth not; and it shall be given him."*

These passages, along with many others, assure us that Divine guidance is ours for the taking. Your faith must boldly anticipate and seek it. You have embarked on this journey of faith, fully surrendering your will to God, trusting Him to lead and guide you. As you learn to identify His voice amidst the noise, remember the promises of His guidance. By His grace and your faith, you will discern His will for your life and walk in it confidently.

In conclusion, dear reader, do not despair when doubt and confusion set in. God's promises stand sure, His guidance is unwavering. As you surrender all to Him, His voice will become clearer, guiding you in the path He has designed especially for you. Let your faith, like a beacon, lead you through this journey, ever closer to the heart of God.

Trusting in the Unwavering Guidance of God

There's a powerful truth at the heart of my faith journey, and it's one that I want to share with you. As stated in *James 1:6-7* in the Bible*, "But let him ask in faith, nothing wavering. For he that wavereth is like a wave of the sea driven with the wind and tossed. For let not that man think that he shall receive any thing of the Lord."* This truth offers reassurance; divine guidance is promised to us, and we are certain to receive it if we ask in faith without wavering.

Next, I learned that God, in His infinite wisdom and knowledge, might guide me along paths that seem perplexing to those around me. He sees blessings hidden from our short-sighted human eyes, waiting for us in unexpected places. I realized that God's thoughts are not as ours, neither are His ways like ours. As the One who knows the end from the beginning, only He can accurately predict the outcomes of our actions.

I've also come to understand that God's love may lead me to make decisions that may not align with the desires of my loved ones, even my dearest friends. I discovered this through passages like *Luke 14:26-33,* which states, *"If any man come to me, and hate not his father, and mother, and wife, and children, and brethren, and sisters, yea, and his own life also, he cannot be my disciple. And whosoever doth not bear his cross, and come after me, cannot be my disciple."*

These passages reveal the possibility that to truly follow Jesus, we may need to forsake all we have and, at times, even contradict our loved ones' wishes. It's important to recognize this because often, a child of God led into a life of obedience might tread paths that those he holds dear might not approve of. Yet, in these moments, we must remain firm in our faith and trust in God's guidance.

Now, this doesn't mean that we neglect our responsibilities towards our loved ones. Far from it. As we draw closer to Christ, we manifest the gentleness and meekness of our Lord more deeply and exhibit more tender consideration for those who guide and counsel us. When we act contrary to the wishes of our loved ones in obedience to Christ, our love and patience should bear witness to our true motivations.

With these truths ingrained, the question remains: how do we discern God's guidance? How do we recognize His voice amongst the cacophony of life? As we delve into this journey of unwavering faith, we must remember, the voice of God is like a gentle whisper, nudging us onto the path that leads to Him.

In conclusion, the journey of faith calls for an unflinching trust in God's guidance, a readiness to follow His path even when it contradicts human reasoning or meets disapproval. When we listen and recognize His voice with a heart full of faith, we find ourselves on a divine navigation, guided by His unwavering love and wisdom. This is the journey of a true disciple of Jesus Christ.

Discerning the Divine Guidance in Life

Once upon a time, there was a humble servant who lived by a simple yet profound understanding. He believed that God speaks to us in four distinct manners: through the sacred voice of Scripture, the gentle impressions of the Holy Spirit within us, the discernment of our own higher judgment, and the guiding signs of our life circumstances, what he referred to as providential circumstances. He held a steadfast belief that when these four voices resonate in harmony, it can be recognized as God's divine voice.

This servant always remembered a foundational principle: God's voice is always consistent, regardless of the many ways it may reach us. For he reasoned, God cannot contradict Himself. If He tells us something in one voice, He wouldn't advise the opposite in another. When he perceived contradictions, he realized the speaker might not be God, hence his rule for distinguishing God's voice was to test its harmony.

Now, let's say this humble servant received an impression or intuition. He would reflect on it and check if it was in accordance with the Scriptures, if it sat right with his own higher judgment, and whether the circumstances of his life allowed for its manifestation. If it didn't pass any of these tests, he wouldn't act upon it but wait in quiet trust for God to reveal the point of harmony. He had an unwavering faith that God would indeed show him, sooner or later, if it was His voice that had spoken.

The Apostle Paul reminds us in his Epistle to the Ephesians, *"And hath raised us up together, and made us sit together in heavenly places in Christ Jesus" (Ephesians 2:6)*. However, he also warns us that there, we will have to fight spiritual battles *(Ephesians 6:12)*. The humble servant understood that our spiritual enemies, whoever they may be, can communicate with us through our spiritual faculties, producing inner impressions just as God does.

In the midst of this spiritual battleground, he was aware of other voices that could confuse and mislead him. The self-serving and clamorous voice of the ego is one such voice, always demanding to be heard. Evil and deceiving spirits also whisper in our ears, looking to trap those venturing deeper into spiritual life. Thus, he realized the crucial need for discernment, to distinguish the divine voice from the misleading ones.

In their eagerness to heed the divine voice, the humble servant saw that some well-meaning Christians had sometimes ignored, or even acted against the teachings of

Scripture, disregarded obvious signs from life's circumstances, and rejected their own higher judgment. God, in His boundless mercy, forgives them, seeing the sincerity of their hearts. However, their choices often led to sorrowful consequences in their worldly lives.

Therefore, the first test to confirm the divine authority of any voice speaking to us should be its moral alignment with the teachings of Christ in the Gospel. The servant knew that anything contrary to this could not be of God, for God cannot contradict Himself. He also held firmly to the belief that until we have found and obeyed God's will as revealed in the Bible, we cannot anticipate a separate direct personal revelation.

In conclusion, life offers us a symphony of voices. To discern God's voice amidst this cacophony requires a keen sense of harmony - harmony between the Scriptures, the stirrings of the Holy Spirit within us, the wisdom of our higher judgment, and the signs presented by our life circumstances. This discernment leads us to peace and clarity, knowing we are guided by God's divine will. As we follow this path, we become, like the humble servant, instruments of divine harmony in a discordant world.

Embracing the Scriptures as Our Beacon in Life33

As I traverse this remarkable journey of life, I find myself reflecting on a simple, yet profound rule which often slips from our collective conscience. As children of our divine Father, we are given the Scriptures, a set of clear instructions guiding our way. It is written, *"Thy word is a lamp unto my feet, and a light unto my path" (Psalm 119:105, KJV).* When He provides such explicit guidelines, we can't expect or desire a special revelation regarding the same.

For example, no man should expect a divine revelation instructing him not to steal. Why, you may ask? The Scriptures explicitly declare, *"Thou shalt not steal" (Exodus 20:15, KJV).* This truth seems self-evident, yet I have encountered brothers and sisters in Christ who overlook this, inadvertently straying into the realm of fanaticism.

The Scriptures provide more explicit guidance on life's intricacies than most people believe. It is remarkable to note that clear directions for many of life's significant matters are carefully inscribed in our Father's book. Consider the discourse on attire; it is written in *1 Peter 3:3-4* and *1 Timothy 2:9-10*, that we should adorn ourselves with modesty and good works, not with extravagant attire or jewels. The topic of conversation isn't overlooked; we find advice in *Ephesians 4:29* and *5:4,* instructing us to use wholesome words that build up, refraining from obscene or foolish talk.

The Scriptures also teach us about responding to injuries and defending our rights. We are told in *Romans 12:19-21, Matthew 5:38-48,* and *1 Peter 2:19-21* that vengeance is the Lord's, and we should love our enemies, blessing those who curse us. Forgiveness is a key theme as well, with *Ephesians 4:32 and Mark 11:25-26* emphasizing that we must forgive each other just as God, for Christ's sake, forgave us.

The Word also implores us not to conform to worldly standards, with *Romans 12:2, 1 John 2:15-17,* and *James 4:4* admonishing us not to love the world or its desires but to be transformed by renewing our minds. Even our anxieties are addressed in *Matthew 6:25-34* and *Philippians 4:6-7,* where we're encouraged to trust in God and not be anxious about anything.

These examples serve to underscore the richness and practicality of the guidance provided by the Bible. In times of uncertainty, we should first seek answers within the Scriptures, pleading with our Father to illuminate His Word through the power of His Spirit, making His will known to us. We must obey whatever teachings appear to be clear within these sacred pages.

Embracing the Scriptures in this manner, our obedience becomes a living testament to a present, living Word. The Bible serves not just as an ancient message sent long ago, but a fresh, present message each time we delve into its pages. As our Lord Jesus Christ proclaimed, *"The words that I speak unto you, they are spirit, and they are life" (John 6:63, KJV).*

However, we must bear in mind that the Bible is a compilation of guiding principles, not disjointed aphorisms. Extracted texts may sometimes seem to endorse things fundamentally at odds with the Bible's overall principles. I once heard of a Christian woman who, inspired by the verse, *"For we walk by faith, not by sight" (2 Corinthians 5:7, KJV),* decided to literalize the text. She blindfolded herself and walked up and down the aisle of a meeting-house, interpreting this as an enactment of the walk of faith.

While her act reflected her commitment, it is crucial to understand that the Scriptures aren't a collection of literal commandments to be performed physically, but rather a compilation of spiritual principles to guide our lives and attitudes. Such wisdom can only be accessed when we approach the Word with a heart of humility and an openness to be guided by the Holy Spirit, who illuminates the teachings within these sacred pages.

As we navigate through the complexities of life, it is wise to regularly immerse ourselves in the Scriptures, seeking divine wisdom and understanding. When we align our thoughts, actions, and decisions with the principles outlined in God's Word, we experience a transformation that transcends human comprehension. We gain clarity, cultivate a heart of compassion, and are equipped to face the challenges of life with faith and courage.

In conclusion, the Bible, God's divine manual, should be our beacon in life, guiding us in the path of righteousness. It is a living message, breathed out by God, and is profitable for teaching, for reproof, for correction, and for training in righteousness *(2 Timothy 3:16, KJV)*. The principles it teaches remain relevant to this day, providing us with a foundation upon which to build our lives. As we continuously and prayerfully meditate on these divine truths, we foster a more intimate relationship with our Heavenly Father, finding peace, joy, and purpose along this journey called life.

Navigating Life through the Divine Guidance

In my journey of faith, I encountered an unexpected trial. I once accidentally tripped, landing against a stove and badly burning myself. In the aftermath, I was bewildered by this peculiar providence. Applying the wisdom from Scriptures and my God-given sense of discernment could have spared me this misapprehension. The first litmus test for our perceptions ought to be our own enlightened judgment or common sense.

As the Bible says in ***Proverbs 4:7 (KJV), "Wisdom is the principal thing; therefore get wisdom: and with all thy getting get understanding."*** This timeless truth is as valid today as when Solomon penned it. The Scripture consistently instructs God's children to employ all their faculties - both external and internal - throughout their earthly sojourn.

Just as we use our physical senses for our external navigation, our inner faculties should guide our spiritual journey. We cannot expect to avoid physical stumbling if we walk blindfolded, just as we cannot hope to evade spiritual stumbling if we abandon our judgment and common sense.

Seeking guidance, I once queried a sound-minded Christian, "How do you distinguish between the voice of false spirits and the Holy Spirit's guidance?" Without hesitation, she responded, "I test them against common sense." It is indeed true that while we shouldn't rely on our unenlightened human understanding in spiritual matters, we should trust our God-enlightened judgment and common sense.

Scripture, too, affirms this principle in *John 10:4 (KJV)*, *"And when he putteth forth his own sheep, he goeth before them, and the sheep follow him: for they know his voice."* Take note of the words "goeth before" and "follow". He precedes us to prepare the way, and we are to follow the path thus laid.

The way of Christ does not involve forcing open doors or bulldozing over obstacles. If the Lord "goes before" us, He will ensure all doors are opened, absolving us of the need to knock them down ourselves. We must listen for and respect the checks in our spirit. As a rapidly maturing Christian once shared, "I always mind the checks."

Ultimately, all truly divine guidance will harmonize four distinct voices - our inward impressions, the voice of Scripture, our sanctified judgment, and providential circumstances. If they seem discordant initially, we ought to wait until they align. Any action should be grounded in the divine sense of "oughtness", borne from the accord of all God's various voices.

The fact that God loves us enough to care about our lives' minutiae is astounding. His willingness to guide us, revealing how to live a life pleasing to Him, is a gift beyond comprehension. Just as our interest in people's lives deepens with our affection for them, God's concern testifies to His love for us.

God desires to guide us in everything - our duties,

pleasures, friendships, occupations, and all we do, think, or say. *Philippians 2:13 (KJV)* says, *"For it is God which worketh in you both to will and to do of his good pleasure."* This implies that God will shape our will, guiding us through internal desires rather than external commands. We will feel an innate desire to act, not a compulsory need, granting us a service of perfect liberty. Despite the accompanying difficulties, doing what we desire always feels effortless.

In conclusion, navigating life under the guidance of the Lord is a precious gift. It is not merely about avoiding physical or spiritual stumbling but learning to walk in the path prepared for us. It is about finding joy and privilege in a life hidden with Christ in God. His divine guidance is not a restrictive force, but a liberating one, filling our hearts with desires aligned with His will.

Remember the harmony of the four voices - our inward impressions, the voice of Scripture, our sanctified judgment, and providential circumstances - which is a testament to God's will. When these voices align, it's a clear indication of divine guidance. However, when there is a discord, we must be patient and wait upon the Lord until they synchronize.

The path of the divine is not one where we knock down doors or trample upon obstacles, but one where doors are opened for us, where a way is prepared before us. In His love and wisdom, God goes before us, guiding us and leading us along the path He wants us to tread.

His care for each detail of our lives - our duties, our

pleasures, our relationships, our occupations - is an overwhelming testament of His love. He doesn't just guide us, He walks with us, guiding our steps and filling our hearts with His desires, making His service a thing of joy and liberty.

As the scripture says in *Philippians 2:13 (KJV), "For it is God which worketh in you both to will and to do of his good pleasure."* His divine guidance works within us, molding our desires and actions according to His will. It's not about compulsion, but about a deep inner desire to walk in His ways.

So, dear reader, as you walk this path of faith, may you always listen for the four voices of divine guidance and always follow in His footsteps. No matter what trials you may face, no matter what obstacles lie before you, know that with God's guidance, you are on a journey of joy, privilege, and perfect liberty. In His love and wisdom, He will guide you every step of the way, leading you into a life of fulfillment and purpose.

Remember that it's not just about avoiding stumbling, but about walking in the way that has been prepared for you. As you do so, may you find the joy and privilege that come from a life lived in harmony with the divine will, a life hidden with Christ in God, and a life under the constant and loving guidance of our Heavenly Father. May you always walk in His footsteps, secure in His guidance and love.

Living the Laws of the Divine in the Spirit of Christ

As a mother, I know the profound wish to guide my child perfectly and effortlessly towards the right path, a path full of righteousness and wisdom. If only I could embody their will, inspiring them to seek and act upon my benevolent intentions. A similar desire is at the heart of our Heavenly Father's divine plans for us, His children, in the new era. As stated in *Hebrews 10:16 KJV, "This is the covenant that I will make with them after those days, saith the Lord, I will put my laws into their hearts, and in their minds will I write them."*

In this divine process, our affections and judgment become the driving forces towards obedience, instead of fear. The Holy Spirit, our eternal guide, often impresses upon us a longing to undertake or forego certain actions, steering our hearts and minds toward our Father's will.

Picture your soul, deep in prayer, when a subtle suggestion, a nudge, arises within you, stirring your consciousness towards a certain duty. "I yearn to do this or that," you ponder. "I wish I could." The Holy Spirit might even present you with a question, urging you to consider, "Should I possibly do this?" It's an inner whisper that gently, yet convincingly, proclaims what the right and best course of action is.

When these stirrings arise, I urge you to entrust them to the Lord, affirming your will to obey Him. As the Scripture teaches us in *Proverbs 3:5-6 KJV, "Trust in the LORD with all thine heart; and lean not unto thine own understanding. In all thy ways acknowledge him, and he shall direct thy paths. "* If these impressions align with the Scriptures, sound judgment, and Divine Providence, obeying them swiftly and willingly is the best path.

When the Holy Spirit beckons, obedience comes easily. If you hesitate and engage in a debate with yourself, the path becomes increasingly challenging. As a rule, the initial convictions, particularly in a heart wholly surrendered to God, are often right. Our Father is faithful and ensures His voice rings loudest amidst the cacophony of worldly voices.

I caution against doubting or questioning these convictions. Maintain an attitude of trust and prayer, but remember, even these should be momentary lest the window for action closes and the blessing slips away. Yet, when the path isn't clear, when doubt or differing opinions from those around you arise, patiently wait for more illumination. As *Romans 14:23 KJV* says*, "For whatsoever is not of faith is sin,"* meaning we mustn't act when uncertainty lingers. Only the clear conviction of righteousness is a safe guide.

Patience must be practiced with faith and absolute surrender. Continually utter your "Yes" to the Lord's will, no matter what it entails. I have come to realize that the absence of a will surrendered to God often lies at the heart of our difficulties. This lack is only second to our doubt in divine guidance. Many of God's children, despite reading the promises and feeling their need, find it challenging to believe that guidance will indeed come to them.

This skepticism leads us to a peculiar predicament: God speaking, but us failing to listen, because we don't believe He speaks to us. *Isaiah 30:21* KJV comforts us with, *"And thine ears shall hear a word behind thee, saying, This is the way, walk ye in it, when ye turn to the right hand, and when ye turn to the left."* Let us hold fast to this promise and tune our hearts to the divine guidance ever present in our lives, always ready to guide us toward the path of righteousness.

My dear brethren and sisters, do not be disheartened when the voice of God seems faint or indecipherable amidst the clamor of life. Remember, our Father, in His infinite wisdom, has inscribed His laws not on stone tablets, but on our hearts and minds. His Spirit continuously interacts with us, stirring desires and convictions that align with His will. These divine suggestions and impulses, gentle though they might be, are the Heavenly Father's way of guiding us.

Consider the words of *John 14:26 KJV: "But the Comforter, which is the Holy Ghost, whom the Father will send in my name, he shall teach you all things, and bring all things to your remembrance, whatsoever I have said unto you."* This scripture reaffirms our belief in the active guidance of the Holy Spirit, a divine entity sent in the name of our Lord Jesus Christ to teach and guide us.

A surrendered heart - one that has willingly submitted to the will of God - is the most receptive to His guidance. It acknowledges that it's not by our strength or intellect that we navigate life, but by the strength of the Lord and His wisdom. The words of *Proverbs 16:9 KJV, "A man's heart deviseth his way: but the LORD directeth his steps,"* remind us of our role - to devise, to plan - and God's role - to direct, to guide.

Dear brothers and sisters, let us set aside our doubts and inhibitions, surrendering our will to our Father and trusting in His divine guidance. Our skepticism should not prevent us from hearing His voice. Let us remember the promise from *Psalms 32:8* KJV, *"I will instruct thee and teach thee in the way which thou shalt go: I will guide thee with mine eye."*

In conclusion, navigating life is like journeying through a labyrinth. The path can often seem unclear and our direction unsure. Yet, if we surrender our will to the Lord, trusting in His divine guidance, we open ourselves to His Holy Spirit. In doing so, we allow Him to write His laws on our hearts and minds, guiding us toward our Heavenly Father's will. Let us strive to listen, to obey, and to trust in Him. For, as Jesus has shown us through His own life, obedience, faith, and love are the keystones to living a life of righteousness and joy in our Father's embrace. Amen.

A Roadmap to Spiritual Growth

No mortal parent or mentor can truly guide their offspring or wards if they adamantly refuse to trust that the words uttered are an authentic reflection of the parent or mentor's intentions. Our Heavenly Father, who "at sundry times and in divers manners spake in time past unto the fathers by the prophets" (Hebrews 1:1, KJV) continues to converse with us, fervently seeking to see if any souls are willing to obey and attune their ears to His divine counsel.

At every juncture of our existence, our Heavenly Father seeks to reveal Himself to us. "I that speak unto thee am He. I that whisper in thy heart, I that manifest in thy circumstances, I that communicate through thy losses and victories, thy sorrows and joys, I am He who speaks everywhere and in all things." With such profound faith, we must hold the assurance that the Lord's voice is constantly speaking to guide us. We should wholeheartedly trust that He will bless us with the wisdom necessary for our journey, and once we've sought illumination, our deepest conviction of "oughtness" must be accepted as the guidance we've sought.

Let me propose a few key principles to aid us in our spiritual journey.

Firstly, we should nurture a steadfast belief in God's guidance. This reminds us of the scriptural assurance that *"Trust in the LORD with all thine heart; and lean not unto thine own understanding" (Proverbs 3:5, KJV).*

Secondly, we must submit our will to His divine guidance. This requires a heart that echoes, *"Not my will, but thine, be done" (Luke 22:42, KJV).*

Thirdly, we need to attune our ears and hearts to listen to the Divine voice. Remember, *"Be still, and know that I am God" (Psalm 46:10, KJV)*.

Fourthly, we should be patient and wait for divine harmony to emerge within us, embodying the truth that *"they that wait upon the LORD shall renew their strength" (Isaiah 40:31, KJV)*.

Lastly, once we are sure of the divine guidance, we must obey without question. As said in *James 1:22 (KJV), "But be ye doers of the word, and not hearers only, deceiving your own selves."*

God is the true home for every creature. While the path might seem rough and narrow, nothing else can quench the love that yearns for God. You might feel that you've journeyed little on this road, my dear soul, but take courage, let the thought of God entice you further. The way towards spiritual perfection might seem challenging to the flesh, but it's not hard to love.

Do not ration your duties towards God. Contemplate deeply on Jesus, His boundless love, and how it was freely bestowed upon you. Strive for a calm heart, all day, every day. This is the key to catching the whispers of the Spirit that guide you from hour to hour. Keep your conscience alive and receptive. Follow where grace leads you - for therein lies the path to perfection.

Be obedient and love your unseen Guide as He loves you. Time and obedience will guide you towards sainthood.

In conclusion, the journey towards spiritual growth involves a conscious effort to listen to, trust, and obey God's divine guidance. As we journey, let us strive to keep our hearts receptive, our ears attentive, and our spirits willing to heed His call. As we nurture our trust in God, surrender our will to His, and remain patient, we shall surely navigate the journey towards spiritual enlightenment and growth.

In this divine voyage, the importance of consistently pouring our hearts into the tasks He has set before us cannot be overemphasized. Just as Jesus unreservedly demonstrated His love for us, so should we freely give our love and service to God. *"We love him, because he first loved us" (1 John 4:19, KJV).* This love isn't merely an emotion, but an active commitment that finds expression in our daily lives.

In maintaining an all-day calmness of heart, we're better equipped to hear the words of the Spirit, which come to us in the quiet moments, in the challenges, and even in the mundane tasks of our day-to-day life. The Scripture states: *"He that hath an ear, let him hear what the Spirit saith unto the churches" (Revelation 2:7, KJV).*

In this journey, we must also ensure our conscience remains sensitive to His call and teachings. We should endeavor not to miss any inward signal and pursue the path where grace encourages us. This pursuit is what ultimately leads us to spiritual perfection. *"Be ye therefore perfect, even as your Father which is in heaven is perfect" (Matthew 5:48, KJV).*

As we learn to love and follow our unseen Guide, our spiritual journey becomes more profound and fulfilling. It is through time and obedience that we develop a deep relationship with Him, eventually blossoming into spiritual maturity, or as we call it, sainthood.

In essence, our journey towards spiritual growth is a path filled with conscious listening, trusting, and obedience to God's divine guidance. It calls us to maintain a receptive heart, an attentive ear, and a spirit ready to heed His divine call. As we cultivate our trust in God, surrender our will to His divine wisdom, and exercise patience, we are certain to progress on our path towards spiritual enlightenment. This journey may challenge us, but in the light of His love and guidance, we will prevail and grow closer to Him.

"For I know the plans I have for you," declares the LORD, "plans to prosper you and not to harm you, plans to give you hope and a future" (Jeremiah 29:11, KJV). So, let us march on, trust in His divine wisdom, and let the thought of God allure us further on. In time and obedience, we shall attain our spiritual goal, and indeed, we shall become saints in His divine kingdom.

Chapter TWELVE

CONCERNING TEMPTATION

In the journey of faith, I have noticed, dear friends, certain misconceptions concerning the trials of temptation. One erroneous belief is the expectation that, once we anchor our soul in God, temptations will evaporate. Some believe the promised deliverance extends not only from succumbing to temptation, but even from the experience of temptation itself. Hence, when they still perceive the 'Canaanite' in the land, and witness daunting, walled cities reaching towards heaven, they grow disheartened, doubting the authenticity of their path, fearing they may have strayed.

Furthermore, they mistake temptation for sin, accusing themselves for what, in truth, is the adversary's scheme. This leads them into a pit of condemnation and discouragement. If this discouragement festers, it eventually morphs into actual sin. The adversary ensnares a disheartened soul with ease; thus, we often falter from the mere apprehension of having faltered.

Addressing the first of these misconceptions, it's important to remember the Scriptural truths. The apostle Paul reminded us in ***Ephesians 6:12 (KJV)*** that, ***"For we wrestle not against flesh and blood, but against*** *principalities, against powers, against the rulers of the darkness of this world, against spiritual wickedness in high places."* Our Christian life is indeed a warfare, and it does not cease when we find our rest in Christ Jesus. In fact, the powers that seek to tempt us in these heavenly places are far superior to any we've previously faced.

Surprisingly, temptations generally multiply tenfold upon entering the interior life. Regardless of their nature or number, they should never make us question our genuine connection to the Divine. More often than not, intense temptations signal abundant grace rather than scarce grace.

Reflecting on the journey of the Israelites in *Exodus 13:17 (KJV), "And it came to pass, when Pharaoh had let the people go, that God led them not through the way of the land of the Philistines, although that was near; for God said, Lest peradventure the people repent when they see war, and they return to Egypt."* God initially did not lead them through enemy territory because they were not yet prepared to trust Him in warfare. But as their faith matured, He allowed their adversaries to challenge them.

Similarly, in their journey through the wilderness, they encountered fewer enemies and engaged in fewer battles than in the Promised Land. The land was populated with seven mighty nations, thirty-one kings to overthrow, fortified cities to conquer, and giants to vanquish. It was only after they entered the land of Canaan that they confronted the Hittites, Amorites, Perizzites, Hivites, and Jebusites.

Take heart, dear Christian, the very magnitude of your temptations might be one of the strongest indications that you truly are in the spiritual land you have been seeking to enter. These trials are distinctive to this spiritual journey.

In conclusion, understanding that temptations are part and parcel of our spiritual journey is the key to enduring and growing through these trials. Do not be discouraged when you face temptations; rather, see them as a sign that you are treading the path towards spiritual maturity. Remember *James 1:12 (KJV), "Blessed is the man that endureth temptation: for when he is tried, he shall receive the crown of life, which the Lord hath promised to them that love him."* Stand firm in faith and press on, for in Christ, victory is assured.

A Journey of Courage and Cheerfulness

In the throes of my journey, I've discovered that one must never let temptation lead to self-doubt or cloud the certainty of having found refuge in God's "heavenly places." Understanding the distinction between temptation and sin is our second challenge and is not as straightforward. It may seem superfluous to assert that temptation is not sin itself, yet a significant portion of our anguish arises from not comprehending this truth.

The mere insinuation of wrongdoing appears to carry contamination, and when the source of this evil is unidentified, we, the tempted souls, begin to perceive ourselves as irredeemably wicked and distant from God for entertaining such thoughts and suggestions. It's as if a burglar intrudes into a man's home intending to steal, and when the master of the house opposes and seeks to evict him, the intruder accuses the owner of being the thief himself. This is the enemy's primary strategy to ensnare us.

The enemy stealthily comes and whispers harmful suggestions to us - doubts, blasphemies, jealousies, envy, and pride. Then, the enemy hypocritically says, "How sinful you must be to entertain such thoughts! It's clear you're not placing your trust in the Lord. If you were, it would've been impossible for these thoughts to invade your heart."

Such reasoning seems so plausible that we often accept it as the truth, and we then find ourselves under condemnation and inundated with discouragement. Consequently, we are prone to succumb to actual sin. Discouragement is one of the most detrimental forces in our journey of faith, whereas cheerfulness is among the most beneficial. A sage once said, regarding overcoming temptation, that cheerfulness is of utmost importance, not just once, but thrice - as the first, second, and third essential things.

We ought to anticipate victory. This anticipation of triumph is why the Lord repeatedly told Joshua, *"Be strong and of a good courage," "Be not afraid, neither be thou dismayed," "Only be thou strong and very courageous." (Joshua 1:6-9, KJV)* He delivers a similar message to us, saying, *"Let not your heart be troubled, neither let it be afraid." (John 14:27, KJV)*

The potency of temptation lies in the weakness of our hearts. The enemy is well aware of this and often launches assaults by sowing seeds of discouragement in any way possible. Sometimes, this discouragement stems from what we perceive as a righteous grief and revulsion at our susceptibility to such temptation, which is actually a disappointment stemming from the fact that we secretly believed ourselves too virtuous or detached from worldly desires to be tempted.

This self-disappointment is a worse state than the temptation itself, presenting as humility but is merely the result of wounded self-love. Genuine humility can bear the revelation of our weaknesses and follies because it doesn't derive expectations from self, but solely from God. This kind of humility, rather than discouraging us from trusting God, propels us towards deeper faith. Conversely, the false humility born out of self-plunges us into the abyss of faithless discouragement, nudging us towards the very sin that causes us distress.

In conclusion, temptation is not the same as sin. Like Jesus, we should strive to understand and apply this wisdom to our lives. As it is written in *1 Corinthians 10:13 (KJV), "There hath no temptation taken you but such as is common to man: but God is faithful, who will not suffer you to be tempted above that ye are able; but will with the temptation also make a way to escape, that ye may be able to bear it."* Therefore, it is essential that we maintain an attitude of courage and cheerfulness while facing temptations, trusting not in our own strength, but in God's.

The enemy may try to discourage us, making us question our faith and feel distant from God, but we must remember the words of Jesus in *Matthew 28:20 (KJV): "Lo, I am with you always, even unto the end of the world."* We need to stand firm in the truth that God is always with us, guiding us through our trials and making a way for us to endure and overcome.

Moreover, we should not fall into the trap of false humility, which stems from self-love and leads to faithless discouragement. Genuine humility acknowledges our weaknesses and foolishness, and drives us towards deeper faith in God. As *Philippians 4:13 (KJV)* reminds us, *"I can do all things through Christ which strengtheneth me."*

In our journey of faith, there will be moments of struggle and moments of triumph. But throughout it all, we should remain steadfast, cheerful, and full of courage, keeping our hearts and minds fixed on God. Remember the words of *Proverbs 3:5-6 (KJV), "Trust in the Lord with all thine heart; and lean not unto thine own understanding. In all thy ways acknowledge him, and he shall direct thy paths."*

So let us face each day, each trial, each temptation, with a heart full of courage and cheerfulness, trusting that God is with us and that through Him, we can overcome. May we never forget, even in the face of temptation, that we are indeed seated in the promised "heavenly places" with

Christ, far above the reach of the enemy.

A Call to Endure with Faith

As a follower of Christ, I have a vivid memory of an enlightening allegory that clearly depicted the cunning tactics of the devil. Picture this: Satan gathers his wicked cohorts for a council. Their despicable mission? To induce sin in a virtuous man.

One diabolical spirit, brimming with vile enthusiasm, proposed, "I'll make him sin by exposing him to the pleasures of sin. I'll speak of its intoxicating delights and the alluring rewards it seemingly offers." Satan, however, dismissed this idea, retorting, "He has sampled those illusory pleasures; he knows their true, corrosive nature."

Next, a different demon suggested, "I will lay bare the hardships and sorrows virtue often brings. I'll try to convince him that righteousness has no joys, no rewards." Yet again, Satan disagreed, *"No, he has tasted the sweet nectar of virtue. He understands that 'her ways are ways of pleasantness, and all her paths are peace' (Proverbs 3:17, KJV)."*

Eventually, a cunning imp offered, "I will sow seeds of discouragement in his soul." At this, Satan rejoiced, "Ah, that's the way! His spirit crushed, he'll be ours." And sadly, they succeeded.

A wise sage once declared, "All discouragement springs

from the devil." This truth, I urge all Christians, must be remembered and used as a protective amulet against despair. Shun discouragement as you would sin itself. However, this is an impossible feat if we fail to discern the true source of temptation.

The Holy Scripture proclaims, *"Blessed is the man that endureth temptation" (James 1:12, KJV),* and further encourages us to *"count it all joy when ye fall into divers temptations" (James 1:2, KJV).* Thus, temptation in itself is not sin. It's no more sinful to hear the whispered temptations of evil in our hearts than it is to overhear the profanity or malicious talk of wicked individuals in the streets. Sin is not in the hearing; it's in the joining.

If, when evil whispers creep into our minds, we turn away and give them no attention, we remain blameless. But if we entertain these thoughts, mull over them, and begin to consider them as potentially true, then we sin.

Temptation may knock on our hearts a thousand times a day without causing us to sin. We cannot prevent these attempts. But if the devil can make us believe his temptations are of our own making, then he has already won half the battle, and total victory is not far off.

I once comforted a distraught woman who had been deceived in this very way. The moment she knelt to pray, repugnant thoughts would invade her mind. She felt guilty, believing that she herself was the source of these terrible thoughts. I assured her that these thoughts were the enemy's ploys, not originating from her. I advised her to pay them no heed and instead to turn her focus to Jesus, entrusting all to Him.

The devil had gained ground by making her feel responsible for the temptations, thus causing her distress and guilt. However, if she chose to ignore them, turning her attention instead to our Lord, I assured her that victory would be hers.

In conclusion, every follower of Christ must remain vigilant against the devil's ploys. Recognize that the evil whispers in your mind are not your own. Instead of being discouraged, place your trust in Jesus and His promise of salvation. You'll find that by enduring temptation, you emerge victorious.

Every battle against temptation is fought and won in the mind. It's within this arena that Satan wages his most insidious war, aiming to distort our perceptions, dishearten our spirits, and detach us from our Savior, Jesus Christ. But, as Christ-followers, we're not defenseless. Armed with the Sword of the Spirit, the Word of God (Ephesians 6:17, KJV), we can refute every lie, rebuke every temptation, and reject every attempt to mar our virtuous journey.

Our resilience in the face of temptation comes from understanding that it is not sin to be tempted. The sin lies in surrendering to the temptation, in letting it steer our thoughts and actions away from the path of righteousness. The apostle James explains, *"But every man is tempted, when he is drawn away of his own lust, and enticed. Then when lust hath conceived, it bringeth forth sin: and sin, when it is finished, bringeth forth death" (James 1:14-15, KJV).*

Furthermore, we must remember that even our Savior, Jesus Christ, was not immune to temptation. During His time in the wilderness, Satan himself tried to tempt Him. However, Jesus resisted, replying, *"Get thee behind me, Satan: for it is written, Thou shalt worship the Lord thy God, and him only shalt thou serve" (Luke 4:8, KJV).*

Jesus, our perfect example, shows us how to handle temptation. He didn't debate with Satan; instead, He immediately turned to Scripture, wielding it as His weapon of choice. In every instance, He demonstrated the power of God's Word to dismiss the devil's schemes. This divine example underscores the importance of embedding God's Word in our hearts, so that we might not sin against Him (Psalm 119:11, KJV).

As Christ's disciples, we are not left alone in our struggles. We can turn to Jesus in our times of need, confident in His love and the promise that He will provide a way of escape from our temptations (1 Corinthians 10:13, KJV).

Therefore, beloved, let us not grow weary or lose heart when temptation arises. Rather, let us stand firm in our faith, draw near to God, resist the devil, and he will flee from us (James 4:7, KJV). Victory over temptation is ours in Christ Jesus. For He has overcome the world (John 16:33, KJV), and in Him, we too shall overcome. Amen.

"Finding Victory in Temptation: Lessons of Faith"

Once upon a time, I came to understand the real truth, and the next time those pesky thoughts entered my mind, I spoke firmly to the intruder, "I see you for who you truly are now. You are the source of these terrible thoughts, and I refuse to accept them. The Lord is my Savior; you can take these thoughts and settle them with Him." Just like that, the intruder, shocked to have been found out, retreated in disarray and my soul was entirely freed.

The enemy, you see, is quite aware that when we recognize an evil suggestion as coming from him, we will reject it much quicker than if we believe it to be our own idea. If each temptation came prefaced with the words, "I am Satan, your unforgiving enemy; I am here to lead you astray," we would most likely not be tempted in the slightest to follow his suggestions. He must conceal his true nature to make his traps appealing. We can claim victory more easily if we are aware of his schemes and identify him at his first approach.

There's a common misconception about temptations: we often believe that time spent battling them is time wasted. Hours slip by while we fight off temptations, making us feel like we have achieved nothing. But you know what? Those hours when we're under attack can often be when we're serving God most truly.

The devil's wrath against God is expressed through

temptation. Unable to harm our Savior, he tries to wound Him by defeating us. Our ruin matters to him only as it accomplishes this aim. When we resist temptation, we're fighting for our Lord. Times of temptation can sometimes be the most valuable for our growth and connection to the divine.

There's a passage in the Bible that talks about this, *"Blessed is the man that endureth temptation" (James 1:12, KJV).* This suggests that being patient under the stress of temptation can nurture the virtue of patience and foster our reliance on Jesus. And most importantly, resisting temptation brings glory to our Savior.

We are also reminded that the test of our faith through various temptations is more valuable than gold. The reward for our patience and faith will be the gift of eternal life, promised by the Lord to those who love Him. Now we understand the exhortation in the Book of James, *"Count it all joy when ye fall into divers temptations; Knowing this, that the trying of your faith worketh patience. But let patience have her perfect work, that ye may be perfect and entire, wanting nothing" (James 1:2-4, KJV).*

Temptations, it seems, are part of God's plan to complete our journey towards spiritual maturity. So, ironically, the enemy's own weapons are used against him, illustrating that everything, including temptations, can work together for the good of those who love God.

How can we overcome temptations, you ask? As you know, our interior life is built upon faith. Our motto remains, "We are nothing, Christ is all." Realizing our own helplessness, we understand we cannot do anything by ourselves. Hence, our only choice is to surrender the temptation to our Lord, trusting Him to overcome it for us.

Committing ourselves to Him for victory over temptation should be as absolute as our initial commitment to Him for salvation. He must do everything for us in both instances. It was only faith then, and it should be only faith now. When we fully trust in Him, the Lord works miracles in defeating the temptations we face, as thousands can testify.

In conclusion, the journey towards overcoming temptation is a journey of faith and trust in the Lord. We must be alert to the devil's tactics, recognizing that he cloaks himself in our thoughts, pushing us toward sin. When we unveil his deceit, his power over us diminishes.

Remember, the enemy's attacks are not just against us; they are attacks against our Savior, Jesus Christ. When we resist temptation, we are not only defending our hearts, but also honoring the Lord. We become His soldiers in this spiritual battle, standing firm in the face of adversity.

The scriptures tell us, *"Blessed is the man that endureth temptation" (James 1:12, KJV).* It might seem strange to feel blessed while under the strain of temptation, but enduring this struggle cultivates patience and strengthens our faith. We are being shaped, molded by the hands of God, becoming better, stronger, more spiritually mature.

In our battle against temptation, we must be firm in our faith. Just as we entrusted our salvation to the Lord, we must entrust our struggle with temptation to Him. Faith, in the beginning, was our saving grace, and it must be our strength in overcoming temptations.

As we hand our battles over to Jesus, it's crucial that we completely leave them in His capable hands. It's His fight now, not ours. This is not a sign of our weakness, but a testament to our trust in His strength and righteousness.

Let us rejoice then when we face diverse temptations, for they are but trials of our faith, designed to work patience in us, and bring us to a state of perfection and completeness, wanting nothing (James 1:2-4, KJV). Every temptation faced and overcome, every battle given to the Lord, strengthens our faith and deepens our connection to Jesus.

The key to victory over temptations is unwavering faith. This faith that saved us, this faith that sustains us, can also deliver us from the power of temptation. It is through faith that our weakness is transformed into strength, our fears into courage, and our temptations into victories.

So, whenever you face temptation, remember the truth, expose the enemy, and place your trust in the Lord. Stand on your faith and let Jesus fight your battles. His victories will truly be miraculous, transforming you and glorifying Him.

In the end, when we stand firm in our faith and resist temptation, we honor our Lord, strengthen our spiritual armor, and contribute to His victory. The enemy may target us, but God uses these attacks to perfect us, showcasing how He turns everything, even temptations, for our good.

" Temptation: Pathway to Spiritual Growth"

In my journey, I've come to realize the immense importance of temptation in shaping our spiritual character. Rather than dwelling on overcoming it, I wish to shine light on the essence of temptation itself. I yearn to free the faithful and conscientious souls from the shackles that bind them when they misunderstand temptation and equate it with sin.

You see, we must not be ignorant of the undeniable truth - temptations, in reality, are invaluable components of our soul's evolution. Regardless of their initial source, they are tools used by the Almighty to shape in us precious traits of character which might otherwise be absent. Whenever temptation is present, God, too, is there, supervising and modulating its intensity. The saint in the desert once questioned, "Where were You, Lord, while I was being tempted?" The compassionate answer came, "Close beside you, my child, always."

Temptations challenge us. If we aren't tried, our worth cannot be realized. They cultivate our spiritual strength, bravery, and wisdom, which are crucial for our growth, the very thing God yearns for us. Without temptations, our spirituality would be superficial. *James 1:12 (KJV) says, "Blessed is the man that endureth temptation: for when he is tried, he shall receive the crown of life, which the Lord hath promised to them that love Him."* The "crown of life" is invaluable, well worth all the trials and endurance needed to achieve it, and it can't be attained without these.

Allow me to share an illustrative story. A sickly lady once acquired the cocoon of a splendid butterfly with extraordinarily radiant wings, hoping to witness its emergence within her chamber. As spring approached, she watched with delight as the butterfly began to emerge, but with great difficulty. Despite its straining and struggling, progress was slow. She thought it needed help and used a pair of fine scissors to snip the restricting cord at the cocoon's opening.

Suddenly, the cocoon opened, and the butterfly escaped without struggle. She felt triumphant, yet soon noticed that something was amiss. Although the butterfly was free from its cocoon, its magnificent wings were lifeless, colorless, and trailed behind like a burdensome load. It lived a feeble, miserable life for a few days before it perished, never having lifted its powerless wings.

In her disappointment, the lady confided in a naturalist, who explained that her intervention was the problem. The struggle to emerge from the cocoon was crucial for the life fluid to flow into the wings. Her misguided kindness in easing the butterfly's struggle had left the wings lifeless.

Our spiritual wings, too, require the struggle and exertion inherent in our battle with temptation and trials. By avoiding these struggles, we would only weaken our souls' power to "mount up with wings as eagles" (Isaiah 40:31, KJV), and would forfeit the "crown of life" promised to those who endure.

In conclusion, let us understand the intrinsic value of temptations. They are not to be feared or avoided but embraced as opportunities for spiritual growth. God is always with us during these trying times, guiding us and using the trials to shape our character. So, when you face temptation, remember - it's not a sign of sin but a path to strength and spiritual development. Stay strong, persevere, and let your spiritual wings unfurl in all their glory.

.

CHAPTER THIRTEEN
Acknowledging and Overcoming Failures

As the title suggests, this piece talks about failures. Some might be surprised, thinking, "Failures? I thought there were none in this life of faith!" True, there should be none, and there need not be. However, sometimes they happen. We must confront realities, not theories.

Teachers of spiritual life don't claim that sinning becomes impossible. They only argue that sin is no longer necessary and that there is a chance for constant triumph. It's rare to find someone who hasn't admitted to occasionally yielding to temptation.

When talking about sin here, I mean known, conscious sin. I'm not addressing unknowing sins or so-called inherent sins, which are all forgiven through atonement and do not disturb our relationship with God. I'm leaving the doctrines about sin to theologians to argue and settle. My focus is on believers' experiences.

Misunderstanding about known or conscious sin can be dangerous in the Christian life. When a believer, who believes they're on the path of holiness, is caught off guard by sin, they're tempted to either give up entirely or hide their sin to protect the doctrine, calling it a weakness and refusing to be open and honest about it. Neither approach promotes real growth in a holy life.

To handle this, one should face the unfortunate reality straight away, correctly identify it, and then seek the cause and solution. Being completely honest with God and oneself is essential for a life united with Him. Dishonest handling of sin can disrupt the communion with Him more than the sin itself.

A momentary failure doesn't mean you should feel disheartened and consider everything lost. Our faith isn't compromised by it. We aren't advocating a state, but a journey. The path of holiness isn't a destination, but a route. Sanctification isn't something we acquire at a certain point and keep forever. It's a life we live daily, hour by hour.

A detour doesn't erase the path. It can be quickly returned to. In this journey of faith, there may be momentary lapses. These are regrettable and should be avoided, but if properly addressed, they need not disrupt the soul's stance on complete dedication and perfect trust, or its joyful communion with God.

The essential thing is to return to God instantly. Sin isn't a reason to stop trusting; it's a compelling reason to trust even more. No matter what caused the lapse, discouragement won't solve it. Just as a child learning to walk doesn't give up after falling, a believer learning to live by faith shouldn't despair after sinning. The only solution in both cases is to stand up and try again.

The children of Israel experienced a major defeat shortly after entering the promised land, against the small city of Ai. The Bible tells us in Joshua 7:5-9:

"Wherefore the hearts of the people melted, and became as water. And Joshua rent his clothes, and fell to the earth upon his face before the ark of the Lord until the eventide, he and the elders of Israel, and put dust upon their heads... O Lord, what shall I say, when Israel turneth their backs before their enemies?"

This verse captures their despair perfectly. However, as we know, the Israelites didn't stay defeated. They learned from their failures and ultimately found victory. Similarly, in our spiritual journey, we must accept and learn from our failures, and with God's grace, continue on our path with renewed vigor.

In conclusion, failures are not permanent roadblocks in our faith journey. They are temporary obstacles that can be overcome with honesty, trust, and steadfast faith in God. Our relationship with God is not defined by our shortcomings but by how we respond to them. When we stumble, the best course of action is to acknowledge our failings, ask for forgiveness, and use the experience to grow stronger in our faith.

This doesn't mean that sin should be taken lightly. It should be avoided at all costs. However, when we do fail, we should not lose heart or fall into despair. Instead, we should turn back to God immediately and trust in His forgiving and restorative nature.

The apostle John provides us with a reassuring message in *1 John 1:9 (KJV), "If we confess our sins, he is faithful and just to forgive us our sins, and to cleanse us from all unrighteousness."* This verse encourages us to confront our sins with honesty and assurance of God's forgiveness.

Living a life of faith is a journey, not a destination. It's about walking the path of righteousness every day, striving to align ourselves with the teachings of Christ. In this journey, we may encounter momentary failures, but these failures are not the end of the path. Like the Israelites, we learn from our mistakes, pick ourselves up, and continue on the path to a holy life.

To sum up, let's take courage in the knowledge that God's grace is sufficient for us. His strength is made perfect in our weakness (2 Corinthians 12:9, KJV). Thus, our momentary failures don't define us; they are stepping stones that can strengthen our relationship with God if handled correctly. Despite the stumbles, our walk of faith should remain steadfast, honest, and trusting, always aiming for growth and maturity in Christ. Let us strive daily to follow Jesus's footsteps and trust in His mercy and forgiveness. Even when we falter, His love for us remains unchanging.

Triumph Over Defeat in the Image of Christ

When faced with defeat, like many children of God, I often feel as though my courage fades into nothingness. I've caught myself yearning for what was once familiar, pleading, "If only we were content and stayed on the other side of Jordan!" I would forecast my own failures, predicting further losses against my foes. Back then, as it often happens now, I believed that despair and discouragement were the only fitting responses to such defeat. However, God had different plans.

In the Bible, we see how God reached out to Joshua in his time of despair, saying, ***"Get thee up; wherefore liest thou upon thy face?" (Joshua 7:10, KJV).*** God was telling Joshua, and all of us, that the right response to defeat isn't surrendering to hopelessness, but rather confronting the problems and moving beyond them. We are called to renew and "sanctify" ourselves right away. God always commands us to "rise up and sanctify the people." On the contrary, the temptation of the enemy is to "lie down and be discouraged."

I've found that we tend to believe that it's almost disrespectful to approach the Lord immediately after we've sinned against Him. We might feel as if we should endure the consequences of our wrongdoings and the accusations of our conscience for a while. It's hard to believe that the Lord would be willing to immediately welcome us back into His loving fellowship. This reminds me of a conversation I had with a young girl who struggled with this very idea.

When I assured her that Jesus always forgives our sins as soon as we ask Him, she couldn't believe it. She felt that

He should make us feel sorry for at least a few days and that we should have to beg for His forgiveness multiple times. She even believed that we should ask Him "in a very pretty way." In reality, however, many Christians act on this very misconception, allowing their remorse and despair to create a chasm between them and God, wider than their sins ever could.

This belief contrasts sharply with how we wish our own children would behave. A mother's heart aches when her child isolates in remorse, doubting her forgiveness. Yet, her heart fills with joy when her child immediately asks for forgiveness. This human expression of love reflects God's infinite love for us, evident in His plea, *"Return, ye backsliding children, and I will heal your backslidings" (Jeremiah 3:22, KJV).*

When we become conscious of our sins, we should also become aware of our immediate forgiveness. This understanding is crucial for our journey on the path of holiness. No separation from God can be tolerated even for an instant on this path. By keeping our eyes on Jesus continually, we remain on this path. However, if we get distracted by our sins and weaknesses, we risk straying off the path.

If sin overwhelms us, we must instantly bring it to the Lord, acting on the promise given in *1 John 1:9: "If we confess our sins, He is faithful and just to forgive us our sins, and to cleanse us from all unrighteousness" (KJV).* We should not make excuses for our sins or try to forget them over time. Like the children of Israel, we should rise early in the morning, go to the place where we've hidden our wrongdoings, and lay them before the Lord. We should confess our sins, and then put them away, building over them a heap of stones so they are forever out of sight. We should believe in the moment that God forgives our sins and cleanses us from all unrighteousness. We must claim forgiveness and cleansing immediately by faith, trusting in God more completely than ever before.

As soon as the sins of Israel were revealed and set aside, God's word came again, providing a glorious encouragement, *"Fear not, neither be thou dismayed... See, I have given into thy hand the king of Ai, and his people, and his city, and his land." (Joshua 8:1, KJV)*

It is a similar message for us. After confronting and casting away our sins, God encourages us to rise above our fear and despair. He assures us that, despite our previous failures, He has given us the strength to overcome the challenges we face. We must not remain wallowing in defeat, but instead, rise in the faith that God has given us the power to triumph.

In conclusion, facing defeat and sin can often lead us to a state of despair and discouragement. However, the divine example set by Jesus Christ encourages us to rise up from our downfalls and face our challenges. We are called to acknowledge our sins, ask for forgiveness, and trust that the Lord will forgive us immediately. By doing this, we not only reaffirm our commitment to walk on the path of holiness but also strengthen our relationship with God. Remember, His yearning love is always ready to heal our backslidings and guide us towards triumph over defeat.

It's time we rise up, trust in His promise, and renew ourselves in His grace.

"Elevating Courage Through God's Forgiveness"

"I must find my courage soaring to new heights, surrendering myself entirely to the Lord so His mighty power can perfectly perform His will in me. Furthermore, once my sin is confessed and forgiven, I should not dwell on it or indulge in a mire of regret and remorse. I mustn't elevate it to a place of importance, inspecting it from all angles, letting it become a looming mountain that obscures my view of God. I should emulate the Apostle Paul, 'forgetting those things which are behind, and reaching forth unto those things which are before,' *I need to 'press toward the mark for the prize of the high calling of God in Christ Jesus' (Philippians 3:13-14).*

To exemplify these principles, let me share two contrasting stories. The first involves a devout Christian man, a pillar of the church, who had been relishing the blessings of full salvation for several months. However, he succumbed to a temptation to treat a fellow believer unkindly. Shocked by his own transgression, he was plunged into profound despair, doubting he had ever embraced the life of full trust in Christ.

His despair swelled day by day, gradually leading him astray into various sins until his existence became a torment to himself and those around him. His physical health declined under this immense burden, and there were concerns for his sanity. After three harrowing years, he encountered a Christian lady well-versed in understanding sin.

In just a short conversation, she unearthed his inner turmoil and immediately suggested, "Undoubtedly, you sinned in that act, and I won't urge you to excuse it. But have you confessed it to the Lord and asked His forgiveness?" The man responded that he had done nothing but confess and plead for God's forgiveness continuously over these three dreadful years.

The lady questioned, "But you've never believed He forgave you?" The man replied, "No, because I never felt He did." To this, the lady countered, "What if God said He forgave you, would you believe it then?" "Oh, yes," responded the man, "if God said it, I would believe it."

The lady then turned to *1 John 1:9* in the KJV of the Bible, which states, *"If we confess our sins, He is faithful and just to forgive us our sins, and to cleanse us from all unrighteousness."* She explained that for three years, he had been confessing his sin while God's word assured him of forgiveness and cleansing, yet he refused to believe. This disbelief made him 'a liar' before God.

After understanding the enormity of his error, the man was struck silent with shock and dismay. However, when the lady proposed that they should kneel, confess his past unbelief and sins, and then and there claim present forgiveness and cleansing, he obediently complied. The outcome was miraculous. His heart was flooded with light, and he broke into praises for the astounding deliverance. It took mere moments for his faith to guide him back to the comfort and joy of Jesus's salvation.

In another instance, a Christian lady, after two weeks of bright and victorious spiritual experience, succumbed to a burst of anger. This immediately led the enemy to cast doubt, claiming her past spiritual growth had been a mistake.

Continuing in the spirit of Christ's teachings, I urge you to remember that sin, once confessed and forgiven, should not become a beacon of remorse or self-doubt. It is essential to trust in the Lord's grace and forgiveness, letting these divine gifts inspire us to rise to the 'high calling of God in Christ Jesus.' By remembering this, our courage can truly soar, and we can face our everyday challenges with strength and peace.

Let us consider the second lady's response to her moment of anger. Instead of sinking into despair as the man did, she chose a different path. With wisdom granted by her recent experience in the land of promise, she managed to quickly regain her footing. She reminded herself that the occasional stumble doesn't negate the journey she had undertaken with Christ. With humility, she sought God's forgiveness and found peace, understanding that His mercy is as boundless as His love.

Both these stories demonstrate contrasting responses to sin. However, what stands out is the magnitude of God's forgiveness and our role in accepting it. When we confess our sins, God is *"faithful and just to forgive us our sins, and to cleanse us from all unrighteousness" (1*

John 1:9). Once this divine pardon is granted, we should not dwell on past transgressions, but rather embrace the gift of forgiveness, allowing ourselves to be cleansed and renewed.

The journey of faith is one of continuous learning and growth. We may stumble along the way, but these missteps are opportunities for us to realize the depth of God's love and mercy. The enemy may use these moments to sow seeds of doubt, but we must remain steadfast, knowing that God's forgiveness is constant and His love unwavering.

In conclusion, the strength of our courage rests on the foundation of our faith in God's forgiveness. We must never let our past sins obscure our view of His divine grace and mercy. Instead, we should allow our transgressions to be stepping stones, leading us closer to Him. For in the end, our courage isn't defined by our ability to avoid falling but by our willingness to rise each time we do, leaning on the "high calling of God in Christ Jesus." May we always remember and take to heart His merciful forgiveness, allowing it to guide us on our path to salvation. In the style of our Savior Jesus Christ, let us press forward, reaching toward the higher call with courage and faith.

A Journey to Spiritual Deliverance

Picture me, deceived about my life, lacking trust, and feeling defeated. Suddenly, thoughts surged through my consciousness, suggesting that perhaps the life of holiness is not meant for me. I had attempted to dedicate myself to it wholeheartedly, to trust without falter, but I felt I could do no more.

Yet, having been well-taught in the ways of God, I quickly reminded myself of His words. As stated in the KJV of *1 John 1:9, "If we confess our sins, He is faithful and just to forgive us our sins, and to cleanse us from all unrighteousness."* Trusting in this promise, I decided not to wallow in self-defeat, but to confess and seek forgiveness.

Riddled with anger, I sought solitude in a quiet room. Kneeling beside the bed, I poured out my heart, "Lord, I confess my sin. In this very moment, I am sinning. I abhor it, but I cannot overcome it. I confess it to You with shame and embarrassment. Yet, I believe that according to Your word, You forgive and cleanse." Saying it aloud seemed to lighten the heavy burden within me.

As the confession left my lips, a sudden peace descended. The Lord, in His mercy, stilled the storm within me. My soul was enveloped in light and joy, the enemy fled, and through His love, I emerged victorious. This victory was swift, taking less than five minutes, and it renewed my resolve to continue on the path of holiness. It was through this experience of defeat and redemption that I found a door of hope in my valley of troubles.

This experience reminded me of the lyrics, "I will sing unto the Lord, for He hath triumphed gloriously." After all, in any crisis, the only remedy is to trust in the Lord.

And if trusting is all we can do, wouldn't it be better to do it immediately? Every time I fail, I am reminded that the path to recovery lies in increasing my faith, not diminishing it. I would urge you, dear reader, let any failures you encounter drive you towards the Lord, with complete surrender and perfect trust.

Now, as we explore the causes of failure in this journey of full salvation, remember it's not about the strength of the temptation, our own weaknesses, or any shortcomings in our Savior's power or willingness to save us. The book of Joshua chapter 1, verse 5 promises us, *"There shall not any man be able to stand before thee all the days of thy life."* We are reminded again in *1 Corinthians 10:13, "God is faithful, who will not suffer you to be tempted above that ye are able; but will with the temptation also make a way to escape, that ye may be able to bear it."*

In the case of the people of Israel who fled before the men of Ai, it was not the strength of their enemy nor a failure on God's part that caused their defeat. The cause was hidden deep within them, a disobedience against God's commandments. This hidden sin weakened them and turned them away from their enemies.

In conclusion, remember that God's promise of forgiveness and cleansing is ever present for us. It is through confessing our sins and trusting in God's word that we are able to overcome our struggles and continue on our path of holiness. Let this serve as an encouragement to you in your walk with God. No matter the sin or the struggle, God's grace and forgiveness are always within our reach. Let us always strive to trust in

Him more fully, especially in moments of failure. For in Him, we find not only the strength to overcome but also the promise of peace and the assurance of His unwavering love.

In the face of temptation or failure, rather than sinking into defeat, let us strive to increase our faith and trust in the Lord. Remember, it is through our trust in His divine promises that we find the strength to conquer our weaknesses.

So, my fellow traveler in this journey of life, let's learn from our failures. Let them serve not as a stumbling block but as stepping stones to greater faith and deeper trust in the Lord. As we navigate through life's valleys, let us remember that hidden within each valley of Achor is a door of hope. Every time we confess our sins, our hearts lighten, and we open this door to let in God's comforting light and joy.

And remember, no matter how deep the sin or how hidden it is, nothing can stand against the power of God's forgiveness and cleansing. Our failures don't define us; rather, it's our faith and our willingness to confess, seek forgiveness, and grow in Him. So let us turn to Him, confess our sins, and immerse ourselves in the bountiful love and mercy of God. For He has triumphed gloriously, and in Him, we find our deliverance and hope.

May our song of deliverance forever echo the triumphant chorus, "I will sing unto the Lord, for He hath triumphed gloriously." Let our lives be a testament to His love, His forgiveness, and His saving grace. May we continually trust in Him and seek His forgiveness, knowing that He is faithful and just to forgive us our sins and to cleanse us from all unrighteousness. In doing so, may we find ourselves walking more firmly on the blessed highway of holiness, continually living a life of faith, trust, and complete surrender to Him. Amen.

The Hidden Sin: A Lesson in Spiritual Diligence

I am reminded of a sobering truth found in the Holy Scriptures. The verse **Joshua 7:13** from the KJV **reads,** *"Up, sanctify the people, and say, Sanctify yourselves against tomorrow: for thus saith the Lord God of Israel, There is an accursed thing in the midst of thee, O Israel: thou canst not stand before thine enemies, until ye take away the accursed thing from among you."*

This profound teaching highlights a crucial spiritual principle. Any behavior, feeling, or thought contrary to God's will - no matter how minor or deeply hidden in our hearts - will lead to spiritual defeat. It could be a grudge harbored against another, a habit of making harsh judgments, reluctance in obeying God's voice, or a dubious habit or situation. Any of these can cripple our spiritual strength.

We might bury this evil deep within our hearts, cover it from sight, and even deny its existence. Yet, its presence lurks in our awareness. Even when we engage more earnestly in our spiritual duties, this hidden transgression can lead us to unexpected failure. The only way to overcome this is to bring the hidden wrong to light and lay it before God.

As followers of Christ striving for a life of purity, when we face defeat, we must examine not the strength of our enemy, but something deeper - a hidden insubordination within us. This internal wrongdoing is like a disease, and the sin it causes is merely a symptom. Even in what appears good at a first glance, evil might be hiding. For instance, beneath what seems like an intense zeal for truth, a judgmental spirit or a subtle reliance on our understanding might hide. Underneath a mask of faithfulness might lie a lack of Christian love, or an unnecessary concern for worldly affairs might mask a significant lack of trust in God.

Our blessed Guide, the Holy Spirit, who dwells within us, helps reveal these hidden wrongs through small prods of our conscience, leaving us without excuse. However, we might disregard His soft voice, assuring ourselves everything is right, allowing the evil to continue within us, causing unexpected defeat.

Let me share an everyday occurrence that aptly illustrates this. I had moved into a new house where I found a seemingly clean and empty cider cask in the cellar. Despite the twinges of my conscience urging me to investigate, I left it undisturbed due to the perceived inconvenience. Over time, moths infested my house, threatening to ruin my possessions. Despite my efforts, I failed to eliminate them.

I share this as a reminder of the importance of spiritual diligence and self-examination in our walk with God. The cask in my cellar is akin to those hidden sins within us that we avoid confronting, and the moths symbolize the consequences of such avoidance, silently but relentlessly causing havoc.

In conclusion, the teaching in *Joshua 7:13* serves as a stark reminder for us to continually scrutinize our spiritual health. It prompts us to acknowledge, confront, and remove any hidden sin within us. For, as in *1 John 1:9 KJV, "If we confess our sins, he is faithful and just to forgive us our sins, and to cleanse us from all unrighteousness."* Only by doing this can we maintain spiritual vitality and stand strong in the face of our spiritual battles.

Lessons From the Moth-Filled Cask

My furniture was old, and I thought it might be the cause of a problem I was facing. So, I got it reupholstered. When that didn't help, I even started thinking about crazy, impossible reasons. Then, I remembered a cask in my cellar. I decided to open it and to my surprise, thousands of moths flew out. It looked like the person who lived in the house before me had put something in that cask that bred these moths. This was the source of my problem.

I realized this moth problem was like a bad habit or an indulgence that might seem harmless, but deep down we know it isn't right. This type of behavior, kept hidden from the view of others, and even from God's watchful eyes, can cause failure in our lives. We hold onto a secret, not letting the Lord into every aspect of our lives. And so, we often find ourselves unable to face our challenges, feeling defeated.

In the Bible, *Psalm 139:23-24 says, "Search me, O God, and know my heart: try me, and know my thoughts: And see if there be any wicked way in me, and lead me in the way everlasting."* This verse teaches us that to avoid failure or to understand why we failed, we need to pray and ask God to show us if there's anything wrong within us, and then guide us onto the right path.

Sometimes, we might be upset with ourselves when we fail. It seems like we're doing this for God's glory, but if we really think about it, it might just be our own pride that's hurting. Realizing that we aren't as good as we thought we were hurts our pride. This disappointment in ourselves can sometimes be a bigger mistake than the original wrong we did.

When we make a mistake, the best thing to do isn't to beat ourselves up or make excuses. Instead, we should calmly talk to God about it. If we do this with peace and love in our hearts, it will help us move forward. People who have spent a lot of time thinking about and studying God's ways say that simply turning back to God helps us more than feeling bad about what we've done wrong. The moment you notice you've done something wrong, turn back to God. His love will help you out of the situation. Looking at ourselves will only make us feel worse because the problem is within us, but turning to God will bring peace to our hearts.

Remember, no matter how many times we mess up, Jesus is always ready to help us out. The Bible says in *Luke 1:74-75, "That he would grant unto us, that we being delivered out of the hand of our enemies might serve him without fear, In holiness and righteousness before him, all the days of our life."*

So, we should always pray, "Lord, keep us from doing wrong. Let us show others how You can help them in every way." We should never be okay with anything less than being so open to God, and having so much faith in Him, that He can make us perfect, doing His will and making Him happy. *Hebrews 13:21 says, "Make you perfect in every good work to do his will, working in you that which is well-pleasing in his sight, through Jesus Christ; to whom be glory for ever and ever. Amen."*

In conclusion, our journey to live a good life, like the moth-filled cask, can be obscured by our own bad habits and mistakes. However, through prayer and turning to God, we can overcome these obstacles and live a life that pleases Him. By submitting ourselves to His divine guidance, we open the doors for His love and mercy to transform us. We allow Him to expose and rid us of the hidden moths of sin and disobedience.

By continually seeking God's examination of our hearts, like in Psalm 139:23-24, we invite Him to reveal our faults. When we allow God to guide us, He leads us on the path of righteousness, the path that is pleasing to

Him.

Our failures can cause disappointment and hurt, but we must remember that these feelings often stem from our own pride. Instead of wallowing in self-pity or self-condemnation, we should view these failures as opportunities to learn and grow.

Turning back to God, time and time again, shows our faith in Him. It is His love and grace that lifts us from our mistakes and sets us back on the right path. In the light of His presence, we find comfort and deliverance.

Ultimately, Jesus Christ is our greatest ally. His sacrifice allows us to serve God fearlessly, *"In holiness and righteousness before Him, all the days of our life" (Luke 1:74-75).* As such, we must always pray for His protection against sin and His guidance to live as faithful testimonies of His power to save.

We should never settle for less but strive towards spiritual perfection by fully entrusting ourselves to God's will. As stated in *Hebrews 13:21,* God is able to make us perfect in every good work, as long as we are willing to surrender to Him and trust in His ways.

Remember, the glory belongs to Jesus Christ forever and ever. It is through Him that we find the strength and courage to overcome our trials and emerge victorious. Let us, therefore, embrace His teachings and strive to live a life that reflects His love and mercy. To Him be the Glory, forever and ever. Amen.

Chapter FOURTEEN

DOUBTS

Overcoming Doubt: Embracing the Life of Faith

Many Christians find themselves enslaved by the habit of doubting. The chains of doubt bind them more tightly than any drunkard's fatal habit. At every step of their Christian journey, they face the daunting odds of doubts that lie in wait, ready to assail them at any moment. These doubts make their lives wretched, hinder their usefulness, and constantly interrupt their communion with God. While embracing a life of faith can often lift believers out of this realm of doubts, there are times when the old tyrant of doubt resurfaces, causing stumbling and a weakened heart, even if he cannot completely drag the believer back into the dreary wilderness.

We may recall the gripping yet horrifying story of Christian's imprisonment in Doubting Castle by the wicked giant Despair. Our hearts rejoiced as he escaped through the massive gates, fleeing from that cruel tyrant. Little did we suspect that we too would be taken prisoner by the same giant and confined in the same castle. I fear that every member of the Church of Christ has experienced this at least once. Take a moment to revisit the account, and you may find your own grievous experiences mirrored there—moments that were difficult to bear and sorrowful to reflect upon later.

It seems strange that those who bear the name "Believers," implying that their primary characteristic is faith, would have to confess to such experiences. Yet, it has become such a universal habit that if the majority of the Church were to be renamed, "Doubters" would be the fitting and descriptive name. Many Christians have resigned themselves to living with doubt, regarding it as an inevitable affliction of life that they must endure. They lament their doubts as one might lament their rheumatism, presenting themselves as "interesting cases" in need of special sympathy and consideration. Sadly, even those who earnestly long to embrace the life of faith and have taken steps towards it often find themselves in this position.

Doubt can be a formidable tyrant, robbing us of joy, hindering our spiritual growth, and undermining our relationship with God. Yet, it is not a necessary part of our journey. As followers of Christ, we are called to be believers, to trust in the promises of God. Overcoming doubt requires a deliberate choice to rely on God's Word, to seek His presence, and to surround ourselves with fellow believers who can encourage and uplift us. Jesus Himself said in *Matthew 21:22, "And all things, whatsoever ye shall ask in prayer, believing, ye shall receive."* By firmly anchoring our faith in Him, we can break free from the chains of doubt and embrace the abundant life of faith that God has prepared for us.

Let us not settle for a life marked by doubt, but instead, let us press forward with unwavering faith. Doubt may attempt to cast shadows on our path, but we have been given the tools to overcome it. The Scriptures serve as a source of light and truth, guiding us in every circumstance.

In the book of Mark, chapter 9, verse 24, a father cried out to Jesus, saying, *"Lord, I believe; help thou mine unbelief."* This humble plea reflects the struggle many of us face. We may have faith, but there are moments when doubt creeps in and threatens to undermine our confidence. Like this father, we must turn to Jesus and ask for His help in overcoming our unbelief.

The apostle Paul, in his letter to the Corinthians, encourages us with these words: *"For we walk by faith, not by sight" (2 Corinthians 5:7).* Walking by faith requires a shift in our perspective. Instead of relying solely on what we can see and understand, we choose to trust in the unseen realities of God's promises. This deliberate choice to trust in God's faithfulness enables us to rise above the doubts that seek to ensnare us.

Moreover, Jesus Himself assures us of the power of faith in *Matthew 17:20*, where He says, *"If ye have faith as a grain of mustard seed, ye shall say unto this mountain, Remove hence to yonder place, and it shall remove, and nothing shall be impossible unto you."* The tiniest measure of faith, when placed in God, can move mountains and conquer doubts.

To overcome doubt, we must immerse ourselves in the truth of God's Word. Meditate on the promises He has given us, such as *Psalm 37:5: "Commit thy way unto the Lord; trust also in him, and he shall bring it to pass."* Memorize these passages and allow them to become the foundation of your faith.

Additionally, we should surround ourselves with fellow believers who can encourage and strengthen us. The book of Hebrews urges us to *"consider one another to provoke unto love and to good works" (Hebrews 10:24).* Through fellowship and shared experiences, we can inspire and uplift one another, reminding ourselves of God's faithfulness in the midst of doubt.

In conclusion, doubt may try to shackle us, but we are not destined to be its prisoners. Jesus Christ, our perfect example, demonstrated unwavering faith throughout His earthly ministry. By seeking His guidance, meditating on His Word, and relying on the support of fellow believers, we can overcome doubt and step into the abundant life of faith God intends for us. Let us cast off the chains of doubt and walk confidently in the truth, knowing that our faith has the power to move mountains and bring us closer to God.

THE WORDS OF JESUS

JESUS: In my teachings, I have noticed that many people, although they believe their sins are forgiven and they are children of God through faith in Me, still struggle with doubt. They may have overcome their old doubts about salvation and reaching Heaven, but they have simply shifted their habit of doubting to a higher platform. They say, "Yes, I believe my sins are forgiven and I am a child of God, but..." This "but" encompasses a never-ending list of doubts about every declaration and promise made by our Father. They wrestle with these doubts, refusing to believe them until they have more tangible proof than God's simple word. Consequently, they wonder why they walk in darkness and view themselves as spiritual martyrs, burdened by ongoing conflicts. I must strongly protest against this entire mindset.

It is as futile as joining a drunkard in lamenting the consequences of his destructive habits and praying for grace to endure them. Instead, I declare to both the enslaved souls and the drunkard the perfect deliverance I have in store for them through Me. I urge them, with all the strength of My being, to avail themselves of this deliverance and be set free. I will not entertain their despairing excuses. They ought to be free, they can be free, and they must be free!

Do you dare to tell Me that it is an inevitable necessity for God to be doubted by His children? Would you tolerate your own children doubting you? Would you allow their doubts to persist even for an hour? Would you not be indignant if your child came to you and said, "Father, I cannot believe your word, I cannot trust your love"?

Hannah: I recall witnessing the profound indignation of a mother when one of her children expressed doubt. She had brought her two little girls to my house and left them in my care while she attended to some errands. One child, filled with the joyful confidence of childhood, immersed herself in the pleasures of my nursery, singing and playing until her mother returned.

The other child, burdened by the cautious mistrust of maturity, sat alone in a corner, wondering if her mother would remember to pick her up, fearing she would be forgotten, and imagining that her mother would be glad to be rid of her because she was a naughty girl. Eventually, she worked herself into a frenzy of despair. I shall never forget the look on that mother's face when her weeping child explained what troubled her. Grief, wounded love, indignation, and pity fought for dominance within her. Indignation triumphed that day, and I doubt that little girl had ever been disciplined so firmly before.

Throughout my life, this scene has taught me a powerful lesson, compelling me to reject doubt concerning My Heavenly Father's love, care, and remembrance of Me whenever it clamored at the door of My heart. I am convinced that doubting is a true luxury for many people, and abstaining from it would require the most challenging self-denial they have ever experienced. This luxury, like all others, brings sorrowful consequences. Perhaps, as you consider the sadness and misery that doubt has caused in your own Christian journey, you may say, "This is no luxury to me, but a fearful trial." However, I urge you to pause for a moment. Try giving up doubt and see for yourself whether it is truly a luxury or not. Don't your doubts come knocking as sympathetic friends, understanding your difficulties and offering condolences? Isn't it a luxury to sit with them, entertain their arguments, and join in their commiseration? Would it not be an act of self-denial to resolutely turn away from them and refuse to listen?

I implore you to embrace faith instead. Doubt robs you of the peace and assurance that faith brings. It hinders your spiritual growth and keeps you bound in a cycle of uncertainty and turmoil. By entertaining doubt, you open the door to fear, anxiety, and a constant questioning of God's faithfulness.

But if you choose to let go of doubt and embrace faith, you will experience a transformation. Faith is the key that unlocks the door to the abundant life I offer. It is the assurance of things hoped for and the conviction of things not seen (Hebrews 11:1). When you trust in Me wholeheartedly, you can rest in the knowledge that I am faithful to fulfill every promise I have made to you.

Scripture reminds us in *Proverbs 3:5-6, "Trust in the LORD with all thine heart; and lean not unto thine own understanding. In all thy ways acknowledge him, and he shall direct thy paths."* It is through unwavering trust in God that you find true guidance and direction in your life.

Remember the words Jesus spoke to His disciples when I walked the earth: *"Take no thought for your life, what ye shall eat, or what ye shall drink; nor yet for your body, what ye shall put on. Is not the life more than meat, and the body than raiment?... Consider the lilies of the field, how they grow; they toil not, neither do they spin: And yet I say unto you, That even Solomon in all his glory was not arrayed like one of these" (Matthew 6:25-29).*

Jesus: Just as I provide for the needs of the birds and the flowers, I will surely provide for your needs as well.

When doubt creeps in, remember the countless times I have shown My faithfulness throughout history. Reflect on the miracles, the answered prayers, and the promises fulfilled. Allow the testimony of others to strengthen your faith, for their stories bear witness to the goodness and power of God.

Let go of the luxury of doubt and embrace the freedom and joy of unwavering faith. Seek Me in prayer and immerse yourself in My Word, for it is a lamp unto your feet and a light unto your path (Psalm 119:105). Trust in My promises, for they are *"yea and amen" (2 Corinthians 1:20).*

In conclusion, doubting may seem like a luxury, offering solace in the face of trials. But in reality, it is a hindrance to your spiritual growth and a barrier to experiencing the fullness of God's love and provision. Instead, choose faith. Trust in God with all your heart, knowing that He is faithful and will guide you in every aspect of your life. Release doubt and embrace the freedom, peace, and joy that come from trusting in the Lord.

Trust in the Lord and Abandon Doubts

Have you ever found pleasure in harboring negative thoughts against those who you believe have wronged you? Have you experienced the allure of dwelling on their unkindness, delving into their malice, and imagining all sorts of wrongdoings against them? It may have made you miserable, but there was a certain fascination in that misery that made it difficult to let go. Doubting can be just as luxurious. When things go awry in your life, when circumstances seem mysterious and temptations unique, it is natural to conclude that God has abandoned you, ceased to love you, and become indifferent to your well-being. It is almost irresistible to believe that you are too wicked for Him to care or too troublesome for Him to handle. You may not intend to blame or accuse Him unjustly, for you feel that your unworthiness fully justifies His indifference and rejection.

This line of thinking allows you to indulge in your doubts, disguised as a just and truthful assessment of your own flaws. But in reality, you are entertaining unjust and misguided thoughts about the Lord, just as you would about a human enemy. He Himself declares that He came not to save the righteous, but sinners. Your very sinfulness and unworthiness are the strongest claims you have on His love and care.

Consider the poor little lamb that strays from the flock and becomes lost in the wilderness. Could it say, "The shepherd does not love me, care for me, or remember me because I am lost. He only loves and cares for the lambs that never wander"? Similarly, could an ill person claim, "The doctor will not come to see me or provide any medicine because I am sick. He only cares for and visits healthy people"? Jesus declares, "They that are whole need not a physician, but they that are sick." He also asks, "What man of you, having an hundred sheep, if he lose one of them, doth not leave the ninety and nine in the wilderness, and go after that which is lost until he find it?" Any thoughts contrary to what He says about Himself are indeed hard thoughts, and indulging in them is far worse than harboring ill thoughts about any earthly friend or foe.

Throughout your Christian journey, from beginning to end, it is always sinful to entertain doubts. Doubts originate from the devil and are always untrue. The only way to confront them is through direct and emphatic denial. This leads us to the practical aspect of this matter, how to find liberation from this destructive habit. My answer is that deliverance from doubts, like any other sin, can only be found in the Lord. You must surrender your doubts to Him, just as you have learned to surrender your other temptations.

Treat them in the same way you handle your temper or pride. Give them up to the Lord. In my belief, the most effective remedy is to make a commitment against doubts, similar to how you would encourage a drunkard to pledge against alcohol, relying solely on the Lord to keep you steadfast. Like any other sin, the stronghold of doubt lies within the will, and the will to doubt must be relinquished, just as you surrender the will to yield to any other temptation. When you surrender your will, God always takes possession.

Conclusion: indulging in doubts is a luxury that leads to misery and wrong thoughts about our Lord. Throughout your Christian life, doubts must be rejected, for they stem from the devil and are always untrue. To find deliverance from this detrimental habit, you must surrender your doubts to the Lord and make a committed pledge against them. Trust in the Lord and abandon doubts, for your sinfulness and unworthiness are the very reasons you can claim His love and care. Just as a lost lamb or an ill person receives the attention and compassion of their caretakers, so too will you find that God diligently seeks after and cares for those who feel lost and unworthy.

The key to overcoming doubts lies in surrendering them to the Lord, just as you would surrender any other temptation. Handing over your doubts requires a conscious decision to trust in God's faithfulness and goodness. It is not a passive act but an active choice to rely on Him alone. Just as you would trust a doctor to provide healing or a shepherd to rescue a lost sheep, trust in the Lord's unfailing love and His promises.

To truly break free from the grip of doubt, consider making a commitment before God to resist doubts whenever they arise. Treat it as a solemn pledge, relying on the Lord's strength and guidance to keep you steadfast. Recognize that doubts are not a reflection of God's character or His love for you, but rather a deceptive tool of the enemy to hinder your faith and growth.

Remember, throughout your Christian journey, doubts will tempt you, but they are not from God. Reject them with boldness and confidence, affirming the truth of God's Word. Fill your mind with Scripture, for it is a powerful weapon against doubts. Take comfort in verses like *Psalm 56:3*, which says, *"What time I am afraid, I will trust in thee,"* and *Matthew 28:20*, where Jesus promises, *"Lo, I am with you always, even unto the end of the world."* These verses remind us of God's unwavering presence and His faithfulness to those who trust in Him.

In conclusion, the luxury of doubting is a deceptive trap that can lead to a distorted view of God's love and care. As followers of Christ, we are called to surrender our doubts to Him, trusting in His goodness and promises. Doubts have no place in our lives, for they are the work of the enemy and are always untrue. Instead, make a firm commitment to resist doubts, relying solely on the Lord's strength and guidance. Fill your mind with His Word and rest in the assurance that He is always with you. Trust in the Lord wholeheartedly, for your doubts can be overcome, and your faith can be strengthened as you walk in His love and care.

An Unyielding Stand in Faith and Trust

Once upon a time, I found myself on the edge of a decision, a decision between doubting and surrendering my deepest fears to Him. Then I chose the path of faith and made a promise. A promise that I would not waver in my faith, that I would allow His blessed Spirit to guide me. And, oh, the transformation it brought in me! His overwhelming power kept my doubts at bay, showing me the remarkable strength of belief.

But, alas, surrender is not always easy. Our souls, ever so complicated, often hesitate to let go of that little space for doubt, seeing it as a safe haven. We say, "I don't want to doubt anymore," or "I hope I won't," but it is quite a challenge to confidently say, "I will not doubt again." Yet, to truly surrender, we must reach that point of saying, "I will not". We must let go of our liberty to doubt, forever.

It is crucial to consciously make this commitment, to surrender doubt once and for all. It's similar to someone struggling with alcohol addiction, taking the leap towards sobriety. It doesn't work in parts or degrees. It's an all-or-nothing deal, total abstinence.

Then, once the surrender is made, we must let go and trust the Lord for every trial and temptation that comes our way. The moment we face an assault, we must raise the shield of faith. The first hint of doubt should be handed over to the Lord. Tell the enemy, "Take it up with Him." Don't entertain doubt for even a moment. Regardless of how reasonable it might seem, simply say, "I dare not doubt; I must trust. The Lord is good, and HE does love me. Jesus saves me; He saves me now."

Repeating these three powerful words – "Jesus saves me" – is enough to scatter the mightiest army of doubts. I know this because I've tried it countless times, and it has never failed. Don't try to argue or prove your doubts wrong. Don't entertain them; rather, dismiss them with contempt. Use the powerful words from scripture, such as in *Isaiah 41:10: "Fear thou not; for I am with thee: be not dismayed; for I am thy God: I will strengthen thee; yea, I will help thee; yea, I will uphold thee with the right hand of my righteousness."*

Keep your faith in Jesus and declare your trust in Him. Even when doubts seem like your closest friends, deny them. Stand strong against their allure, just as the Israelites did against the temptations of Egypt.

Just this morning, I faced an army of doubts, trying to break down my door of faith. Everything felt unreal, as if I, wretched and miserable, couldn't possibly be loved or cared for by the Lord. Yet, I dared not let these doubts in, for I had made a pledge against doubting. I raised my shield of faith, handed over my doubts to the Lord, and kept repeating, "The Lord does love me. He is my present and perfect Savior; Jesus saves me, Jesus saves me now!" And the victory was mine.

Indeed, the enemy had come in like a flood, but the Lord lifted up a standard against him, according to *Isaiah 59:19, "So shall they fear the name of the LORD from the west, and his glory from the rising of the sun. When the enemy shall come in like a flood, the Spirit of the LORD shall lift up a standard against him."* My doubts were defeated, and my soul burst into the song of Moses and the children of Israel.

In *Exodus 15:1*, it is written, *"Then sang Moses and the*

children of Israel this song unto the Lord, and spake, saying, 'I will sing unto the Lord, for He hath triumphed gloriously: the horse and his rider hath He thrown into the sea.'" I found myself echoing these very words, celebrating the triumph of the Lord and His glorious victory over the waves of doubt that sought to overcome me.

In our lives, we face many trials and tribulations, many moments where we question our worth and our place in the Lord's plan. Doubts may seem as plentiful as grains of sand on a beach, each one seeking to erode our faith. Yet, we must remember that in the face of all this, there is a beacon of hope, a Savior, Jesus Christ, who loves us unconditionally and is our constant deliverer.

Even when the storm of doubt is raging, even when the waves of uncertainty are crashing around us, we must never forget this truth: "Jesus saves me, Jesus saves me now." This affirmation, this steadfast belief, is our shield against doubt, our strength in the face of adversity.

In conclusion, as we journey through life, let us dare not to doubt, but rather, to trust. Let's surrender our fears and uncertainties to the Lord, and let His love guide us. For He is our Savior, our guide, and our protector. So, raise your shields of faith high and stand against the waves of doubt, for Jesus saves us, He saves us now.

A Testament to the Strength in Trusting God

Hello friends, I want to tell you a story about strength.

But it's not the kind of strength you get from lifting weights or running. It's the kind that comes from inside, the kind that can only come from God. The Bible says, *"The Lord is my strength and my song, and he is become my salvation. The Lord is a man of war; the Lord is his name" (Exodus 15:2-3, KJV).*

Now, there are times when we might question or doubt. But we need to remember that doubting is not what God wants for us. God tells us, *"Let not your heart be troubled, neither let it be afraid" (John 14:27, KJV).* In the Bible, God always encourages us to trust Him, without any exception. If we read the Book of Psalms, it becomes clear that the person who trusts God, no questions asked, is the one who pleases Him.

Remember how the people of Israel angered God? It was because *"they believed not in God, and trusted not in His salvation" (Psalms 78:22, KJV).* But Isaiah tells us, *"Thou wilt keep him in perfect peace, whose mind is stayed on thee: because he trusteth in thee" (Isaiah 26:3, KJV).* It hurts us when our friends doubt us, and it's the same with God. Our doubts hurt Him too.

One evening, my dear child, who's now with the Lord, told me, "Mother, I've had my first doubt." She said Satan had tried to convince her that the Bible wasn't true. But she responded with faith, telling Satan, "I will believe it. So there!" I was so proud of her for standing strong in her faith, reminding her that all doubts and discouragements are lies from the enemy.

The very next night, as I was putting her to bed, she said,

"Mother, Satan's been at it again." This time, Satan had tried to make her feel unloved by Jesus because of her naughtiness. But once again, she held on to her faith, telling Satan, "Shut thy mouth!" She smiled as she told me, "He can't make me unhappy one bit." She had won a great victory of faith, proving that even a little child can overcome doubt.

Friends, let's take a lesson from my child. Let's decide never to doubt God again. Let's make a promise to God and ourselves that we'll always trust Him. It's okay to tell Him about your doubts, your weakness, your struggles. But also tell Him that you trust Him to help you, to keep you from falling. Keep your eyes fixed on Jesus, ignore your doubts, and hold tight to your faith because He is faithful and He has promised to help us.

And if you can do that, if you can hold onto your faith and trust in Jesus, you'll find yourself winning every battle, no matter how big or small. You will be more than a conqueror through His love.

In conclusion, let's remember to always trust in God, to reject doubt, and to stay strong in our faith. Just like my little child did, we can also overcome and emerge victorious. The strength and victory we seek are found in unwavering trust in God. Amen!

CHAPTER FIFTEEN

PRACTICAL RESULTS IN THE DAILY WALK AND CONVERSATION

"Christ Within: The Transformative Power of Faith"

In the radiant heart of our spiritual journey, as we delve into the profound mystery of life wrapped in Christ and immersed in God's love, we should anticipate transformative changes in our daily lives. These changes ought to mark us, truly making us a unique people, passionate about good deeds.

My son, a college student, once wrote a profound statement to a friend, something that has lingered in my mind ever since. He wrote that we Christians are, by default, God's witnesses. Why, you may ask? The world around us may not necessarily delve into the sacred scriptures of the Bible, but they most certainly observe our lives, our actions. Our conduct, therefore, significantly influences their belief in the divine essence of the religion we follow.

We live in an era that venerates facts and craves evidence. If our faith is to gain ground, it needs to surpass the realm of theory. It must demonstrate itself in the tangible transformation of lives, vividly illustrating the formidable power of God orchestrating His divine will within us. Our contemporary scholars, scientists, and critical minds demand "forms of life" as proof. And when we, the Church, can exhibit the embodiment of a holy life in each member, we would have conquered their final bastion of skepticism.

Before I conclude this narrative, I would like to speak earnestly about the inevitable results of a faith-filled life. I aim to evoke in my dear readers their duty to live a life that corresponds to their high calling in Christ. I believe that through our journey in this book, a bond of friendship and mutual longing has developed among us. We share a desire to reflect the magnificent light of Him who has pulled us out of darkness. So, as a friend among friends, I trust I can be frank and specific about the aspects of life and character essential to authentic Christian growth.

Sadly, the benchmark for holy living among Christians has been disappointingly low. Even a modest display of true dedication and righteous conduct often evokes surprise and disapproval from a considerable segment of the Church. Regrettably, many who profess to follow Jesus Christ barely reflect Him in character or action, leading to a disconcerting disparity.

But you and I, who have responded to God's call for a life of total dedication and unwavering trust, must tread a different path. We must rise above the worldly norms and standards. We must distinguish ourselves, avoiding the trap of conforming to the world in character or intention.

Scripture in the KJV says, ***"Wherefore come out from among them, and be ye separate, saith the Lord, and touch not the unclean thing; and I will receive you." (2 Corinthians 6:17).*** We are called upon to be separate, to live differently from the world, and to reflect the light of Jesus Christ in all we do.

In conclusion, as we continue to experience the transformative power of faith in our lives, let us remain vigilant in living out the teachings of Christ. This is more than a religious duty; it's a privilege and an opportunity to be a living testimony of God's love and power. Let's embrace it wholeheartedly, not just for ourselves, but for the world that keenly watches us, and most importantly, for the glory of God.

A Call for Holiness in Everyday Life

My dear friends, we must break away from the spirit and ways of this world. Like citizens of Heaven, our focus should be on the things above, where Christ sits at God's right hand. Just as ***Colossians 3:1*** in the says, ***"If ye then be risen with Christ, seek those things which are above, where Christ sitteth on the right hand of God."***

Our journey through life should mirror that of Christ. We must embody His mindset, the very same that He carried. We are pilgrims and strangers, and we must reject earthly desires that fight against the soul. We are soldiers of Jesus Christ, and we must avoid worldly affairs to please

Him, our Commander who chose us to serve.

In line with *1 Thessalonians 5:22, KJV, we must "Abstain from all appearance of evil."* Kindness should flow from us to others; we should be tender-hearted, forgiving one another, just as God, for Christ's sake, has forgiven us. *Ephesians 4:32, KJV,* instructs us to *"Be ye kind one to another, tenderhearted, forgiving one another, even as God for Christ's sake hath forgiven you."*

We must never hold grudges or respond to cruelty with the same. Instead, we should return evil with good, and offer our other cheek when someone strikes us. Humility should guide us to the lowest position among our peers, prioritizing their honor over ours. We must be gentle, humble, and flexible; not defending our rights but standing for the rights of others.

Whatever we do should be for the Glory of God. To sum it up, *1 Peter 1:15-16, KJV,* commands, *"But as he which hath called you is holy, so be ye holy in all manner of conversation; Because it is written, Be ye holy; for I am holy."*

Living in this way, my dear friends, is practical and means living differently than most around us. It means fully turning our backs on our own selfish motives and aims. It shows we are a peculiar people, not only in God's sight but also to the world.

Our money will no longer feel like ours, but the Lord's, and should be used in His service. We won't be driven to chase worldly gains but will seek first God's kingdom and His righteousness, trusting *Matthew 6:33, KJV, "But seek ye first the kingdom of God, and his righteousness; and all these things shall be added unto you."*

The world's frivolous pursuits won't entice us anymore. Instead, our hearts will be set on heavenly matters rather than earthly ones. Our days will be spent in service to our Lord, and we will accomplish our rightful duties even more perfectly, for *Ephesians 6:6, KJV*, instructs us to do so, *"Not with eyeservice, as menpleasers; but as the servants of Christ, doing the will of God from the heart."*

We will be led to all these things by the blessed Spirit of God, if we surrender to His guidance. However, without understanding the true standard of a Christian life, we might miss His call due to ignorance.

In my observation, those who follow the Lord with a devoted heart invariably develop certain virtues over time. These include a calm spirit, acceptance of God's will as it unfolds daily, flexibility to God's purpose, patience during provocation, serenity amid chaos, respect for others' wishes, and indifference to insults. Freedom from worry or fear and a lack of concern for earthly things become the norm.

A Journey Towards Godly Transformation

In my home, I begin to care less about fancy furniture

and the luxury of my surroundings. I start to value the things of God above personal decoration. I use my voice not for idle chatter, but to speak and sing in God's honor. I dedicate my wealth, placing it in service to Him. I use my pen to write His words, my lips to speak His truth, and my hands and feet to fulfill His commands. As the years pass, I become less interested in worldly matters. Instead, I grow more heavenly-minded, more transformed, resembling Christ. Even my countenance radiates the inner divine life so visibly that everyone around me can tell that I am living with God, and remaining in Him.

I am certain that each one of you has felt a hint of the life I'm describing. Haven't you felt a faint whisper of God's voice speaking to your heart about these things? Haven't you recently felt uncomfortable upon realizing your missteps? Hasn't your soul been stirred with uncertainty and anxiety about your past actions and habits? Haven't you felt a growing discomfort with certain life habits, yearning for a different way? Aren't there paths of dedication and service opening up before you, filling you with a deep desire to walk in them?

These yearnings, doubts, and inner conflicts are the voice of the Good Shepherd in your heart, calling you away from all that opposes His will. Please, don't ignore His gentle entreaties. You might not comprehend the hidden paths He is guiding you towards, or the abundant blessings awaiting at their end. If you did, you would leap forward, joyously complying with His every command.

Christian perfection can only be attained by faithfully following our Guide. He illuminates your path, one step at a time, through the teachings and circumstances of your daily life, asking only that you surrender to His guidance. So, if you feel a conviction of sin in anything, know it is the voice of your Lord, and yield it promptly to His command, rejoicing that He has begun to guide you. Be entirely receptive in His wise hands. Follow where He leads, avoid what He warns against, obey Him entirely, and He will swiftly guide you towards a life of remarkable conformity to Himself, a living testament to those around you, beyond what you can imagine.

I once knew a person who surrendered herself to follow the Lord wherever He led. Within three short months, she journeyed from utter despair into the blissful realization of union with Jesus Christ. Amidst her darkness, she devoted herself to the Lord, surrendering her will so He could work His own good pleasure in her. Immediately, He began to speak to her through His Spirit, prompting her towards acts of service for Him, guiding her away from un-Christlike dispositions. Recognizing His voice, she yielded to His every request, fearlessly following His lead, her only concern being disobedience to Him. Day by day, He led her swiftly towards His will, making her life a testimony to those around her, converting even the most skeptical into believers through her transformation.

In conclusion, this is the path of devotion, a journey towards Godly transformation, where your voice, pen, wealth, hands, and feet are used in His service. It requires surrender, obedience, and a willingness to follow God's guidance in all things. This way may not always be easy, but it leads to a deep, fulfilling union with Christ and an abundant life that stands as a beacon of God's transforming power.

The Path of Surrender: Journey Towards Divine Love

In the blink of an eye, after three short months of unwavering devotion, a remarkable thing happened. Her Savior, in His infinite wisdom and love, revealed to her the profound mysteries of His affection. The promised blessing from the Book of Acts 1:5 was fulfilled, as she was baptized with the Holy Spirit.

The scripture reads, *"For John truly baptized with water; but ye shall be baptized with the Holy Ghost not many days hence" (Acts 1:5, KJV).*

Do you think she has ever regretted her devoted path? Has anything but gratitude and joy filled her heart as she looked back on the journey that led her to such blissful place? Although certain steps might have been challenging at the time, she saw them now as necessary for reaching this place of divine blessedness.

My dear friend, if you yearn for such a blessing, surrender yourself completely to our Divine Master. Do not shy away from any sacrifices He may ask of you. "The perfect way is hard to flesh, It is not hard to love; If thou wert sick for want of God, How swiftly wouldst thou move."

Trust Him entirely! If He asks for what may seem insignificant to you, remember His vision is far greater than ours. What may seem small to you could be crucial in His divine plan for you. To mold you according to His divine will, He requires your total flexibility. This obedience is often more quickly developed by submitting in little things rather than the greater.

Your greatest desire is to follow Him wholeheartedly. Can you not, then, continuously say, "Yes, Lord!" to all His loving commands, whether they seem big or small, and trust Him to guide you on the quickest path to your most abundant blessings?

My friend, this is what you committed to, whether you knew it at the time or not. It meant utter obedience. It meant your will aligns with God's will under all circumstances, at all times. It meant you surrendered your liberty of choice, entrusting yourself entirely to your Lord.

It meant a daily commitment to follow Him wherever He may lead you, with no thoughts of turning back. Now, I implore you to uphold your promise. Surrender everything else to embody the divine life within you through your everyday actions and conversations.

You are connected to your Lord through an incredible bond; walk, then, as He walked. Show the world the reality of His power to save, by allowing Him to save you fully. Do not fear this commitment, for He is your

Savior, and it is within His power to fulfill it all. He does not expect you, in your human weakness, to achieve this on your own. All He asks is for you to submit to Him, so He can work in you to fulfill His divine will by His own mighty power.

In conclusion, the path to divine love involves surrender, trust, and obedience to our Lord's will. It may not always be easy, and it may require sacrifices that at times seem insignificant or even difficult. But remember, it is in these moments of surrender and obedience that we allow God's love and power to work within us, leading us to our fullest blessings. As we walk this path, we become living testimonies of God's saving power, revealing the reality of His love to the world.

Heaven, a living illustrations of His love and grace

Living a Christlike life doesn't merely involve saying the right words, attending church regularly, or even reading the Bible daily, important though these practices are. More fundamentally, it involves an inner transformation that reshapes our values, priorities, and actions to mirror those of Christ.

Just as a mirror reflects the image of a person standing before it, we, as Christians, are meant to reflect the image of Christ in our daily lives. It means treating others with the same love, kindness, and humility that Christ demonstrated. It means having the courage to stand for truth, just as Christ did, even when it is unpopular or challenging to do so.

This transformation into Christlikeness is not a one-time event, but a lifelong journey. And it's not a journey we have to undertake alone. Our loving Lord not only guides us through His Word and Spirit but also equips us with the strength and grace we need to become more like Him each day.

Being a Christian, then, is about embodying Christ's selfless love in our lives. It's about being a little more patient, a little more forgiving, a little more generous, just as Christ would have been under our circumstances. It's about making our lives an epistle of Christ, a living letter of God's love to the world.

To paraphrase the little girl's profound insight, it's about being the kind of person Christ would be if He were in our shoes. This is what it means to be a Christian - not just in name, but in truth and in deed.

In conclusion, let us strive to be Christlike Christians, embodying His teachings in our daily lives, and reflecting His love to the world around us. For as the Apostle Paul wrote in *Romans 8:29, KJV: "For whom he did foreknow, he also did predestinate to be conformed to the image of his Son."* This is our calling, our journey, and our destiny. May we all find the strength and courage to embrace it fully.

Chapter SIXTEEN

THE JOY OF OBEDIENCE

When I was younger, I came across a remarkable saying that stuck with me, "Perfect obedience would be perfect happiness, if only we had perfect confidence in the power we were obeying." This phrase sparkled with the promise of a unique kind of joy I had yet to experience. As I stumbled through my own willful, unruly life, this saying echoed back to me time and again, suggesting the possibility of a calming, yet enriching pathway to true satisfaction. I yearn to share with you this revelation, which I now hold as my reality.

I found this rest in Jesus Christ, our Lord, the Master to whom we can offer our absolute obedience. In doing so, we may carry His yoke, finding our most profound peace. My dear friend, you might not yet comprehend the joy you are foregoing. The Master has shown Himself to you, and He beckons for your total surrender. Yet, you recoil, full of hesitation.

You might be inclined to offer some degree of surrender, considering it a fitting tribute. But the thought of absolute surrender, without any reservation, may appear overwhelming, perhaps even frightening. It seems to you an enormous undertaking. The prospect of perfect obedience terrifies you.

Furthermore, you observe others who seem to tread a wider path with clear consciences than what you perceive as your designated track. You might wonder why there are these disparities. You may find it puzzling, possibly unjust, that you must undertake tasks they are not required to or refrain from activities they are free to enjoy.

Remember this, dear Christian: this perceived difference is not a burden, but a privilege, although you may not perceive it as such now. Your Lord Jesus Christ stated in *John 14:21 (KJV): "He that hath my commandments, and keepeth them, he it is that loveth Me; and he that loveth Me shall be loved of my Father, and I will love him, and will manifest Myself to him."*

You hold His commandments; those you envy do not. You are aware of your Lord's will in many aspects of life, while they, regrettably, wander in ignorance. Isn't this a blessing? Is it not a privilege that you have been chosen for such a close relationship with your Master that He shares with you insights hidden from those more distant? Do you grasp the level of intimacy and tenderness this involves?

Life presents us with numerous relationships requiring varying degrees of commitment. However, I implore you to see that our relationship with our Lord Jesus Christ is unlike any other.

In conclusion, my dear friend, I encourage you to embrace this path of perfect obedience to our Lord. It may seem challenging and intimidating initially, but it is a road lined with the promise of perfect happiness and profound peace. Let go of your hesitations and surrender completely to His will. Your path may be narrower than others, but remember, it is a path of privilege that leads to an intimate relationship with the Lord. Embrace this unique privilege, and you will indeed experience an indescribable joy.

"United in Love: An Echo of the Divine Union"

Friendships can be delightful, akin to a refreshing breeze on a warm day. We can share joyous moments and congenial thoughts with friends, and even when we part ways, the separation does not greatly distress us. In these relationships, we respect boundaries and don't interfere in each other's most private affairs. However, sometimes, these friendships evolve into something deeper, something more profound—love.

In love, two hearts intertwine so tightly they become one, echoing the beautiful words of the Bible: *"And they twain shall be one flesh: so then they are no more twain, but one flesh" (Mark 10:8, KJV).* This bond of love blurs the lines of individuality. Our separate paths merge into a shared journey, and our interests interweave into a common tapestry of life. Suddenly, things we once deemed permissible become unacceptable due to the intensity of the bond we share.

In the realm of love, there's no room for the reserve and distance typical in mere friendships. Love is an offering, an all-inclusive gift, that expects a similar whole-hearted reciprocation. The desires of our beloved become our binding obligations, and our deepest wishes are to understand every longing of our partner, ready to fulfill them with an eagerness that defies the speed of the wind.

But does this love, with its obligations, weigh heavy on our hearts? Do we long for the easy, unaffected friendships we once had, wishing to lessen the intense proximity of our souls? Or, do we rather revel in the privileges that this close bond affords us, looking at the less intense relations around us with a mix of compassion and triumphant joy?

Each new understanding of our beloved's mind becomes a treasured delight and privilege. The paths we tread for the sake of love, no matter how challenging, become light under our feet. If you've experienced this deeply satisfying love, even briefly, with someone on this earth, if you've found joy in sacrificing and serving for their sake, if the notion of surrendering your will to another has ever appeared to you as a precious reality or a desirable privilege, then I urge you to carry these feelings forward in your relationship with God.

God's love for you is more than a mere friendship. It mirrors the words in *Isaiah 62:5 (KJV): "For as a young man marrieth a virgin, so shall thy sons marry thee: and as the bridegroom rejoiceth over the bride, so shall thy God rejoice over thee."* His love demands a full surrender, and anything less will dishearten Him. He has given you everything, and in return, He asks for your complete devotion. He spared not Himself in His love for you; how then can you withhold any part of yourself from Him?

In conclusion, the earthly love that we experience is but a reflection of the divine love that our Heavenly Father has for us. It's a journey that requires a wholehearted commitment, a surrender that signifies not the loss of freedom, but a union in love. It is the path towards oneness, echoing our relationship with the Almighty, a bond that asks for all and gives all in return.

A Journey Towards Complete Surrender

Imagine, dear reader, a magnificent love story where one gives everything they have to the other, pouring out in lavish generosity all they hold. This is not merely a tale from a book; it's our journey with the Lord. Just as He bestowed upon us everything in boundless love and sacrifice, we too are called to present to Him our undivided devotion.

Remember, He has given all for you! In your turn, shower upon Him your unmeasured devotion. Embrace the joy and eagerness in plunging into His open arms, and yield to His divine guidance. Let Him have every part of you. Abandon all that separates you from Him, relinquishing your personal choice, and take delight in the intimate closeness that makes this love not only possible but essential.

Haven't you ever desired to express your love to someone far away, someone you couldn't approach closely? You might have felt an intense need for surrender and dedication, an inner fire, but found no heart upon which to pour out this passion. You may have even felt your hands full of the most precious gifts, but lacked the opportunity to bestow them.

As you hear the gentle voice of your Lord, calling you into a closer relationship with Him, you realize this dedication is not just possible, but necessary. Will you hold back, or will you respond without hesitation? Will you find it burdensome that He shows you more of His heart than He does to others and that He won't let you be content with anything that separates you from Him?

Psalm 37:4 (KJV) says, "Delight thyself also in the LORD; and he shall give thee the desires of thine heart." Is there anywhere you wish to go where He cannot accompany you? Do you have any ambitions that He cannot share? The answer is a resounding 'no'. You respond to His every desire with joyful eagerness. Even His smallest wish becomes an inviolable command to you, disobedience to which would shatter your heart.

The road He traces for you may seem narrow, but you take joy in its constraints and look with boundless compassion upon those who have missed this invaluable joy. The obligations of love transform into its sweetest privileges. The right to express your limitless devotion to your Lord elevates you to an unspeakable glory. The sheer delight of absolute obedience awakens within you, and you start to understand Jesus' words in *Psalms 40:8 (KJV), "I delight to do thy will, O my God: yea, thy law is within my heart."*

This ecstatic joy is not one-sided. Doesn't the Lord also take pleasure in those who surrender entirely to Him and love to obey Him? We might feel overwhelmed to ponder this, but the Scriptures offer glimpses of the delight, the satisfaction, the joy our Lord finds in us. These revelations of blessedness captivate our souls and fill us with awe.

In conclusion, our boundless devotion and complete surrender to the Lord bring a unique joy not only to us but also to our Heavenly Father. It's an intimate dance of divine love where we offer all of ourselves, responding with unmeasured passion to His limitless love for us. Let us then continue to 'delight to do His will', expressing our immeasurable devotion and finding joy in our journey towards complete surrender.

"An Unreserved Love: Embracing the Call of Christ"

Being in need of Him is something we can all grasp easily; yet, the notion that He might need us seems beyond our understanding. Our yearning for Him is instinctual, but His longing for us defies our comprehension. However, He repeatedly expresses this desire, and we are left with no option but to believe Him.

As it is written in the book of John, Chapter 14, Verse 21, (KJV), *"He that loveth me shall be loved of my Father, and I will love him, and will manifest myself to him."* He has fashioned our hearts to harbor this profound, overwhelming affection, and has presented Himself as the recipient of this love. This love is invaluable to Him.

Day in, day out, He approaches every heart, seeking acceptance as the ultimate object of affection. He poses numerous questions to the believer, inquiring if we are ready to accept Him as our Beloved, to endure suffering and solitude for His sake, to relinquish our wills entirely to Him, and to find contentment in pleasing only Him. He proposes a bond so intimate that it necessitates a separation from worldly desires, calling us to pledge ourselves solely to Him.

These calls to unity with Him are extended to all believers, yet not all respond with an affirmative "Yes". For some, other affections and pursuits seem too precious to surrender. These individuals will not be denied Heaven because of this, yet they will miss out on an indescribable joy.

But you are different. You have joyously and eagerly accepted His calls, saying, "Yes, Lord; yes!" Your love for Him compels you to separate from the world, a concept incomprehensible to those with fainter hearts. You joyfully embrace sacrifices and services that are unfathomable to those with less commitment. This life you've chosen allows you the privilege to shower Him with your love and devotion.

Though this may distance you from others, remember His words in *Luke 6:22-23 (KJV): "Blessed are ye, when men shall hate you, and when they shall separate you from their company, and shall reproach you, and cast out your name as evil, for the Son of man's sake. Rejoice ye in that day, and leap for joy: for, behold, your reward is great in heaven."*

You will partake in His glory, for you share in His suffering. He finds satisfaction in seeing the fruits of His labor in your love and devotion. Your love is His reward for everything He has done for you.

Therefore, do not hold back from expressing your wholehearted devotion to Him. While others may not understand, remember that His approval is the only one that truly matters. Give your all - body, soul, and spirit, time, talents, voice, everything - to Him without reservation. Open up your entire life to His control.

In conclusion, embracing the call of Christ is more than a mere agreement. It is an act of unrestrained love, surrender, and devotion. It's a life dedicated to His glory and service. Embrace this call, and experience a joy beyond measure - a joy that comes only from the unreserved love for our Savior, Jesus Christ.

"A Daily Walk in His Steps: Guided by God's Love"

Dear reader, every day when I awake, I ask myself,

"Lord, how should I shape this day to bring joy to You? Where should my path lead? What should I do? Whom should I visit? What words should I speak?" I surrender my mind to His guidance and implore, "Lord, guide my thoughts so they may be pleasing to You."

I ask Him to guide my reading, my activities, and my friendships. I implore, "Lord, grant me the wisdom to judge all things in accordance with Your wisdom." There isn't a single day, not even an hour, in which I don't strive to understand His will and to follow Him wholeheartedly.

This personal dedication to Him brings a divine glow to life, illuminating even the most ordinary existence with a heavenly light. Have you ever mourned the loss of the enchanting charm of youth, which seems to fade in the harsh light of reality? Invite God into your life and its myriad details. This will ignite an enthusiasm in your soul far greater than the liveliest days of youth ever could. When God's love illuminates your life, nothing appears hard or harsh anymore. Even the humblest life is sanctified by His presence.

There have been times when I've watched a woman toiling at her wash-tub. I have pondered over the disheartening aspects of such a life and wondered why such lives must exist. But then, I am overcome with a wave of joy as I remember the possible sanctification of this existence. I reassure myself that even this life, if lived in Christ and with Christ, following Him wherever He may lead, can be filled with an enthusiasm that makes every hour glorious.

It comforts me to know that God's most astonishing blessings are available to all, regardless of wealth, age, or status. As our Lord Himself declared, *"For whosoever shall do the will of God, the same is my brother, and my sister, and my mother" (Mark 3:35, KJV).* Reflect for a moment on these profound and astonishing words - His brother, sister, and mother! What wouldn't we give to be one of these!

So, I urge you, dear Christian, come and experience for yourself how good the Lord is. Discover the extraordinary blessings He has prepared for those who *"keep His commandments, and do those things that are pleasing in His sight" (1 John 3:22, KJV).*

For He has promised, *"And it shall come to pass, if thou shalt hearken diligently unto the voice of the Lord thy God, to observe and to do all His commandments which I command thee this day, that the Lord thy God will set thee on high, above all nations of the earth; and all these blessings shall come on thee, and overtake thee, if thou shalt hearken unto the voice of the Lord thy God" (Deuteronomy 28:1-2, KJV).*

In conclusion, I invite you to embrace a life lived in the footsteps of Christ. When God guides our actions, decisions, and thoughts, even the simplest lives can be imbued with divine purpose and glory. So, let's seek His wisdom in all things, for His blessings are abundant and everlasting. Let our daily prayer be to serve Him in all aspects of our lives, to follow His commandments, and to do what is pleasing in His sight. Such a life, dear reader, is the true essence of a daily walk in His steps, guided by

His unwavering love.

A Journey of Spiritual Blessings

Once, in a time long ago, the Lord spake unto His children, the Israelites. His words were a promise, a covenant of blessings that would come upon them if they faithfully kept His commandments. I remember His words in the book of Deuteronomy, Chapter 28, and they still ring true to my heart today:

"Blessed shalt thou be in the city, and blessed shalt thou be in the field. Blessed shall be the fruit of thy body, and the fruit of thy ground, and the fruit of thy cattle, the increase of thy kine, and the flocks of thy sheep. Blessed shall be thy basket and thy store. Blessed shalt thou be when thou comest in, and blessed shalt thou be when thou goest out. The Lord shall cause thine enemies that rise up against thee to be smitten before thy face; they shall come out against thee one way, and flee before thee seven ways. The Lord shall command the blessing upon thee in thy storehouses, and in all that thou settest thine hand unto; and He shall bless thee in the land which the Lord thy God giveth thee."

And it continued,

"The Lord shall establish thee a holy people unto Himself, as He hath sworn unto thee, if thou shalt keep the commandments of the Lord thy God, and walk in His ways. And all people of the earth shall see that thou art called by the name of the Lord, and they shall be afraid of thee. And the Lord shall make thee plenteous in goods, in the fruit of thy body, and in the fruit of thy cattle, and in the fruit of thy ground, in the land which the Lord sware unto thy fathers to give thee. And the Lord shall make thee the head, and not the tail; and thou shalt be above only, and thou shalt not be beneath; if that thou hearken unto the commandments of the Lord thy God, which I command thee this day, to observe and to do them."

For the Israelites, these blessings were visible, and they touched upon their daily lives in a tangible way. But for us, today, these blessings are deeper. They touch our hearts, our spirits. They're a light that brightens our souls from the inside, making our spirits shine brighter, infinitely more glorious.

Yet, these spiritual blessings aren't just given freely. They come with a condition. We have to listen, observe, and follow the commandments of the Lord. Just as He promised the Israelites, so He promises us. We, too, can experience the richness of His blessings if we surrender our wills to Him and strive to walk in His ways.

To conclude, these promises, written ages ago, still hold their weight today. The blessings promised to the Israelites are ours to claim, not in material goods, but in the form of spiritual prosperity. As we strive to keep His commandments, we'll find ourselves richly rewarded in the ways that truly matter. Embrace these promises in all their fullness, and find your life touched by the hand of the Lord, as He promised all those years ago!

CHAPTER SEVENTEEN

ONENESS WITH CHRIST

As a believer, every interaction I have with God has a sacred purpose. It is designed to lead me towards unity with Him. The very words of Jesus Christ in the Holy Bible reflect this divine aspiration: *"That they all may be one; as thou, Father, art in me, and I in thee, that they also may be one in us:...I in them, and thou in me, that they may be made perfect in one, and that the world may know that thou hast sent me, and hast loved them, as thou hast loved me." (John 17:21-23 KJV).*

Before the world was formed, God had this grand design for His people: a profound connection of souls, an intimacy as close as the bond between God the Father and Jesus, His Son. This divine mystery, once hidden throughout time, was revealed through the incarnation of Christ and the Scriptures.

Yet, this glorious experience of unity with God is not embraced by all believers. Though this blessing is available for everyone, many, due to dim vision or lack of faith, fail to grasp it. At this moment, God is calling all believers to surrender entirely to Him so that His will may be fulfilled in their lives.

My life as a Christian has been a journey, leading me toward this divine union. God created me for this intimate fellowship with Him. Unless I comprehend this and willingly embrace it, neither God's yearning for me nor my heart's search for final rest will be satisfied.

Reflecting on the disciples' journey in the Bible, I see a parallel with my own Christian experience. The disciples first recognized their spiritual need and accepted Jesus as their Lord. They served Him, had faith in Him, and yet, they weren't like Him. They quarreled over who was the greatest, they fled from the cross, they misunderstood His teachings, and they even abandoned Him in times of peril. Despite their faults, they preached His word, showing faith in Him, but they only knew Jesus as an external figure, their Lord, and Master, not yet their Life.

The Pentecost marked a significant transformation in the disciples' lives. They experienced the Holy Spirit's power and presence and understood Jesus as a deeply personal and internal force, an indwelling Life. From then on, they recognized Christ within themselves, helping them to will and to act according to His good pleasure. This revelation liberated them from the bondage of sin and death, leading them toward a life of divine unity.

In conclusion, as a believer, my journey towards the Divine Union is a progressive awakening of my soul. By surrendering myself entirely to God, I move towards the realization of this spiritual unity. This is the ultimate purpose of my faith: to experience Christ within me, guiding me, working in me, and helping me fulfill His divine will. Through this intimate relationship, I find liberation from sin and a profound sense of oneness with the Divine. This is the magnificent plan that God had in mind for all His children, and it is my earnest endeavor to realize this union in its fullest sense.

"Becoming One with Christ: The Path to True Union"

My journey with the Lord was never a power struggle or a battle of interests. It gradually became clear that only His will mattered to me, only His interests were precious. He and I became one, just as He had always intended. Now, dear reader, perhaps you've walked a similar path. You've left many things behind to follow Christ. You've placed your faith in Him, served Him, and loved Him, yet you may not fully resemble Him. You understand what loyalty and trust mean, but perhaps you're yet to experience complete union with Him. It's as if there are two separate wills, two distinct interests, two different lives. You may not have given up your life entirely to live solely in His.

Our journey may have started with "I and not Christ," then progressed to "I and Christ," and possibly now it's "Christ and I." But have you reached the point where it's "Christ only, and not I at all?"

Perhaps the concept of oneness with Christ feels unclear to you. Some people assume it comes as an overwhelming emotion or a profound sense of unity, so they delve into their feelings, hoping to understand their bond with God through their emotional state. However, this can lead to a dangerous misinterpretation. Our unity with Christ isn't about emotions, but about leading a Christ-like life, about our character reflecting His. No matter how fervent or passionate our feelings may be, without the likeness of character with Christ, without shared goals, thoughts, and actions, we cannot claim true oneness. This is plain wisdom and aligns with Scripture too.

In the Bible, in the Gospel of John, Jesus prayed, *"That they all may be one; as thou, Father, art in me, and I in thee, that they also may be one in us: that the world may believe that thou hast sent me" (John 17:21, KJV).* When we speak of two people being 'one,' we imply that their goals, actions, thoughts, and desires align. If a friend showers us with love but their perspectives and actions contradict ours, we won't truly feel united, despite our mutual affection.

To achieve true unity, we must share the same passions and aversions, joys and sorrows, hopes and fears. As it is commonly said, we should see the world through each other's eyes and think with each other's minds. This is simple wisdom, and it holds true for our relationship with Christ. We can't be one with Him unless we reflect His nature, character, and life. Unless we are Christ-like in our thoughts and ways, we cannot claim to be one with Him, no matter what our feelings may suggest.

I've encountered Christians who, despite lacking Christ-like attributes, claim a deep connection with Christ due to their intense emotions. Yet, they lack the true essence of unity with Him.

In conclusion, oneness with Christ isn't about an emotional high. It's about striving to mirror Christ's character, embody His teachings, and living according to His will. This is the true path to unity, the path that leads us to say, "Christ only, and not I at all." May we all seek to walk this path, growing ever closer to our Lord, Jesus Christ, in character and in truth.

"The Path of True Disciple: Living a Christ-like Life"

In my experience, I can barely recount a sight more sorrowful. I strongly believe that our Lord Jesus Christ sought to address such matters when He declared in Matthew 7:21, "Not every one that saith unto me, Lord, Lord, shall enter into the kingdom of heaven; but he that doeth the will of my Father which is in heaven." In uttering these words, He wasn't imposing an arbitrary dictate of God's will. Rather, He was shedding light on the essence of spiritual life. It's like declaring, "No one can join the circle of astronomers unless they truly practice astronomy." Just feeling an emotional connection doesn't qualify someone as an astronomer—it's their actions and dedication to the practice that matters.

In much the same way, unless we emulate Christ in

character, in life, and in action, we cannot truly unite with Him. There simply isn't another way. We need to adopt His virtues, His "nature," or we cannot share His divine life, because His life and His nature are indivisible. Some of us, swept up in emotional fervor, might overlook this. We feel so close to Christ, so united with Him, that we mistakenly take these feelings for reality.

Forgetting the essential demand for Christ-likeness in character and lifestyle, we may pin our hopes and assurance on our euphoric emotions and spiritual sensations, mistakenly believing we must be united with Him because we are privy to such uplifting spiritual experiences. However, it is crucial to remember that these feelings could be evoked by other factors than divine influence, and are often subject to our individual temperament and physical state. Placing these feelings as a barometer of our spiritual union with Christ can be a dangerous path, potentially leading to the profound self-deception our Lord warned against in Luke 6:46-49, "And why call ye me, Lord, Lord, and do not the things which I say?"

In our hearts and among friends, we may find comfort in declaring Him as our Lord, but are we truly living out His teachings? This, as He reminds us, is what truly matters. If we claim to abide in Him, driven by our emotions, we should deeply contemplate these words, "He that saith he abideth in Him, ought himself also so to walk, even as He walked."

Despite our feelings, we cannot possibly be dwelling in

Him unless we are walking His path. If you are truly united with Christ, you will respond with kindness to those who confront you harshly. You will endure all tribulations without complaint; you will not retaliate when scorned, but instead respond with love, as Christ did. You will prioritize the well-being of others above your own, embody humility, and serve others, following in the footsteps of Christ. You will genuinely love your enemies, show kindness to those who use you spitefully, and, in essence, live a Christ-like life, exhibiting outwardly what you feel inwardly. The way you live among your fellow beings should mirror how Christ lived among us.

In conclusion, embracing the path of the true disciple involves not merely feeling a connection to Jesus but living as He lived, acting as He acted, and loving as He loved. It is in this Christ-like life and action that we find true union with Him, disregarding fleeting emotional highs in favor of sincere, meaningful imitation of His nature. By living as Jesus did, we can truly say that we are abiding in Him.

"One with Christ: The Test of True Faith"

My dear friends, let's delve into the profound mystery and beauty of being one with Christ. If this unity doesn't shape your life, regardless of how intense or extraordinary your emotions might be, then you are not truly united with Him. Achieving oneness with Christ surpasses any fleeting feeling. It's a profound, humbling, and life-altering experience. He was and is holy. Those who find unity with Him will also embrace holiness. We can't ignore this simple truth.

When Jesus sought to explain His oneness with God, He said, *"I do always the things that please Him" (John 8:29, KJV). "Whatsoever He saith unto me that I do" (John 12:50, KJV). "The Son can do nothing of Himself, but what He seeth the Father do; for what things soever He doeth, these also doeth the Son likewise" (John 5:19, KJV). "I can of mine own self do nothing; as I hear I judge, and my judgment is just; because I seek not mine own will, but the will of Him that sent me" (John 5:30, KJV). "If I do not the works of my Father, believe me not. But if I do, though ye believe not me, believe the works; that ye may know and believe that the Father is in me and I in Him" (John 10:37-38, KJV).*

Jesus proved His unity with God through His actions. This remains the test of oneness today. If Jesus could say that if He did not do His Father's works, then He should not be believed, regardless of His declarations or promises, His followers should follow the same path. It's true that *"a good tree cannot bring forth evil fruit, neither can a corrupt tree bring forth good fruit" (Matthew 7:18, KJV).* It's not a matter of will, but a question of ability. A soul in union with Christ will naturally bear a Christlike life, just like a grapevine yields grapes, not thistles.

I'm not arguing against emotions. Emotions are valuable gifts when they come from God and should be cherished. What I caution against is using emotions as the sole measure of spiritual maturity. We should not base our faith on fleeting emotions. Whether they come or go should not sway us. We must focus on the essential signs of oneness with Christlikeness in character, conduct, and life. Then, we can confidently say, *"he that saith I know Him, and keepeth not His commandments, is a liar, and the truth is not in Him. But whoso keepeth His word, in him verily is the love of God perfected: hereby know we that we are in Him"* (1 John 2:4-5, KJV).

You may have been struggling with a lack of emotions. You yearn for the feelings others speak about, but they seem elusive. You fervently pray for them and sometimes feel let down by God for not granting them. You worry that your lack of emotion signals a lack of unity with Christ. Please, my dear friends, release your concerns about feelings. They are not the measure of your relationship with Christ.

In conclusion, oneness with Christ is not about lofty emotions, but about a life transformed, mirroring the life, character, and works of Christ. Our unity with Him is evidenced by our actions, our love for His word, and our obedience to His commands. This is the heart of our faith and the true test of our unity with Him. Our emotions may come and go, but the foundation of our faith remains unshakeable: oneness with Christ in heart, mind, and action.

Remember, dear friends, that emotions are not the arbiter of our faith or our unity with Christ. Instead, they are fleeting, sometimes accompanying our spiritual journey, sometimes absent. Emotions are not the substance of our faith; our life, character, and obedience to Christ's teachings are.

Don't despair if you can't feel the emotions others seem to experience. Your faith is not any less. Oneness with Christ is not an emotional state but a transformation of life. The real test lies in whether we bear the fruit of the Spirit: love, joy, peace, patience, kindness, goodness, faithfulness, gentleness, and self-control. The fruit we bear in our lives testifies to our union with Christ more than any emotion ever could.

If you abide in Christ, His words abide in you, and your life bears Christ-like fruit, then be assured, you are one with Him. This is the true measure of unity, not fleeting feelings. In the words of Jesus, *"If ye keep my commandments, ye shall abide in my love; even as I have kept my Father's commandments, and abide in his love" (John 15:10, KJV).*

The pursuit of oneness with Christ calls for humility, obedience, and a commitment to live a life pleasing to God. Remember, our union with Christ is not judged by the intensity of our emotions, but by our love for Him, manifested in our obedience to His commands and our willingness to live a life mirroring His own.

Keep your heart steadfast in this pursuit, dear friends. Let the true measure of your faith be your transformed life, echoing the life and teachings of Christ. This is the pathway to real, unshakeable unity with Christ. For, as He said, *"He that hath my commandments, and keepeth them, he it is that loveth me: and he that loveth me shall be loved of my Father, and I will love him, and will manifest myself to him" (John 14:21, KJV).*

In closing, being one with Christ transcends mere emotional experiences. It demands a life aligned with the teachings and example of Christ. Hold steadfast to your faith, living out the commandments, and you will find genuine unity with our Lord and Savior, Jesus Christ. Trust in Him, live as He did, and you will truly be one with Christ.

The True Measure of Spiritual Union with Christ

When assessing your spiritual state, it's essential to recognize that emotions aren't reliable indicators. They reflect your temperament or your current physical state, not necessarily your level of grace. I've seen this firsthand. There was a woman, a servant of mine, who would become utterly overwhelmed during revival meetings at her church. But at other times, she displayed little to no evidence of spiritual life. She even fell short of basic morality.

Certainly, the Bible, teaches us that a Christ-like life and walk should accompany a true spiritual experience born of His spirit. The book of *Ephesians (5:1-2) says, "Be ye therefore followers of God, as dear children; And walk in love, as Christ also hath loved us, and hath given himself for us an offering and a sacrifice to God for a sweetsmelling savour."* Therefore, we can't separate spiritual experiences from moral character.

Take the example of a congregation from the Southern States. They were a nuisance to their neighborhood because they disregarded common moral principles. Yet, their nightly meetings were filled with powerful emotions and fervor. Someone eventually addressed the issue with their preacher, urging him to sermonize about morality. His response was, "Ah, missus, I knows dey's bad, but den it always brings a coldness like over de meetings when I preaches about dem things."

This example highlights that while emotions might be beyond your control, character isn't. A life filled with Christ can lead to Christ-like behavior. Thus, your oneness with Him depends on your character, not your emotions.

Upon understanding the true meaning of oneness with Christ, the next step is understanding how to attain it. To do this, we must first recognize the facts of our spiritual life and our relation to these facts.

Reading *1 Corinthians 3:16* reveals a powerful truth: *"Know ye not that ye are the temple of God, and that the Spirit of God dwelleth in you?"* These remarkable words are directed to "babes in Christ," who are yet to mature in their faith. This means that the soul-union, the glorious mystery of an indwelling God, belongs to even the weakest and most failing believer.

It isn't a new thing you need to ask for, but rather, realize and embrace that which you already possess. It's an absolute truth that the body of every believer is the temple of the Holy Ghost.

I see it like this: Imagine Christ living in a house, confined to a distant closet, unseen and unacknowledged by the home's dwellers. He yearns for recognition, for companionship in their daily lives. However, He won't force Himself upon them as only a voluntary companionship can satisfy His love.

In conclusion, true spiritual union with Christ isn't measured by the intensity of our emotions during spiritual experiences. It's gauged by our Christ-like character that should pervade our lives every day, regardless of our feelings at any particular moment. And every believer already possesses this connection; we only need to realize it, nurture it, and let it manifest in our actions. After all, our bodies are the temples of the Holy Ghost, the dwelling place of Christ.

A Heartfelt Call to Union with Christ

Day in, day out, as the sun rises and sets, a favored family lives in blessed ignorance of the great gift they possess. They proceed with their daily tasks, completely oblivious of the divine Guest who resides within their dwelling. Decisions are made, plans are formulated, without considering His wisdom or inviting His protection. They wade through days and weeks steeped in loneliness and melancholy when they could be basking in the radiant warmth of His presence.

Then, in an enlightening moment, the proclamation rings out, "The Lord is in this house!" How would the head of the household react to this news? Would he express profound gratitude and open every door wide to welcome this divine Visitor? Or would he recoil, overcome by fear and uncertainty, seeking a hidden corner as refuge from the Lord's all-knowing gaze?

Beloved friend, I bring you the same joyous news: the Lord dwells within your heart. Since the moment of your conversion, He has made His home within you. You could have spent every moment basking in His holy presence, taken every step under His guidance. Yet, your ignorance of this blessed reality has left you alone and met with failures.

"Now that I reveal this truth to you, how will you accept it? Will you rejoice in His presence? Will you open your heart to welcome Him? Will you entrust your life's journey into His capable hands? Will you seek His counsel in every matter, allowing Him to guide your every step? Will you invite Him into your innermost secrets, making Him a part of your most private experiences? Will you answer His longing for union with you, entrusting yourself and all that you are into His loving care?

If you willingly embrace this truth, then you shall start to experience the sublime joy of oneness with Christ. Yet, even this image falls short of the magnificent reality. To be one with Christ, sharing one will, one purpose, one life, transcends the beauty of simply hosting Christ within your heart. Human language fails to capture this wondrous phenomenon.

Such a union means that you share His life, His will, His interests. You partake in His joy and His sorrow, mirroring His very being. You strive to think, feel, act, and walk as Christ did. Does your soul not leap at the prospect of such a destiny? This is no fantasy; it is real and within your reach.

Will you accept this divine union, dear soul? The Lord will not impose this unity upon you; He desires your companionship, your friendship. It must be your choice. Just as a bride must give her consent to the bridegroom, you must willingly choose unity with Christ.

So, what will be your response? First, understand that this divine union is promised in Scripture. Second, surrender your entire being to Him, allowing Him to take possession. Finally, believe that He has taken up residence within you. This realization is the beginning of your path to truly experiencing the joy of unity with Christ.

And so, I ask you once more: will you welcome Him in, not as a guest, but as an integral part of your very being, becoming one with Christ? May your answer reflect the deep longing of your soul, the desire for divine companionship and unity that transcends the mundane world. Let the joy of this spiritual union fill you, granting you peace, strength, and immeasurable happiness.

A Journey of Spiritual Transformation

As I embarked on a new journey in my life, I began to consider myself as no longer living, but rather, it was Christ who lived in me. This mindset, this faith, I upheld without wavering. Each day and night, I continually reminded myself, ***"I am crucified with Christ: nevertheless I live; yet not I, but Christ liveth in me" (Galatians 2:20, KJV).*** This phrase, like a spiritual mantra, became the rhythm of my soul, the habit of my existence.

I strived each day to let go of my earthly life through faith and in reality, while embracing the life of Christ. This action, through consistent repetition, shaped the entire framework of my being. Day by day, I realized I was carrying in my body the death of Jesus, so that His life could be revealed in me. I learned the true meaning of salvation and, to my amazement, discovered aspects of the Lord that were beyond my wildest dreams.

My realizations left me astounded! I thought to myself, "God is my true home and He is right here with me. Why have I been searching so far and wide for Him when He is nowhere but near?" Yet, I recognized an even deeper truth: God isn't merely close to me, He is within me. My spirit is the place He cherishes most.

For so long, I believed I was without a home, feeling lonely and tired. I thought I was missing my joy as I traversed this Earth, but all the while, I was God's sanctuary.

To conclude, the journey of self-discovery and spiritual transformation has taught me that it's not my earthly self that lives, but Christ who lives within me. The closer I get to Him, the more I understand my role in His divine plan. This path of spiritual transformation isn't always easy, but it's worth every step, for it leads to an understanding of God's love and presence in our lives that surpasses all human understanding.

I have come to realize that God is never distant; He is within me. In accepting this truth, I find myself at home in His love, becoming a sanctuary where His spirit dwells. Through this journey, I discovered my life in Christ and the endless joy of His constant presence within me.

Chapter EIGHTEEN

A LESSON IN THE INTERIOR LIFE

In the heart of winter, as Christmas time adorns our streets, a particular sight in the store windows often captures my attention. I see a compelling portrait, laden with profound symbolism, a testament to resilience in the face of hardship. It depicts a stark, chilly winter scene –

an ominous sky overhead, snow-dusted bare trees, brown grass and wilted weeds speckled with white, the remnants of the season's first snowfall.

Upon a leafless tree in this desolate scene, an empty, snow-filled nest serves as a solemn reminder of the life that once blossomed there. Nearby, a small bird perches with an air of determined tranquility. Despite the surrounding cold and gloom, this bird's spirit remains unbroken, its tiny head uplifted towards the heavens, its throat prepared to deliver a melody of fortitude and hope.

This picture, forever placed on my shelf, serves as a silent sermon to me. It whispers a tale of resilience and faith using two powerful words, "Although" and "Yet." These words evoke the essence of a verse from the King James Bible, Habakkuk 3:17-18, "Although the fig tree shall not blossom, neither shall fruit be in the vines; the labour of the olive shall fail, and the fields shall yield no meat; the flock shall be cut off from the fold, and there shall be no herd in the stalls: Yet I will rejoice in the LORD, I will joy in the God of my salvation."

Indeed, life often mirrors this winter scene. There are moments when our souls, like the little bird, find themselves in the cold embrace of despair, bereft of external and internal comfort. It is as if everything we once trusted crumbles before us, with promises unfulfilled and prayers unanswered. It feels as if there's no solid ground to stand on, whether in this world or the heavens.

However, it is precisely in such times that we must

remember the message of the brave bird perched amid the winter. The promise that, "Although" circumstances may seem dire, "Yet" there remains one constant – God, the source of our salvation. The God whose nature never alters, who was, is, and will forever be a beacon of goodness, love, and tenderness.

In Him, we can always find joy, regardless of the adversities we face or the comforts we lack. Just as the bird continues to sing its winter song amidst the bleak surroundings, we too can celebrate the God of our salvation amidst our trials. For even in the most brutal winter, He provides the warmth of hope and the promise of eventual spring.

In conclusion, let this tale of the little bird and its winter song serve as a reminder of the enduring presence and unchanging nature of God. In the face of adversity and trials, His love remains a constant source of joy and salvation. As it is written in Hebrews 13:8 in the King James Bible, "Jesus Christ the same yesterday, and today, and forever." May we remember this, singing our own winter song with faith and hope, as we navigate the snowy landscapes of our lives.

A Journey from Self to the Savior

Speaking in the style of Jesus, let us discuss the unique joy found in God alone. When I say, "rejoice in Him," I am not suggesting that you find joy in your own accomplishments, emotions, or experiences. Sadly, it seems this is often misunderstood. If such things are unsatisfactory, many believe there's no cause for happiness.

However, God tirelessly teaches us the lesson of self-denial. He calls us to shift our focus away from self, our experiences, our personal feelings, and to count our egos as irrelevant. We should not be concerned with our desires but only with God.

Just as a caterpillar is destined to become a beautiful butterfly, it must let go of its former life for a transformation to take place. Similarly, God has designed a higher life for us than the one we're currently living. As the caterpillar must shed its grub form to emerge as a butterfly, our self-life must cease so that a divine life can begin.

Understand this: we must die to our self-life and be reborn in a life focused only on God. This is essential in our spiritual journey, and so we must learn to find joy in the Lord, not in ourselves. At some point, every growing soul must learn to trust in God, just because of His divine nature, not merely for His promises or gifts.

The key to this transformation, I believe, lies in the soul experiencing loss – the loss of everything that isn't God. This doesn't necessarily mean losing friends or wealth, but it means experiencing a sense of desolation, an emptiness devoid of all consolation, whether from within or from outside sources. It's about reaching the end of everything that is not God.

This might sound harsh. It might feel like you're stuck in a slough, like falling off a cliff, or being swallowed by a vast ocean. But in these difficult times, in the midst of all struggles, you will discover the ever-present, ever-loving, and all-powerful God!

Only when you experience this can you truly understand and share in the prophet Habakkuk's triumphant cry: *"Yet I will rejoice in the LORD, I will joy in the God of my salvation." (Habakkuk 3:18 KJV)*

In doing so, you'll also realize the depth of the following verse: *"The LORD God is my strength, and he will make my feet like hinds' feet, and he will make me to walk upon mine high places." (Habakkuk 3:19 KJV)*

Often, we walk on self-created high places that are driven more by our emotions than by God. In times of loss, failure, and darkness, these high places can quickly become cliffs of despair. But by embracing God, even in the midst of life's challenges, we can transform our struggles into opportunities for growth and joy.

In conclusion, God desires us to journey from self-centered living to a life focused on Him. In doing so, we can find true joy, not in our experiences or emotions, but in the Lord alone. This journey may involve loss and hardship, but it leads to the discovery of a divine life filled with joy and strength, provided by our loving and ever-present God. Rejoice in Him, for He is the source of our salvation and our strength.]

"The True Worth of Christ's Sacrifice "

In the splendid kingdom of heaven, there is a deep misunderstanding that needs to be addressed. It is the notion that Jesus Christ, our Lord and Savior, surrendered His life because we humans were worth it.

You see, the death of Christ on the cross wasn't about our worth at all. Let me draw you a picture. Imagine you have a mountain, a large and terrifying mountain, and that mountain is the weight of our sins. The sins we committed, the ones we are committing now, and the ones we will commit in the future.

It's a heavy burden, isn't it? Yet, Christ, in His divine love and mercy, chose to bear this mountain for us. He didn't do it because we were worthy of such an act, but because of how steep and deep our sins were.

Scripture tells us in *Romans 3:23, "For all have sinned, and come short of the glory of God."* Our sins have separated us from the presence and glory of God. But God, in His boundless love, had a plan to bring us back to Him. And that's where Jesus comes in.

Now, let's talk about the demands of God's justice. The same book*, Romans, says in 6:23, "For the wages of sin is death; but the gift of God is eternal life through Jesus Christ our Lord."* Sin demands payment, and that payment is death. It's a law written by God Himself, who is just and righteous.

So, Christ's death wasn't about our worthiness. Instead, it was about fulfilling God's justice, a justice that demanded death for sin.

And finally, let's discuss God's eternal glory. 1 Corinthians 10:31 tells us, "Whether therefore ye eat, or drink, or whatsoever ye do, do all to the glory of God." Everything is for His glory, including the death and resurrection of Christ.

The death of Christ was an act of obedience, a fulfillment of God's will that brought glory to the Father. Jesus told us Himself in *John 12:27-28, "Now is my soul troubled; and what shall I say? Father, save me from this hour: but for this cause came I unto this hour. Father, glorify thy name."*

In conclusion, remember this: The sacrifice of Christ was not about our worth. It was about the depth of our sins, the demand for God's justice, and His eternal glory. We can never earn such a sacrifice, but we can gratefully accept it, live in obedience to His word, and strive to glorify Him in everything we do.

"Unwavering Faith: Finding Joy in the Lord Alone"

In the highest places, the Lord guides those souls who find joy only in Him. These places are untouched by shadows or losses, because their very foundations are built amidst the utter loss and death of everything that is not of God. If we seek an unswerving faith, we must find it solely in the Lord—excluding everything else. We must find joy not in His gifts or blessings or anything that can change with the varying circumstances of our earthly life.

We may perceive our prayers as answered today and unanswered tomorrow. The promises that once seemed brilliantly fulfilled might not appear as a reality to us anymore. The spiritual blessings that once brought us immense joy could be completely lost. We may find ourselves bereft of everything we once trusted, except for the longing memory of those times. Yet, when everything else fades, God remains. God doesn't change. As *Hebrews 13:8* states in the *(KJV), "Jesus Christ the same yesterday, and to day, and for ever."*

The soul that finds joy in God alone can experience no fluctuation. Trusting in His promises is indeed wonderful, but placing your trust in God, the Promiser, is even more glorious. The promises could be misunderstood or misapplied, and when we rely on them, they may seem to let us down. But, no one who trusted in God, the Promiser, has ever been let down. The God behind His promises is infinitely greater and can never fail us in any situation. Hence, a soul anchored in Him experiences perfect peace.

A little child may not always comprehend its mother's promises, but the child knows its mother. The child's trust is based not on her words, but on her existence. Similarly, for us who have learned this lesson, God is always there, even if we don't perceive an answered prayer or a fulfilled promise. Behind the prayers and promises, there is God. As in *Hebrews 11:6 (KJV)*, *"...he that cometh to God must believe that he is..."*

A child rejoices in the mother, not in her promises, but in her very existence. And while God exists, His children must be cared for, and we, His children, should recognize this fact and rejoice in it. God's attributes make neglect, indifference, forgetfulness, or ignorance impossible. He knows everything, cares about everything, can manage everything, and He loves us. What else could we possibly ask for?

Regardless of our circumstances, let us look up to our God, like a fearless little bird, and even amidst our darkest times, sing a joyful and triumphant song. All of God's saints throughout the ages have done this. Job, in his deepest sorrow and trials, said in *Job 13:15 (KJV)*, *"Though he slay me, yet will I trust in him."* David, during his most painful moments, proclaimed in *Psalm 23:4 (KJV)*, *"Yea, though I walk through the valley of the shadow of death, I will fear no evil: for thou art with me."*

In conclusion, the unwavering faith that we must strive for is found solely in the Lord. We should trust in Him, not in His promises, but in His very existence, for God is unchanging. Let us face our trials with steadfast faith, echoing the brave declarations of God's saints throughout history. For, in Him alone, we find our unwavering joy.

"A Testimony of Strength and Joy in the Lord"

I can recall the words that the Lord Himself spoke, assuring us of His constant presence and aid. The Bible in *Psalm 46:1-5* goes like this:

"God is our refuge and strength, a very present help in trouble. Therefore, we will not fear, even though the earth be removed, and though the mountains be carried into the midst of the sea; though the waters thereof roar and be troubled; though the mountains shake with the swelling thereof. God is in the midst of her; she shall not be moved; God shall help her, and that right early."

Just like King David, Apostle Paul also stood strong amidst his trials. He stated his conviction in *2 Corinthians 4:8-9, 16-18:*

"We are troubled on every side, yet not distressed; we are perplexed, but not in despair; persecuted, but not forsaken; cast down, but not destroyed... for which cause we faint not; but though our outward man perish, yet the inward man is renewed day by day. For our light affliction, which is but for a moment, worketh for us a far more exceeding and eternal weight of Glory; while we look not at the things which are seen, but at the things which are not seen; for the things which are seen are temporal; but the things which are not seen are eternal."

With such spirit, we understand that spiritual joy is not a

mere emotion hidden in our hearts. Instead, it's the gladness from knowing Christ, and embracing the blessing of having such a divine God and Saviour. We don't rejoice in our joy itself, but in the cause of it. When we "rejoice in the Lord, and joy in the God of our salvation", no human nor evil force can take this away from us. Our earthly sorrows become irrelevant to this heavenly joy.

Think about our spiritual journey as a pathway through different regions. The first is filled with joy, fervor, and emotional experiences, as well as secret revelations from God. The second, a vast wilderness, teems with trials and temptations, losses and dryness, and darkness both inside and outside. Finally, if we brave the wilderness, we find ourselves on the mountain heights, experiencing unbroken communion with God, detachment from earthly concerns, contentment with His divine will, and miraculous transformation into the image of Christ.

While I can't confirm if this order is accurate for all, I know many who, after tasting the joy of the beginning, found themselves lost in the wilderness. It's a learning curve, teaching us to detach from everything except God, aiming for complete oneness with Him.

Just like a caterpillar must pass through a phase of death to transform into a butterfly, we also need to journey through the harsh wilderness to reach the serene mountain peaks. If we remember this, we can confidently navigate even the darkest times, knowing that everything is fine because God is God.

In conclusion, the Christian journey is one of immense faith and perseverance. As we traverse from a place of new spiritual discoveries through trials and tribulations, we ultimately reach a divine union with God, signifying a metamorphosis in our spiritual life. Through these trials, we learn to embrace the joy of knowing and trusting in God's unwavering presence and love, which is a foundation stronger than any adversity we may face. In the end, we stand firm, just as King David and Apostle Paul did, radiating the joy of knowing and serving the Lord.

"The Song of Faith: Through Sunshine & Storm"

In the silent spaces of many hearts who read this book, I am certain, resides at least one of these desert "Althoughs." For some, there may be many. My beloved friends, is the "Yet" also present there? Have you absorbed the wisdom of the prophet's teachings? Is God sufficiently all-encompassing for you? Can you sing with conviction, "Thou, O Christ, art all I want, More than all in Thee I find," as penned in the hymn by Charles Wesley? If not, you may need the allegorical little bird to serenade you. Its song, echoed from a barren, leafless tree, amidst the winter tempest, must become your anthem as well.

"Though the rain may fall and the wind may howl,
And the biting chill of the winter's scowl;
Though the sky above grows ever cloudier,
And fallen leaves declare summer's departure;

Yet, I raise my face to the storm-ridden heaven,
My heart as serene as a summer's haven;
Joyfully accepting what my God hath given,
Whatever it be.

When I feel the cold, I can say, 'He sends it,'
And His wind, I know, blows blessings amid the grit;
For there's not a need that He doesn't tend,
And my heart stays warm, even as the winds blow unspent.
The gentle, sweet summer was vibrant and glowing,
Bountiful were the blossoms, each bough overflowing;
I trusted Him when the roses were growing,
I trust Him now.

Small would be my faith, should it falter weakly,
Now that the roses no longer bloom meekly;
Frail would be the trust, should it alter now,
Questioning His love as the storm clouds plough.
If I trust Him once, I must trust Him forever,
His path is best, whether I stumble or never.
Through gale or tempest, He will forsake me never,
For He sends all."

As recounted in the book of Proverbs, chapter 3, verses 5-6: *"Trust in the LORD with all thine heart; and lean not unto thine own understanding. In all thy ways acknowledge him, and he shall direct thy paths."*

As we traverse through life's varying seasons, we must remember this divine truth. Our trust in Him must not waver with the changing weather. Whether amid the blooming roses or the howling winds, we must sustain our faith. His love remains steadfast, unwavering in every storm.

In conclusion, remember this eternal song of faith. It reminds us to hold firm in our trust and faith in God, regardless of our circumstances. Despite the storms, despite the desert "Althoughs," our hearts must echo with the unwavering "Yet." As it is written in the book of Isaiah, chapter 40, verse 31 (KJV), *"But they that wait upon the LORD shall renew their strength; they shall mount up with wings as eagles; they shall run, and not be weary; and they shall walk, and not faint."* May this truth guide us all, and may our hearts forever sing this song of unwavering faith and trust.

Chapter NINETEEN

KINGS AND THEIR KINGDOMS; OR, HOW TO REIGN IN THE INTERIOR LIFE

Many years ago, the Pharisees asked Jesus when the Kingdom of God would come. His response was profound and enlightening. As written in the the Bible, *Luke 17:20-21, "And when he was demanded of the Pharisees when the Kingdom of God should come, he answered them and said, The Kingdom of God cometh not with observation: neither shall they say, lo here! or, lo there! for, behold, the Kingdom of God is within you."*

You may have come across the terms "Kingdom of God" and "Kingdom of Heaven" in the Bible. But what do they mean? Simply put, these expressions refer to a divine state, a condition where God reigns supreme and His will is carried out. It is an inner Kingdom, not an outer one.

The thrones in this Kingdom are not made of gold or glittering gems. They're not located in grand castles or lavishly decorated palaces. Instead, they're in our hearts, symbolizing our internal rule over things of time and sense.

The Kings and Queens of this Kingdom don't wear royal robes of purple and fine linen. They dress themselves in the spiritual attire of purity and truth. The reign of this Kingdom isn't displayed by physical might or worldly power. It exists and rules within us with quiet strength and invisible authority.

This Kingdom is not in a specific location, nor does it favor one form over another. It's not a place you can point out on a map, nor is it confined to a particular religious structure or place of worship. Rather, it is a state of being.

In this Kingdom, everyone who earnestly seeks God and strives to live a righteous life will find the divine presence within themselves. However, many fail to understand this. We often get caught up in the literal and physical interpretation of a Kingdom and thus, expect the Kingdom of Heaven to be a place of outward victory, seen and observed by all.

We may imagine that sitting on a throne with Christ would entail a public display of power and glory. But as our understanding of Scripture deepens, we realize that such an interpretation falls short of the profound spiritual reality these symbols represent.

In conclusion, let's remember that the Kingdom of God isn't a far-off place we should aspire to reach. It's not about physical wealth or grandeur. It's an inner Kingdom, a state of being that exists within us. As we seek God and strive to live righteously, we find this Kingdom within us, guiding us towards a life of purity and truth. This is the profound teaching that Jesus gave to the Pharisees, and it's a lesson we can take to heart today.

"The Kingdom Within: Discovering the Divine Truth"

The more I look, the clearer it becomes. This powerful vision strengthens before my very eyes, reminding me of the true meaning of our Lord's words. Now, they seem truer than I had ever imagined. He once told us that *"the kingdom of God cometh not with observation; neither shall they say, lo here! or, lo there! for, behold, the kingdom of God is within you" (Luke 17:20-21, KJV)*.

The words in Daniel 2:44 and Isaiah 9:6,7 proclaim this truth loudly:

"And in the days of these kings shall the God of heaven set up a kingdom, which shall never be destroyed: and the kingdom shall not be left to other people, but it shall break in pieces and consume all these kingdoms, and it shall stand forever." (Daniel 2:44, KJV)

"For unto us a child is born, unto us a son is given: and the government shall be upon his shoulder: and his name shall be called Wonderful, Counsellor, The mighty God, The everlasting Father, The Prince of Peace. Of the increase of his government and peace there shall be no end, upon the throne of David, and upon his kingdom, to order it, and to establish it with judgment and with justice from henceforth even forever. The zeal of the Lord of hosts will perform this." (Isaiah 9:6-7, KJV)

This divine kingdom will outshine all other kingdoms, showing its strength from within. If your heart is at peace, no outward chaos can disturb your soul. Even in troubling times, a joyful heart remains triumphant. Your inner self determines your happiness, not the world outside.

The wise man Diogenes understood this. When a king tried to degrade him, he responded, "Yes, but I am not degraded!" His message was clear: No ruler can harm a soul that holds onto its dignity. No oppressor can control a man who is free at heart.

Having this divine kingdom within us means we are no longer at the mercy of external forces. Instead, we rule over them with dignity and freedom. Fashion, fear, or ease - none of these can control us. We rise above all, free from sin, temptation, and discouragement. Even the most deeply ingrained sinful habits cannot chain us.

In this divine kingdom, we are kings. Outwardly, men may be kings by circumstance, but in this inward kingdom, we rule over our circumstances. No matter how much the world tries to constrain us, we stand strong, unaffected by it all. For the true King in this kingdom is One who is beyond all circumstances. He is the maker of all.

In conclusion, the Kingdom of God is not an external entity; it exists within each of us. Our inner strength and peace, our ability to rise above hardships and temptations, and our invincibility against external powers reflect this Kingdom. Let us strive to keep this kingdom thriving within us, for it is our true path to freedom, joy, and divine guidance.

The Divine Kingdom: Shouldering the Burdens for Us

As one of His subjects, I can attest to this profound truth: the governance of His divine kingdom rests solely upon His shoulders. There is no room for doubt. He administers His realm with such discerning judgment and justice that leaves no desires unfulfilled for anyone within His kingdom. In the phrase "the government shall be upon His shoulder," lies the hidden essence of this wondrous kingdom. Upon His shoulder, not upon mine or yours. The concerns are His, the burdens are His, the responsibility is solely His, even the safeguarding lies with Him. The strategy, supply, direction, and oversight — all rest in His capable hands.

Who can question His perfect fulfilment of each obligation that comes with His kingship? Therefore, those within His kingdom are completely liberated from any anxiety, burden, confusion, or worry. By this deliverance, they themselves become royals. Governance doesn't lie on their shoulders; they have no reason to intervene. Their King has taken on the entire responsibility. As long as His subjects are happy and thriving, He willingly bears the weight and worries of kingship.

We often speak of earthly monarchs' responsibilities, feeling pity for the burdens imposed by their role. Even on a human level, we understand that being a king should mean carrying the burdens of even the least of his subjects. At this very moment, countless hearts ache in sympathy for the newly enthroned Czar, burdened with the mighty Russian Empire's governance. From this innate understanding within every human heart about the rightful duties of kingship, we can discern what it means to be in a kingdom where God is King. He Himself proclaimed that everything shall be managed with judgment and justice from this point forth, and forever. Surely, no worries or anxiety can infiltrate here, if the heart truly knows its kingdom and its King!

In John 18:36, our King outlines His kingdom's approach: "Jesus answered, My kingdom is not of this world: if my kingdom were of this world, then would my servants fight, that I should not be delivered to the Jews; but now is my kingdom not from hence." Unlike earthly kings and kingdoms, which maintain their supremacy through outward conflict, God's kingdom conquers with inner strength. Earthly kings quell enemies; God quashes enmity. His victories must first be internal before they can be external. He does not subjugate, but He conquers.

Even we, in our earthly realm, recognize this principle. We don't value a victory over another if it only affects the body and doesn't subdue the heart. No true mother is satisfied with mere outward obedience; she yearns for her child's inner surrender. Unless the fortress of the heart is won, the victory seems worthless. This is even more valid with God, for we are told that *"He seeth not as man seeth; for man looketh on the outward appearance, but the Lord looketh on the heart"* (1 Samuel 16:7, KJV).

In conclusion, we exist in a divine kingdom, guided and protected by a King who willingly bears all burdens for His subjects. He seeks not external victories but the conquest of hearts. As we journey in this kingdom, we must allow our King to govern, trusting His judgement and surrendering our hearts to Him. Only then can we fully appreciate the joy of living in a kingdom where all burdens are shouldered by the King, ensuring peace and prosperity for all.

Subduing Hearts Through Inner Transformation

In the spiritual dialogue, we often mention the phrase "subduing hearts." But let's clarify; this doesn't mean overpowering or enforcing a compulsory surrender on unwilling souls. Instead, it implies winning hearts over and inspiring them to voluntarily submit to divine control. This, my friends, is the exact manner in which God subdues hearts. Thus, when the scripture tells us that "His kingdom ruleth over all" (Psalms 103:19), it signifies that all hearts willingly serve Him with joyful surrender.

God's reign, I must stress, must first be inward before it can be outward. Indeed, it is not a reign at all unless it is within. In the grand scheme of things, it's clear that God cannot rule a kingdom where the subjugation extends only to the external actions of His subjects. His kingdom is not a worldly one but exists within a spiritual realm where His power influences souls, not bodies. Only when the soul is conquered, can His kingdom be truly established.

With this understanding, we find love and blessings in declarations and prophecies stating that God will subdue His enemies under His feet and rule them with righteousness and power. The voice of the great multitude heard by John in Revelation becomes a glorious beacon of hope: "Alleluia! For the Lord God omnipotent reigneth!" (Revelation 19:6).

For further understanding, we look at two scriptures: Romans 14:17 and 1 Corinthians 4:20. They illustrate the essence of God's kingdom: "For the kingdom of God is not meat and drink; but righteousness, and peace, and joy in the Holy Ghost." (Rom. 14:17) and "For the kingdom of God is not in word, but in power." (1 Cor. 4:20).

These scriptures make it clear that God's kingdom isn't about externalities, but internal transformation. It's not about what we consume, where we live, our nationality, or cultural customs, but it concerns the innate traits of our nature and the power of our spiritual life. It's not our actions, but our inner being, that determines our belonging to His kingdom.

His kingdom becomes a reality only when inward righteousness, peace, joy, and power are granted and experienced. Thus, it's only through the inner workings of God's all-subduing Spirit that such transformative results can be accomplished.

An illustrative story comes from Greek mythology. Ulysses, on his journey past the enchanting sirens, filled his crew's ears with wax to block their enticing music, binding himself to the ship's mast. They sailed past safely. Yet, Orpheus, sailing the same route, charmed his crew with his music, superior to the sirens'. They passed the sirens safely, even disdainfully.

Ulysses depended on external measures - wax and bonds - to avoid temptation. In contrast, Orpheus relied on inward joy, captivating his crew with his music, to overcome temptation. Similarly, God's kingdom doesn't require an external law. It rules by the strength of its internal life, just as it is said in Galatians, "Against such there is no law" (Galatians 5:23).

In conclusion, the essence of God's reign is an inward transformation that moves beyond mere outward subjugation. This divine conquest of the heart prompts us towards righteousness, peace, joy, and power in the Holy Spirit. As we surrender our hearts willingly to God, we not only belong to His kingdom but also begin to live and reign in His kingdom. Remember, the Kingdom of God is within you (Luke17:21). It is about the inward transformation that comes when God's Spirit takes up residence in our hearts.

Let's reflect on the story of Orpheus again. The inward joy of his music was powerful enough to overpower the external temptation of the sirens. That's the kind of power God wants us to possess. The power that springs from inward righteousness, peace, and joy. The kind of power that allows us to navigate the world, not with fear of its siren songs, but with a sense of divine purpose and conviction.

This power doesn't require external laws or rules to hold it in check. It operates from the inward law of the Spirit of Life in Christ Jesus. It is a kingdom where the subjects are not forced into compliance but are willingly submitted to God's will. It's a kingdom that doesn't need to subjugate bodies because it has won over hearts.

Living in this kingdom means living with the King's rule in our hearts, making choices that align with His will, and experiencing the power, joy, peace, and righteousness that come from His Spirit dwelling in us.

So let us open our hearts, let us allow God to do His

transformative work within us. Let's seek His kingdom and His righteousness, and all these things will be added unto us (Matthew 6:33). Let us willingly surrender our hearts to the loving rule of our Heavenly Father and experience the inward transformation that marks us as citizens of His eternal kingdom.

Remember, the Kingdom of God is not something external we need to search for, it is internal, waiting to be discovered within us. Let God subdue your heart, not with force, but with His love and righteousness. Experience the joy, peace, and power that comes from living in His Kingdom, the Kingdom that truly reigns over all.

And so we join the multitude heard by John, raising our voices in triumphant declaration: "Alleluia! For the Lord God omnipotent reigneth!" Let His reign be established within us. Let His kingdom come, let His will be done, on earth as it is in heaven (Matthew 6:10). This, dear friends, is the true meaning of divine conquest. This is what it means for God to subdue hearts, our hearts, through inward transformation.

Reigning in The Kingdom of Kings: A Walk of Faith

We exist in a realm of supreme majesty. Imagine, my dear reader, a grand chorus of voices uplifting a song that we ought to already be singing here, even as we tread this earthly life. This song declares: *"Unto him that loved us, and washed us from our sins in his own blood, And hath made us kings and priests unto God and his*

Father; to him be glory and dominion for ever and ever. Amen" (Revelation 1:5-6, KJV).

Think of this! We who have embraced this spiritual kingdom, or rather, within whom this kingdom has taken root, sit upon the throne alongside our Heavenly King. His dominion becomes our dominion. The world, His footstool, becomes ours as well. He overcame the confines of time and sense by the strength of a life lived in a realm far above them, and we are invited to do the same.

Have you ever heard someone say, "They rise superior to their surroundings?" When we say this, we are recognizing a power within that person that masters their surroundings, rather than being mastered by them. This was the essence of our King, and He shares this power with us. However, like Him, our kingship is not flaunted in outward appearances but held firmly in inward strength.

His reign was not displayed through earthly treasures and riches. On the contrary, He had none of these, and yet, He didn't need them. That's the true essence of our reign. We won't have everyone bowing down to us, and not everything will bend to our will. But, even when faced with opposition and adversity, our soul will march in royal triumph.

There is an idea of kingship that seems contrary to human thinking. We often think that to truly reign, our outward circumstances must obey our will. Friends must approve, enemies must be silenced, obstacles must be overcome, and affairs must prosper. That, in our minds, is true reigning.

If we could change the stories of Daniel and the three Hebrew children—Shadrach, Meshach, and Abednego— we might think the victory would have been for Daniel to not be thrown into the lions' den or for the three Hebrews to avoid the fiery furnace altogether. But God's way was infinitely grander.

Daniel was indeed cast among the lions, but through God's power, he reigned triumphant over them. Likewise, Shadrach, Meshach, and Abednego were cast into the fiery furnace. Yet, they walked unharmed through the fire, not even carrying the smell of smoke upon them.

The Kingdom of Kings is not about the absence of challenges. Instead, it's about the power of God working within us to overcome them, just as Jesus did. This reign, my friends, is not marked by earthly riches, but by a profound triumph of soul that enables us to rise above our surroundings, just like our King did. This is the secret to a perpetual reign. This is the divine mystery of our kingship in Christ.

In conclusion, the message of the Kingdom of Kings is a message of triumph over adversity, of strength in the face of challenges. It is a call to rise above our circumstances, to embrace the power that God has granted us and to become one with Christ in His reign. It is not an easy path, but it is a path of victory, and it is open to all who choose to walk it.

The Unseen Kingdom of Inner Peace

In life, we are not promised a journey void of perilous dragons and venomous serpents. Instead, we are guided to walk amidst these treacherous creatures, yet assured that we will "tread them under our feet." What a magnificent kingdom this is—greater than any earthly power or influence! Such is the spiritual realm wherein we become inwardly sovereign, even when outwardly bound.

This majestic kingdom of righteousness, peace, and joy in the Holy Spirit is a gift from God, suitable for those with hearts mirroring His. It's a realm where we can face adversity and still reign with tranquility. We might be *"destitute, afflicted, tormented, to be stoned, and slain with the sword; to wander in sheepskins and goatskins, and in deserts and mountains, and in dens and caves of the earth" (Hebrews 11:37-38, KJV),* yet we stand as regents in the unseen kingdom.

Our world has been graced with such luminaries, those whose souls reigned even in their trials. The story of one such soul resonates from the monks at the monastery of St. Cyr.

This community of monks, known for their piety, provoked resentment from the surrounding monasteries and wrath from their superiors. Ostracized for their faith, one monk was dispatched to a hostile monastery as a prisoner. Despite his noble birth and his previous position as an abbot, he was relegated to degrading tasks and reviled publicly.

Despite this, his spirit remained unshaken; his inner tranquility undisturbed. His response to his persecutors was only kindness and Christ-like love. Such divine meekness he possessed that he won over the hearts of his enemies, becoming their beloved guide. His story echoes the words of Jesus Christ, *"Blessed are the meek, for they shall inherit the earth" (Matthew 5:5, KJV).* Through his meekness, he indeed conquered and reigned in the hearts of those around him.

At one point, a violent offender was confined to the monastery. This man was so ferocious that chains could not bind him, nor human strength subdue him. The monks, recognizing the power of divine meekness, left the offender in the care of the monk from St. Cyr.

The offender met the monk's gentleness with hostility, even to the point of physical abuse. The saintly monk, however, offered no resistance, countering the offender's aggression only with words of love. His gentle spirit, steadfast amidst the fury, seemed to extend a loving invitation, seeking to embrace the offender in a comforting bond of compassion.

In conclusion, trials and tribulations are not to be feared. They are, rather, a passage to prove our inner strength and reveal the beauty of our divine calling. As we walk through the valley of shadow and death, we are assured of God's protection and guidance: *"Yea, though I walk through the valley of the shadow of death, I will fear no evil: for thou art with me; thy rod and thy staff they comfort me" (Psalm 23:4, KJV).* Like the humble monk, we too can manifest this unseen kingdom of inner peace, shaping the world around us through our divine character, reflecting the spirit of Jesus Christ in all we do.

"The True Nature of Divine Dominion"

It became unbearable for the hardened criminal. He could retaliate with anger, revenge, and hatred, yet he found himself defenseless against this display of love and humility. Conquered, he wept at the saint's feet, pleading forgiveness for his cruelty and pledging eternal loyalty to his savior. From that point forward, the criminal ceased to cause trouble. Like a devoted dog, he stuck close to the saint, fulfilling any wish the saint desired. When his prison sentence ended, he chose to stay, unwilling to part from the man who'd shown him the transformative power of love. Such is the power of leadership in the Kingdom of Heaven. Each of us can apply this truth to our lives without needing further explanation.

In Matthew chapters 5, 6, and 7, our King portrays His kingdom's attributes and lays down His laws for His followers. *"Blessed are the poor in spirit: for theirs is the kingdom of heaven" (Matthew 5:3 KJV).* Not the wealthy, mighty, wise, or learned, but the poor in spirit, the meek, merciful, pure in heart, mourners, and those hungering and thirsting for righteousness. Those who endure persecution, revilement, and slander - these are the rightful citizens of this Kingdom. Gentleness, tolerance, humility, and love embody these monarchs, and they govern through these virtues.

A Christian once sought advice on gaining respect. The wise response was, "Command their respect." This command wasn't about authoritative proclamations, but about living in a manner that naturally commands respect. Some may gain a façade of respect through domination, but to rule hearts, one must embrace a different strategy.

Jesus Himself gave insight to those desiring to share in His rule. *"Ye know that they which are accounted to rule over the Gentiles exercise lordship over them; and their great ones exercise authority upon them. But so shall it not be among you: but whosoever will be great among you, shall be your minister: and whosoever of you will be the chiefest, shall be servant of all. For even the Son of man came not to be ministered unto, but to minister, and to give his life a ransom for many" (Mark 10:42-45 KJV).* Worldly leaders exercise authority, yet in the divine perspective, the one who serves reigns supreme. Not the one who demands most, but the one who relinquishes most, achieves this inner kingship.

Imagine the grandeur of the kingship Jesus presents in the Sermon on the Mount: *"But I say unto you, That ye resist not evil: but whosoever shall smite thee on thy right cheek, turn to him the other also. And if any man will sue thee at the law, and take away thy coat, let him have thy cloak also. And whosoever shall compel thee to go a mile, go with him twain" (Matthew 5:39-41 KJV).* Only a soul in harmony with God can ascend such a throne of dominion!

But that's our calling. We are born of a royal lineage, inheritors of this magnificent kingdom, *"heirs of God, and joint-heirs with Christ" (Romans 8:17 KJV).* If only we could grasp this truth and view every act of service or surrender as a step upward towards our kingdom and throne, in a very tangible way.

In conclusion, the Kingdom of Heaven operates differently from earthly kingdoms. It is a domain where meekness, service, and love are the true currencies of power. As heirs of this divine dominion, we must strive to embody these virtues in our lives. Being humble in spirit, pure in heart, and thirsting for righteousness elevates us to our destined thrones in this ineffable Kingdom. It's not about enforcing our will, but about nurturing a spirit of service and surrender. It's about transforming the world, not through dominion but through love, just like the saint who touched the heart of the hardened criminal.

Therein lies our calling to be servant leaders, just as Christ was. *"For even the Son of man came not to be ministered unto, but to minister, and to give his life a ransom for many" (Mark 10:45 KJV).* The true measure of greatness, as defined in the Kingdom of Heaven, is not in how many serve us, but in how many we serve. It's about laying down our lives in service to others, just as Christ did for us.

When we understand this truth, we begin to see every act of service or sacrifice not as a loss, but as a gain. Each is a step towards our ultimate purpose, a step closer to our throne in the Kingdom of Heaven. Such is the true nature of divine dominion, a dominion that is won not by force or authority, but by love, meekness, and mercy.

Let us remember this as we go about our lives. Let us strive to embody these virtues, not to gain worldly respect or authority, but to become true heirs of the Kingdom of Heaven. And as we do so, let us not forget the power of love and humility, as demonstrated by the saint and the transformed criminal.

In the end, the Kingdom of Heaven is not about power or authority, but about love, service, and humility. It's about ruling not over others, but over our own spirits. It's about embodying the virtues Christ taught us and living in a way that naturally commands respect. And in doing so, we become not only heirs to the Kingdom of Heaven but also leaders in the truest sense, guiding others towards this divine dominion.

A Journey in Humility and Service

I want to tell you a little secret. The everyday tasks that we perform and the small sacrifices we make each day can, if done with full dedication, be the steps on the ladder that leads us to our heavenly thrones. I want you to understand that if we remain faithful to our small earthly responsibilities, we will be entrusted with greater heavenly responsibilities. The scripture says, *"He that is faithful in that which is least is faithful also in much..."*

(Luke 16:10, KJV).

For those who follow Christ in this life of service and sacrifice, they will reign with Him in the glory of absolute self-sacrifice and will be the greatest in His divine kingdom of love. Understanding this, wouldn't anyone gladly offer the other cheek, knowing that by doing so, a kingdom can be won, and a throne can be achieved?

Consider the story of Joseph. Whether he was a slave or in prison, he ruled like a king, just as he did when he sat on Pharaoh's throne or rode in Pharaoh's chariot. Genesis 39:6, 22, 23 (KJV) shares his story. Joseph became the greatest by being the least, the highest by being a servant to all. Now, think about this. Are you ruling in this manner, in this unique kingdom? Are you the greatest in your world of home, church, or social circle by being the least and the highest by being the servant of all? If not, your kingdom isn't Christ's kingdom, and your throne isn't shared by Him.

Partaking in this internal kingdom and its heavenly power isn't a theoretical victory or imagined supremacy. It's a real and actual reigning, enabling you to rise above the world and its elements, to walk through it indifferent to its approval or disapproval. You can dwell in an area of heavenly peace and heavenly triumph that the world cannot give nor take away. The Bible tells us, *"For the kingdom of God is not in word, but in power" (1 Corinthians 4:20, KJV).* It's not merely about talking; it's a reality, and those who are in it recognize their kingship and demonstrate it by ruling.

But maybe you're wondering, "How can I be part of this kingdom if I'm not already in?" Jesus provides the answer: "At the same time came the disciples unto Jesus, saying, Who is the greatest in the kingdom of heaven? And Jesus called a little child unto him, and set him in the midst of them, And said, *Verily I say unto you, Except ye be converted, and become as little children, ye shall not enter into the kingdom of heaven. Whosoever therefore shall humble himself as this little child, the same is greatest in the kingdom of heaven" (Matthew 18:1-4, KJV).* It's a kingdom of childlike hearts, and only such can enter.

To be a "little child" is to be just that. Little children are simple, trusting, lighthearted, and unquestioningly obedient to their elders. To be the greatest in this divine kingdom is to have the most innocent, tender, trusting, selfless, obedient heart of a child.

Matthew 7:21 (KJV) tells us, *"Not everyone that saith unto me, Lord, Lord, shall enter into the kingdom of heaven; but he that doeth the will of my Father which is in heaven."* It's not about speaking, but about acting. We must become like children, or we won't ascend to the child's throne. Becoming a child means doing the Father's will, as true childhood combines a spirit of obedience with a spirit of trust.

Therefore, become a little child by setting aside all your pretensions, self-confidence, independence, wisdom, and strength. Agree to let go of your self-centered life and be reborn into the kingdom of God. The scripture reminds us, *"Verily, verily, I say unto thee, Except a man be born again, he cannot see the kingdom of God" (John 3:3, KJV).*

Just like the tale of Joseph, we must be prepared to be a servant to all. It is through service and humility, traits exemplified by children, that we draw closer to Christ's kingdom. This is not an imaginary victory or supremacy; it is a practical reality that enables us to rise above worldly concerns. It's a kingdom where being the least makes you the greatest, and the humblest person reigns. It's a kingdom that transforms you, allowing you to live in peace and triumph that the world can't grant or take away.

In conclusion, our path to divine kingship is through a life of humility, service, and obedience, just as Christ showed us. We can't win a kingdom or gain a throne through greatness, wisdom, or strength, but through the humble, trusting, and obedient heart of a child. It is a journey of self-sacrifice and selflessness, filled with everyday tasks and small sacrifices made with love and dedication. And by faithfully fulfilling these, we ascend our heavenly ladder, step by step, towards the kingdom of God. Let us always strive to live by these principles, in honor of our Lord, who modeled the perfect example of humility and service for us.

The Path from Death to Life

In truth, the journey from one existence to another necessitates death in one and rebirth into the next. It echoes the oft-repeated narrative of transition from death to life. As I declare unto you, the invitation is to die, so that you may live. Surrender your personal life to discover Christ's life. Just as a caterpillar can only transform into a butterfly by leaving its previous existence and embracing its newfound life, we too can only gain access to the kingdom of God through the rejection of self and the embrace of Christ's resurrection life.

Therefore, relinquish all that pertains to the earthly existence: your perceptions, strategies, tendencies, and notions. Embrace, instead, God's designs, methods, and insights. Pursue this course with consistency and fidelity, and you will eventually ascend His throne, ruling alongside Him in an internal kingdom that will shatter and subsume all other kingdoms, persisting into eternity. There is no alternative path. This kingdom isn't accessible through grandeur, spectacle, or power, but through humility, frailty, childhood innocence, and mortality. As it is written, *"Whosoever therefore shall humble himself as this little child, the same is greatest in the kingdom of heaven." (Matthew 18:4 KJV).*

In this kingdom, the humble alone are exalted; to ascend the throne with Christ, we must first endure His suffering, loss, and crucifixion. As written in *2 Timothy 2:12 (KJV), "If we suffer, we shall also reign with him."* This is not an arbitrary reward for our suffering, but an inevitable outcome. Inevitably, Christ's loss results in Christ's gain; Christ's death brings Christ's resurrection, and following Him in renewal will surely lead the faithful to His crown and throne.

For example, consider a poignant anecdote from a book of children's sermons. A young boy from an English Refuge risked his life to save a friend, and Queen of England honored his bravery with a medal, delivered by an esteemed Earl. Despite his nerves and shyness, the boy stood among his peers to receive the award. The Earl, a member of the House of Lords, was visibly moved as he had the honor to pin the medal onto the boy's jacket. His heart was full as he recognized the true glory of this child's selfless act of courage.

The little boy had braved the current, shared the imminent danger with the drowning child, and emerged from the water hand-in-hand with the saved boy. His glory was not one of fame or power, but of selflessness and life-saving courage. That is the glory that surpasses the honors of successful statesmen, warriors, and lawyers.

It compels one to ask, why does self-forgetfulness possess such immense power? It is because, as Jesus Christ taught in the scriptures, *"Greater love hath no man than this, that a man lay down his life for his friends." (John 15:13 KJV).* Through such selfless acts, we demonstrate the love of Christ, and through such death to our own desires, we find the resurrection life of Jesus Christ.

In conclusion, the path to the kingdom of God is paved with humility, selflessness, and death to our earthly desires. By embracing these attributes, we transition from our earthly existence to a life lived in Christ. We must remember that in death to our old self, we discover the resurrected life of Christ within us, a life marked by selflessness, love, and eternal glory.

Embracing the Glory of Selflessness and Sacrifice

Have you ever wondered how a twelve-year-old boy could humble an assembly of mature men? What bestowed that tiny head, with its shock of bright hair, a majesty and honor that surpassed the gleam of gold and gems? How could that small body in its modest clothes, brushing away tears with a coarse sleeve, capture the hearts of thousands, turning them into devoted subjects of his dominion? What was the source of this magic?

The secret lies in the spirit of the boy, a spirit that echoed the selfless sacrifice of Christ. In this, he held a fragment of the divine beauty we're all designed to adore; the splendor that makes angels shout in awe and all heavenly beings bow in reverence, proclaiming, ***"Worthy is the Lamb that was slain!" (Revelation 5:12, KJV).*** The "Lamb that was slain" is the mightiest King our world has ever known, and those who embrace His spirit partake in His kingdom.

Bear in mind, this kingdom is not a location but a character. Therefore, those lacking this character can't possibly belong. When we say, "Thy kingdom come," during our daily prayers, do we fully understand our request? Can we grasp the transformative power it will have within us? Are we ready to embrace such change?

The kingdom of God is the rule of God, which is the will of God. Therefore, when we pray, *"Thy will be done on earth, as it is in heaven," (Matthew 6:10, KJV),* we've discovered the heart of the matter. Barbarians might seize a civilized kingdom using raw power, yet to conquer its civilization, they must yield to its influence. It's the same with the kingdom of heaven, which extends its royal scepter only to those who obey its laws.

As it says in *Revelation 3:21 (KJV), "To him that overcometh will I grant to sit with me in my throne, even as I also overcame, and am set down with my Father in his throne."* An ancient scholar proclaimed, "He who reigns sides with God," and "He who fully accepts the will of God, dwells in a perpetual kingdom."

Do you rule in this manner, in this kind of kingdom? Are you the "greatest" by being the "servant of all"? Are you a sovereign over your circumstances, or do they rule over you? Do you conquer your temptations, or do they conquer you? Can you maintain inner peace in the face of outward loss and defeat? Can you triumph by surrendering and become the greatest by being the least?

If your answers to these questions are all affirmative, then you have entered your kingdom. No matter what your exterior situation might be or how others perceive you, in truth, you are among those whom the Lord pronounces *"the same shall be called greatest in the kingdom of heaven" (Matthew 18:4, KJV).*

In conclusion, the true essence of the kingdom lies in embodying the spirit of Christ - selfless sacrifice for others. When we genuinely pray, "Thy kingdom come," we seek an inner transformation that aligns us with the will of God, making us part of His divine kingdom, a kingdom not defined by earthly riches or worldly power but by selflessness, sacrifice, and servitude. It is in this kingdom that we find our true glory and honor.

Chapter TWENTY

THE CHARIOTS OF GOD FOUNDATION TEXT

I am drawn to the profound words of Psalm 68:17, "The chariots of God are twenty thousand, even thousands of angels: the Lord is among them, as in Sinai, in the holy place." This verse paints a picture of the divine chariots - not just any chariots, but God's chariots. These conveyances are designed for movement and progress. Just as earthly chariots transport riders over distances or obstacles to their desired destination, God's chariots transport our souls. The glorious destinations that await those who travel in God's chariots are beyond words. Moreover, these chariots are "very many," ready and waiting for us.

But oh, how we often fail to see them! Earthly chariots

are plainly visible, while God's chariots are not. They are invisible to all but the eye of faith. Let's recall the tale from 2 Kings 6:14-17, "Therefore sent he thither horses, and chariots, and a great host: and they came by night, and compassed the city about. And when the servant of the man of God was risen early, and gone forth, behold, an host compassed the city both with horses and chariots. And his servant said unto him, Alas, my master! how shall we do? And he answered, Fear not: for they that be with us are more than they that be with them. And Elisha prayed, and said, LORD, I pray thee, open his eyes, that he may see. And the LORD opened the eyes of the young man; and he saw: and, behold, the mountain was full of horses and chariots of fire round about Elisha."

The servant of the prophet saw only the visible Syrian horses and chariots, prompting him to exclaim in worry, "Alas, my Master! how shall we do?" But Elisha, the prophet himself, remained calm and unafraid, for his eyes had the gift to see the invisible. His prayer for his servant was for God to grant the same sight, "Lord, I pray thee, open his eyes that he may see."

We need to pray for the same gift, for ourselves and each other. We should plead, "Lord, open our eyes that we may see." For God's horses and chariots fill our world, ready to transport us to a glorious victory. Yet, these chariots may not appear as we expect them to.

Indeed, they may seem to be our adversaries, our trials, and our sufferings. They might appear as misunderstandings, disappointments, or acts of unkindness. We may perceive them as Juggernaut cars of misery and wretchedness, ready to overrun and crush us. Yet, they are truly God's chariots of triumph, ready to transport us to the victories our souls have been longing and praying for.

Deuteronomy 32:12-13 assures us, "So the Lord alone did lead him, and there was no strange god with him. He made him ride on the high places of the earth, that he might eat the increase of the fields; and he made him to suck honey out of the rock, and oil out of the flinty rock." If we wish to "ride on the high places of the earth," we need to board the chariots that can carry us there. Only God's chariots can take us on such a majestic journey.

Isaiah 58:14 also reminds us, "Then shalt thou delight thyself in the Lord; and I will cause thee to ride upon the high places of the earth, and feed thee with the heritage of Jacob thy father: for the mouth of the LORD hath spoken it." If we surrender ourselves to the divine design and step into the seemingly daunting chariots of God, we are promised a journey to unimaginable heights of victory.

To wrap things up, my dear friends, I want you to remember that the trials and tribulations you encounter in your life are not there to destroy you. Instead, think of them as divine chariots, ready to carry you to a place of triumph and glory. It may be difficult to perceive them in this light, especially during trying times. However, by turning to God and asking Him to open our eyes to see His divine plan, we can change our perspective.

In the spirit of Psalm 68:17, 2 Kings 6:14-17,

Deuteronomy 32:12-13, and Isaiah 58:14, let's learn to see our struggles as God's chariots, vehicles of triumph that can transport us to the victories our souls yearn for. Our prayer should always be, "Lord, open our eyes that we may see." This, I believe, is the secret to riding in God's chariots and experiencing the true victory that awaits us. Let's journey together, riding high in God's chariots of triumph!

Riding with God: Navigating Life's Trials

From a personal perspective, I see that every occurrence in our lives can either be a crushing Juggernaut, or a victorious chariot. It hinges on how we confront these events; whether we succumb to our tribulations allowing them to overwhelm us, or instead ascend into them as if boarding a chariot, transforming them into vessels that convey us triumphantly forward and upward. As written in 2 Kings 2:11-12, "And it came to pass, as they still went on, and talked, that, behold, there appeared a chariot of fire, and horses of fire, and parted them both asunder; and Elijah went up by a whirlwind into heaven. And Elisha saw it, and he cried, My father, my father, the chariot of Israel, and the horsemen thereof. And he saw him no more: and he took hold of his own clothes, and rent them in two pieces."

Whenever we ascend into God's chariots, we experience a spiritual translation akin to Elisha's. We are not lifted to the heavens as he was, but rather transported to the heaven within us - a transformation arguably as majestic as his. From the mundane plane where suffering is rife, we ascend into the "heavenly places in Christ Jesus," victoriously soaring above all worldly concerns. As mentioned in Ephesians 2:6, "And hath raised us up together, and made us sit together in heavenly places in Christ Jesus."

These "heavenly places" are not external but internal, and the path leading to them is internal as well. The vehicle that transports the soul on this journey often takes the form of external loss, trial, or disappointment. Such hardships, while seemingly grievous, later yield the peaceful fruits of righteousness to those who endure them, as described in Hebrews 12:5-11. These trials, regardless of their severity, should be viewed as God's chariots, dispatched to elevate your souls to the "high places" of spiritual accomplishment and enlightenment. The chariots are "paved with love," as stated in Song of Solomon 3:9-10.

The trials you face might appear harsh. They might stem from tense relationships, human malice, cruelty, or neglect. However, every chariot sent by God is inevitably paved with love, for God is love. And the love of God provides the sweetest, softest, and most tender solace any soul could ever find. It is this divine love that sends the chariot, as illustrated in Habakkuk 3:8, 12, 13.

The obstacles in the path of God's people are what invoke His rescue, riding in His "chariots of salvation." Everything becomes a "chariot of salvation" when God commands it. The "clouds" that darken our skies and seemingly block the rays of righteousness, are indeed His chariots, into which we may join Him and "ride prosperously" over all darkness, as referred to in Psalms 45:3-4, Psalms 18:10, and Deuteronomy 33:26.

An insightful writer recently suggested that we can't dispel the clouds with even the most strenuous effort, yet we can rise high above them to reach the clear skies overhead. Whoever rides with God navigates the heavens, soaring high above all earthly clouds, as Psalms 68:32-34 describes. This concept may appear fanciful, yet when we start to incorporate it into our daily lives, it becomes eminently practical.

Consider a personal acquaintance who was constantly irritated by her servant's sluggishness. The servant was otherwise exemplary, a valuable member of the household, but her pace was a ceaseless source of annoyance to her quick-moving mistress. The mistress frequently lost her temper with the servant, only to regret her anger moments later. Despite her determination to master her anger, she consistently fell short. Her life became a battleground of conflict and remorse.

One day, this lady decided to view the situation differently. Instead of seeing her servant as a source of aggravation, she started viewing her as a chariot of God, sent to test her patience and help her rise above her quick temper. This new perspective transformed their relationship. What was once a cause of daily anguish became a means of spiritual growth, allowing her to ascend into a more serene, patient version of herself.

The trials we encounter, no matter how seemingly small, offer us the chance to transcend our limitations, to climb into God's chariot and rise above. Remember Psalm 45:3-4: "Gird thy sword upon thy thigh, O most Mighty, with thy glory and thy majesty. And in thy majesty ride prosperously because of truth and meekness and righteousness; and thy right hand shall teach thee terrible things."

To conclude, God's chariots may appear in various forms, often as trials and tribulations in our life. They might seem overwhelming, even destructive at first. However, by viewing them not as obstacles but as vehicles of transformation and growth, we can harness their power to rise to new spiritual heights. In these heavenly places within us, we are closer to God, embodying His teachings of love and patience, and thus truly riding with Him in victory.

"The Chariots of Patience"

Have you ever wished for patience, prayed for it day in and day out, only to be met with a slow, meandering servant? I too once felt the frustration that arose from this situation. But one day, I had a sudden realization - this slow servant might just be the divine chariot that the Lord sent to carry my soul towards patience. I began to see this person in a new light, and used their slowness as a means to cultivate my patience. The outcome? A victory of patience so profound, no slowness could ever agitate me again.

Let me share another tale with you. I once attended a

convention where due to the crowd, I had to share a room with two others. I longed for sleep, but they desired conversation. The first night, I laid awake, restless and irritable. However, the following day, I heard of God's chariots and that night, I chose to accept these chattering sisters as my chariots to patience and peace. I lay peacefully, my inner tranquility not disturbed by their chatter. Finally, as the hour grew late and the need for sleep imminent, I whispered to them, "Sisters, I am lying here riding in a chariot." Their conversation ceased instantaneously. My journey in God's chariot had not only brought me inner victory, but external victory as well.

Woe unto them that go down to Egypt for help; and stay on horses, and trust in chariots, because they are many; and in horsemen, because they are very strong; but they look not unto the Holy One of Israel, neither seek the LORD! (Isaiah 31:1, KJV)

We often fall into the temptation of trusting in the "chariots of Egypt", the tangible, visible aids that seem so substantial. But God's chariots are invisible, and it's hard to believe they exist, for our eyes are not opened to see them. We put our faith in the multitude of our own chariots, relying on one thing after another to enhance our spiritual growth and achieve our victories.

God often must dismantle our chariots, those we've grown reliant on - a close friend, a beloved preacher, a prayer meeting, or a Bible study group - before we can ascend into His. We must surrender these visible crutches, for it's only through this surrender that we find

God's chariot, the divine instrument found in the very deprivations we mourned over.

"Because ye have spoken this word, behold, I will make my words in thy mouth fire, and this people wood, and it shall devour them." (Jeremiah 5:14, KJV)

God must burn our personal chariots with the fire of His love, those which prevent us from climbing into His. Therefore, let us express gratitude for every trial that assists in the destruction of our chariots, pushing us towards the chariot of God that is always ready and waiting beside us.

"He only is my rock and my salvation; he is my defence; I shall not be moved." (Psalm 62:6, KJV)

Conclusion:

Finally, we must reach the place where all other refuges fail us, to arrive at the realization that it's "He only." Too often, we pair God with something else - an experience, a relationship, a work. But we must learn that it's not "He, and something else", it's "He only." As long as we have our visible chariots, we will not mount the invisible ones. Our journey towards spiritual triumph truly begins when we willingly climb into God's chariot, allowing His love and wisdom to guide us.

"Sing unto God, sing praises to his name: extol him that rideth upon the heavens by his name JAH, and rejoice before him." (Psalm 68:4, KJV)

Often, we find solace and comfort in our tangible chariots - friends, mentors, routines - and tend to rely on them. They feel real and immediate, capable of solving our earthly troubles. But these earthly chariots can only take us so far, while the chariot of God promises to carry us to unimagined spiritual heights. When our worldly chariots fail us or are taken away, it's a divine invitation to ascend into God's chariot, to trust Him fully, and to seek refuge in His love and wisdom.

The real victory is not merely in achieving patience or peace, but in realizing that every trial, every challenge is a divine chariot waiting to carry us towards spiritual growth and victory. It's about realizing that the invisible chariot of God is always by our side, waiting for us to climb aboard. It's about understanding that the path to spiritual victory lies not in the multitude of our chariots, but in the solitary chariot of God.

I implore you, next time you face a challenge, do not despair. Instead, see it as God's chariot, sent to transport your soul over into patience, peace, and ultimately, spiritual victory. Abandon the visible, earthly chariots and dare to mount the invisible, divine chariot of God. Only then can we truly attain the spiritual heights that we seek.

So, let us joyfully embrace the trials and tribulations that come our way, for they are God's chariots, waiting to carry us into His love and light. Let us rid ourselves of our earthly chariots and ascend into God's. For it is in "He only" that we find our salvation, our peace, and our victory. It is in "He only" that we find the spiritual prosperity we seek. So, let's join our hands, mount His chariot, and journey together towards spiritual triumph.

A Journey Towards Divine Triumph

In order for us to travel with God "upon the heavens," we must first put to an end all journeys on the earth, as the Psalmist writes in Psalms 68:24, "They have seen thy goings, O God; even the goings of my God, my King, in the sanctuary." Seeing God's divine workings requires us to be in the sanctuary of His presence, and to join Him in His "goings" and journey with Him, we must let go of all worldly activities and ventures. This is also expressed in Proverbs 20:24, "Man's goings are of the LORD; how can a man then understand his own way?"

When we mount ourselves in God's chariot, our path becomes firm and "established," as obstacles fail to hinder our triumphant progress. All losses are in fact gains if they bring us closer to God. As Paul reminds us in Philippians 3:7-9, "But what things were gain to me, those I counted loss for Christ... and do count them but dung, that I may win Christ."

Paul further understood this truth, celebrating the losses that provided him with immeasurable blessings. Even the painful "thorn in the flesh," the messenger of Satan sent to torment him, became a chariot for his accepting soul, propelling him to heights of victory he could not have otherwise achieved. This is written in 2 Corinthians 12:7-10. Taking pleasure in our trials is like transforming them into the most magnificent of chariots.

Take Joseph, for example. He had a vision of his future victories and reign. But the chariots that bore him towards these triumphs initially seemed like the harshest failures and defeats. His journey to kingship was through slavery and imprisonment—a peculiar path indeed. Yet, no other path would have led Joseph to his victory. This is beautifully illustrated in Genesis 37:5-10, 37:19, 20, 27, 28; 39:19, 20; 39:1-6, 21-23; and finally, his triumph in Genesis 43:38-43.

So, how do we climb aboard these chariots? My answer is simple: Seek God in each of them and find solace in Him. It's like a small child who runs to their mother's arms when facing trouble. The real chariot that guides us through successfully is God's enduring support, as prophesied in Isaiah 46:4, "And even to your old age I am he; and even to hoar hairs will I carry you: I have made, and I will bear; even I will carry, and will deliver you."

Therefore, accept each problem in your life as God's chariot for you. No matter who caused the issue, whether humans or devils, by the time it reaches you, it's God's chariot, intended to transport you to a heavenly place of triumph. Seek the Lord in your trials, and echo the words, "Lord, open my eyes that I may see, not the visible enemy, but Thy unseen chariots of deliverance."

In conclusion, life's trials can be your chariots. They can carry you to the heights of divine patience, long-suffering, and ultimate victory. These trials could be a misunderstanding, mortification, unkindness, disappointment, loss, or defeat. All these are chariots waiting to lift you to the very summit of the victory you have long yearned for. Climb aboard them with thankful hearts, and lose sight of all secondary causes in the radiance of His love. God promises to "carry you in His arms" safely and triumphantly through it all.

There's no doubt in my mind that if we could truly see, we'd find our homes, workplaces, and even the streets we walk, teeming with "the chariots of God." As it's written in Psalms 68:17, "The chariots of God are twenty thousand, even thousands of angels: the Lord is among them, as in Sinai, in the holy place." Therefore, there's no reason for any of us to trudge through life without a chariot.

That one difficult person in your life, who's been making your existence tough, can be transformed from a daunting Juggernaut car into a splendid chariot, carrying you towards the peaks of divine patience and perseverance. That misunderstanding, that embarrassment, that harsh word, that disappointment, that loss, that defeat—all of these are God's chariots, ready to lift you to the heights of victory you've been yearning for.

So, hop on these chariots with a grateful heart. Focus not on secondary causes, but rather, bask in the shine of His divine love that will "carry you in His arms" safely and victoriously over all obstacles. Surrender to His will, trust in His love, and let Him transform your trials into your chariots.

In the end, you'll find yourself "riding upon the heavens"

with God in a way you never imagined possible. Embrace the journey, mount your chariots, and embark on the path towards divine triumph, guided by His love and carried in His arms. After all, in every trial, in every challenge, and in every moment, there are chariots of God waiting to take us on our heavenly journey towards triumph.

Chapter TWENTY ONE

"WITHOUT ME YE CAN DO NOTHING" CONCERNING THE LIFE OF DIVINE UNION IN ITS PRACTICAL ASPECTS.

One day, not too long ago, I found myself on a peaceful drive through the stunning Philadelphia Park with a Quaker preacher. As we admired the natural beauty around us, we began to discuss a concern that weighed heavily on our hearts. We wondered why a lot of the preaching in the church today seemed to yield little fruit.

Naturally, we considered the lack of the Holy Spirit's power as a possible cause. But this didn't seem to account for everything. We both knew many ministers who, although truly anointed with the Spirit, struggled to see the impact of their ministry.

I suggested an idea that had been stirring in my heart: What if the issue was the disconnect between the tone used during preaching and everyday conversation? It struck me that when ministers preach or discuss religious matters, they often adopt a different demeanor. This change can unintentionally push religion away from the sphere of everyday life, making it harder for it to resonate with people whose lives are filled with ordinary tasks and simple pleasures.

"I imagine," I said, turning to my companion, "if you were to use your natural, current tone while preaching, your words might carry a greater impact."

His response was swift, "Oh, but I could not do that, because the preacher's gallery is so much more solemn than this."

"But why is it more solemn?" I questioned. "Isn't it the presence of God that instills the gallery or the pulpit with a sense of solemnity? And don't we have God's presence here as well? Isn't our everyday life just as solemn as preaching, and shouldn't we strive to glorify Him in everything we do?"

As we drove further, the truth became clearer to me. I believe the heart of the problem is the unnatural separation we've created between our so-called religious life and our temporal life. It's as if we've come to see our faith as a removable garment, something to wear or discard depending on the situation.

"But seek ye first the kingdom of God, and his righteousness; and all these things shall be added unto you" (Matthew 6:33, KJV). This scripture urges us to weave our faith into the fabric of our lives, not to treat it as a detachable accessory.

We should remember that God is omnipresent – in the pulpit and the park, in the sacred and the mundane. His divine presence is not confined to religious settings; it permeates every moment of our existence.

In conclusion, it is our responsibility to align our religious practices with our daily lives. To make our faith more meaningful and impactful, we must integrate it into the ordinary and the everyday, so it becomes a natural extension of who we are, rather than a separate entity. After all, God's presence is not just in the church or during a sermon; He is with us always, in every step we take, and in every word we speak.

"Living in Constant Union with Christ"

I am, like you, a faithful servant of God. As such, I partake in the customary Sunday worship, where we earnestly seek God, offering our heartfelt praises and services to Him. Our religious life takes center stage, cloaked in a sober and solemn demeanor. Yet, this austere gravity sometimes reduces the potency of our religious fervor. Then, as Monday dawns, we shift our focus to personal pursuits, donning our everyday life with a sigh of relief. We then live this temporal life with such ease and naturalness, seemingly infusing it with more power.

These observations set my mind pondering and growing stronger with time. Once, while attending a meeting, the leader initiated with a reading from John 15, where the words of Jesus stood out in blazing glory, *"Without me ye can do nothing" (John 15:5, KJV)*. I felt as if I had never truly perceived the depth of these words despite numerous previous readings. I mused, "Jesus Himself declared that without Him, we lack genuine life— temporal or spiritual—and any living or doing apart from Him is considered 'nothing' by God, the seer of all realities."

This revelation prompted me to ponder whether any soul genuinely accepts this truth or, despite theoretical belief, makes it practical in their daily life. I was hit with the realization that the secret of divine union isn't just in interior revelations or experiences but also in its practical application. If I indeed do nothing—literally nothing— apart from Christ, then my union with Him is unceasing and undeniable. Conversely, if I live much of my daily life and do much of my work independently of Him, my union with Him cannot be said to be real, regardless of how profound and delightful my emotions about it may be.

It is this perspective of our spiritual journey that I wish to delve into in this discourse. I firmly believe that the stark segregation between the spiritual and the temporal, a phenomenon all too common, significantly hinders the realization of an interior union with God. It relegates religion so far from our common life that it appears almost unreachable to the majority. Further, it brings an unnatural rigidity and formality into Christians' experiences, potentially depriving them of the joyful, carefree ease that rightfully belongs to God's children.

I implore us, therefore, to comprehend the significance of this matter. It is of paramount importance to bridge the gap between the spiritual and the temporal and to embed our religious life into our everyday existence. By doing so, we will live in continual union with Christ, whether it be Sunday, the day of worship, or Monday, the day of earthly pursuits. Let the teachings of Jesus resonate in our actions, for only then can we truly say we live in Him.

In conclusion, the union with Christ is not a weekly affair nor a theoretical concept. It is a practical and daily lived experience, transcending the boundaries of days and personal interests. As His followers, we must seek to live out His teachings and embody His love every day, for, as He Himself stated, "Without me ye can do nothing." As we strive to make this a reality in our lives, may we experience the joy and peace of being in constant union with Christ.

" Living a Faith-Infused Life"

Looking upon my own life, I've found the concept that underscores everything else is our oneness with Christ. In essence, this idea of unity encapsulates everything. If we are genuinely united with Him, it stands to reason that we can do nothing without Him. It's impossible for two things to behave as one if they act separately. Therefore, if I accomplish anything without Christ, it suggests that I am not unified with Him in that action. It's akin to a branch cutting itself off from the vine, becoming shriveled and useless.

To illustrate, imagine a vine branch recognizing its connection with the vine, its reliance on it for growth, fruit-bearing, and climbing. Now, suppose the branch feels it can grow and climb a certain fence or around a tree trunk by itself. In attempting to live independently, it severs its connection with the vine. Naturally, the branch seeking this independent life would wilt and die. This metaphor perfectly reflects our situation as branches of Christ, the True Vine.

Attempting any action, big or small, independently will lead to spiritual decay and death, just like a natural vine branch. Recognizing this fact highlights how harmful any action is that separates us from our oneness with Christ.

Surely, we've all understood, to varying degrees, that without Christ, we cannot live our spiritual life. Yet when it comes to conducting everyday activities like managing a home, running a business, making calls, darning socks, sweeping a room, or entertaining guests, rarely do we consider these tasks as acts done for Christ. And yet, they can only be performed correctly when we remain in Him, drawing from His strength.

Take a moment to reflect on the Scripture in *John 15:5 (KJV)* where Jesus says, *"I am the vine, ye are the branches: He that abideth in me, and I in him, the same bringeth forth much fruit: for without me ye can do nothing."*

In the same vein, if Christ works in the Christian who leads the prayer meeting, it follows that Christ should work in and through the Christian conducting household tasks or business transactions. Every duty, therefore, holds the same religious significance. The individual determines the action, not vice versa.

Inviting Christ into every facet of life will infuse even mundane tasks with a sense of profound purpose and joy, equating them with spiritual practices. If we *"acknowledge God in all our ways" (Proverbs 3:6 KJV)* and perform all tasks - even eating and drinking - to His glory, we imbue our everyday activities with spiritual significance.

1 Corinthians 10:31 (KJV) reiterates, *"Whether therefore ye eat, or drink, or whatsoever ye do, do all to the glory of God."*

If we perceive our religion as our actual life - and not an additional component - it must necessarily permeate all aspects of our existence. No act, no matter how mundane, can escape His guidance. If God is always with us, His presence is as tangible during business hours or social events as it is during our religious practices. Every moment becomes sacred.

In conclusion, maintaining an inseparable oneness with Christ in every facet of our lives is paramount. This unity with Him transcends religious obligations and transforms our everyday tasks into spiritual practices. As branches of the True Vine, let us commit to living a life firmly rooted in Christ, consistently drawing from His strength in all that we do. Remember, it's not the action that makes the person, but the person who gives meaning to the action. Each moment spent in His presence is a divine gift.

Unveiling the Divine in Everyday Living

Walking this earthly path, I find myself immersed in a profound truth. This truth, firm and unyielding as the bedrock beneath our feet, is this: In Him we exist, in Him we find motion and life itself. This is an unassailable fact. It implies an equally irrefutable reality - without Him, we can do nothing.

God's words, as recorded in the Book of Psalms, echoes this truth with compelling clarity. *Psalms 127:1-2 (KJV)* states: *"Except the Lord build the house, they labour in vain that build it: except the Lord keep the city, the watchman waketh but in vain. It is vain for you to rise up early, to sit up late, to eat the bread of sorrows; for so He giveth His beloved sleep."*

In these verses, the Psalmist illustrates two instances - what we might call secular or worldly activities - that hold no merit without God's involvement. These verses teach us spiritual lessons, but their true weight stems from the fact that God's presence is a part of our temporal, everyday life.

The Bible is replete with this truth, yet it is astounding how often believers overlook it. Whether we are building cities, counting the hairs on our heads, or observing a sparrow's fall, God's presence permeates everything we do. Even in activities as mundane as eating and drinking, we are called to honor Him and bring Him glory.

And so, I encourage you to live your life in His light, knowing every action is touched by Him. You will find a comforting solace in this truth, for it transforms our everyday existence into a divine sacrament. The kitchen, the workshop, the nursery, and even the parlor become places of service to the Lord, as holy and significant as prayer meetings, mission boards, or acts of charity.

Once, a young Christian mother, burdened by her seemingly unspiritual daily life, shared her sorrows with me. "My life," she lamented, "seems void of spirituality from one week's end to the other."

Yet, what she didn't realize was that God's presence doesn't end with Sunday sermons. It extends to every crumb swept, every child consoled, every room tidied. By recognizing His presence in our daily lives, we can transform seemingly mundane moments into opportunities for worship, turning every corner of our life into a hallowed ground of divine connection.

In conclusion, let us remember that the presence of God is not just for the grand, spiritual moments, but for every single heartbeat of our lives. His divine hand shapes not only the universe but our daily activities too. Every task, every responsibility, every moment is a chance to witness His work and bring glory to Him. So, let's continue to live, move, and have our being in Him, knowing that each breath we take is a testament to His ever-present love and guidance.

A Journey Towards Inner Transformation

As I look around at my large family of vibrant children, I am completely consumed by their needs. Every day seems to blend into the next with a never-ending list of responsibilities. I am fully committed to caring for them and managing the household tasks that demand my constant attention. At the end of each day, as I lay my head down, my heart aches with a deep yearning. I realize that in the midst of all the bustle, I have failed to connect with my Lord. I've felt distanced from Him, not having had a single moment to serve His purpose.

But one day, a revelation dawned upon me. I realized the divine presence was intertwined with my everyday duties. I acknowledged that I was utterly dependent on Him, even in the mundane tasks of my daily life. I welcomed this newfound understanding with joy, and from that moment, life took on a new, glorious hue. The constant, comforting presence of the Lord filled my days, transforming every task into a delightful act of service to Him.

I once met a young lady, from a high-class family, who expressed a similar sense of separation from God. She was deeply troubled by the apparent chasm between her worldly obligations and her spiritual connection. She believed that her everyday duties were pulling her away from God, even though she wasn't engaged in any sinful activities.

"For instance," she said, "I have a duty to accompany my mother on social visits. But strangely, nothing seems to distance me more from God than these visits."

I asked her to reconsider her perspective. "What if you viewed these visits as a service to the Lord, performed for His glory?" I challenged.

She was startled at the idea. "Make social visits for God? I've never heard of such a thing," she responded.

I explained, "As a Christian, we are commanded to do everything for the glory of God. If paying visits is right, it should be done for Him. Conversely, if it's not right, you should not be doing it. You must not engage in any activity that you cannot perform for Him."

Her eyes lit up with understanding. "I see now," she exclaimed, "Everything appears different! It's not sin that separates me from Him, but every act performed for His glory will only bring me closer and make His presence more real."

These experiences offer insight into a simple, yet profound truth. A multitude of burdened and weary lives could undergo a beautiful transformation if this truth was realized and lived by. An ancient spiritual writer once said that to become a saint, we don't need to change our deeds. We only need to infuse an inward intention towards God in all our actions. We must strive to perform all tasks for His glory, relying on His strength, rather than our own.

This belief aligns with our Lord's teachings. As it is written in the Bible, *"Without me ye can do nothing."* *(John 15:5).*

The Psalmist further expands on this comforting truth. As Psalm 127:2 states, "It is vain for you to rise up early, to sit up late, to eat the bread of sorrows." These words pose a simple question: Why worry and strain ourselves over tasks that will yield nothing without God's involvement? If God is part of our deeds, why fret and carry unnecessary burdens? His presence signifies His caring guidance, taking responsibility for our actions.

In conclusion, as we navigate our earthly duties, it's essential to recognize the divine presence in our everyday tasks. This conscious acknowledgment has the power to transform mundane duties into acts of divine service, bridging the perceived gap between our worldly responsibilities and our spiritual connection. With this understanding, we no longer need to feel separated from our Lord in the midst of our busy lives. Instead, we can relish His constant, comforting presence, which transforms our daily tasks into acts of worship.

In this journey of life, let us remember that God is our companion in every task, big or small. All we need is a shift in our perception. When we start seeing our daily tasks as services to Him, our lives become a continual act of devotion, and His presence more palpable.

This belief also gives us immense comfort and peace. It eases our burdens, reminding us that our efforts will bear no fruit without God's blessing. As **Psalm 127:2** states in the, **"for so he giveth his beloved sleep."** This signifies that with God's blessing, we can find peace, rest, and contentment amidst our efforts. He doesn't want us to strain ourselves or to live in constant worry. He wants us to trust in His care, lean on His strength, and to find peace in His presence.

To live by this truth is a calling to every Christian. We are asked to bring God into the center of our lives - not just in our prayers, but also in our daily tasks. Whether we are caring for our children, paying a social visit, or performing a mundane chore, we are called to do it for God's glory and with a complete reliance on His strength.

In the words of the Apostle Paul, **"And whatsoever ye do, do it heartily, as to the Lord, and not unto men."** **(Colossians 3:23, KJV)** We must infuse every task, no matter how small or large, with a profound sense of purpose and a deep love for God.

In doing so, we transform our lives into a continuous act of worship, drawing ourselves closer to God, experiencing His divine presence in every moment of our lives. We will find that, indeed, there is no room for feeling separated from our Lord, but rather an opportunity for continual communion with Him in our daily duties.

In conclusion, the key to an unbroken communion with God lies in acknowledging His presence in our daily lives. By infusing our tasks with the intention of serving Him, we transform our worldly obligations into divine service. Through this perspective, we can experience a profound sense of peace, joy, and purpose, carrying out our duties with a joyful heart, secure in His presence, and under His divine guidance.

And so, let us each day pray, as Christ taught us, *"Thy kingdom come, Thy will be done in earth, as it is in heaven." (Matthew 6:10, KJV).* Let us seek His presence in every task, live for His glory, and find our peace in His ever-abiding presence. With this attitude, no duty seems mundane or burdensome, but rather a beautiful opportunity to draw closer to our Lord and experience His divine presence.

"Resting in the Embrace of Divine Love "

Oh, how I wish every child of God could understand this truth! As mothers, we often bear the weight of understanding. Our daily experiences with our children should shed light on this truth if only we pay attention.

Many mothers rise early and sleep late, carrying burdens and responsibilities, only to grant their precious children some peaceful rest. It grieves their hearts when their children refuse to find rest despite their efforts. I am confident that some mothers reading this can deeply connect with my sentiments.

Let me paint a picture for you. Imagine a little boy, flushed and tanned from his day's play or work. His knees are dirty, and his coat is torn. Now, picture a mother, devoted and loving, taking painstaking efforts to mend everything for her child, just so he could enjoy a peaceful sleep, untouched by worry or care. How pointless it would be if the child stayed up late or woke up early to worry about these matters when his mother is already handling it all!

If this is true for our earthly mothers, how much more it is for our Heavenly Father, the One who created all mothers. He came to earth in human form to carry our burdens and sorrows, to work for us, just so that we could "enter into His rest". As written in the Bible, in *Hebrews 4:10, "For he that is entered into his rest, he also hath ceased from his own works, as God did from His."*

Dear ones, have we entered into this divine rest? It's when we recognize that we can do nothing without Christ, yet through Him, we can do all things. We lay aside self-effort, surrendering ourselves completely to God. This surrender allows God to work in us, guiding us according to His divine plan. This is the ultimate rest waiting for God's people.

Scientists are always striving to identify one fundamental force behind everything in nature. They argue that all forms of energy - light, heat, sound - originate from one central force, motion. But the Bible tells us of a more profound origin, the force behind all motion, the "God-force". God is at the core of everything, He is the source and explanation of everything. *John 1:3 (KJV) says, "All things were made by Him; and without Him was not anything made that was made."* Hence, when Jesus said, *"Without me, ye can do nothing" (John 15:5 KJV),* He wasn't revealing a hidden mystery, but stating a simple, evident fact.

He Himself said, *"I can of mine own self do nothing" (John 5:30 KJV),* emphasizing that He and His Father are one, rendering independent action impossible. Thus, when He says we can do nothing without Him, it indicates our profound union with Him, making independent action as impossible for us towards Him, as it was for Him towards His Father.

Dear Christian, doesn't this revelation guide you to an area of exceptional glory?

Conclusion:
In the grand tapestry of life, let us not forget our place and purpose. Like the child trusting his mother's love and care, we too, as God's children, must trust in His providence. Surrender yourself to His divine will and rest in His embrace. As you walk this path, understand the divine union and the glorious rest that awaits in His presence. Remember, we are not meant to navigate life independently; our strength lies in union with Christ. May we rest in His divine love, ceasing our own works as God did from His, and finding peace and rest in His eternal care.

"Walking Daily in Divine Union with Christ"

Ever truly, I tell you, without Him, we can do nothing. We ought to embrace this truth, for it stands as undeniable. Yet, let's go beyond mere acknowledgement. From this moment forward, let us wholeheartedly renounce a life lived apart from Christ. Let us make every moment, every act, an offering to Him, carried out in His service and for His glory, leaning on Him alone for wisdom, strength, serenity, patience, and all that we need to live rightly.

The Book of Proverbs tells us, *"In all thy ways acknowledge him, and he shall direct thy paths" (Proverbs 3:6, KJV)*. It's not so much a transformation of deeds that is needed as it is a shift in motive and dependence. Perhaps, on the surface, your home will be cared for, your children tended, your work conducted just as before. Yet, within, God will be acknowledged, depended upon, and served, leading to a glorious shift from a life of strenuous striving to a life basking in His divine presence.

This divine acknowledgment, this faithful dependence, will invite extraordinary wisdom into your affairs, leading to their swift and efficient accomplishment. Expect a fertile growth of resources, an enhanced understanding of things, and an expansion that will astound your previously constrained soul. I speak this in all sincerity - your home will be tidier, your children better nurtured, your tasks completed swifter, your guests more content, your deals more satisfying, and your life will flow with an ease and harmony never experienced before. For God will be in every moment of it, and where He is, all must indeed go well.

John 15:4 (KJV) tells us, ***"Abide in me, and I in you." Thus, the soul will form a holy habit of "abiding in Christ,"*** and His presence will become the most real and profound aspect of our lives. A constant, silent, and secret conversation with Him will yield continuous joy.

Beloved reader, if you yearn to know the quickest path to the greatest degree of unity and communion with God achievable in this life, look no further than the ordinary path of daily duties done in God and for His glory. The most sublime heights are attainable not as a reward, but as a natural outcome of dwelling in Him. As Jesus said, ***"If a man abide not in me, he is cast forth as a branch, and is withered; and men gather them, and cast them into the fire, and they are burned" (John 15:6, KJV).***

Start today. Begin with each moment, each act of your living. Offer them to God, repeating constantly, "Lord, I am doing this in Thee and for Thy Glory. Thou art my strength, my wisdom, my all-sufficient supply for every need. I depend solely upon Thee." Refuse to live for even a single moment or perform a single act without Him.

Persist in this until it becomes the habitual pattern of your soul. Soon, you will find the longings of your soul satisfied in the abiding presence of Christ, your dwelling Life. This, dear reader, is the essence of walking daily in divine union with Christ. May your path be illuminated with His eternal light as you continue your journey towards everlasting communion with Him.

Chapter TWENTY TWO

"GOD WITH US"; THE ONE HUNDRED AND THIRTY-NINTH PSALM

In the bounty of your great hospitality, we find ourselves enveloped as if in a boundless sea. We cannot lose our way, for wherever we are, we are at home. Nor can we drift away, for we are always anchored in You.

Often, we may not fully comprehend the profound meaning of the words found in Matthew 1:23: "Behold, a virgin shall be with child, and shall bring forth a son, and they shall call his name Emmanuel, which being interpreted is, God with us." Within this verse lies the grandest truth humanity could ever comprehend: God, the Almighty Creator of Heaven and Earth, does not exist as a distant entity in an unreachable heavenly glory. Rather, He lives among us in this world, enveloped in our everyday lives, as close to us as our own hearts.

This truth may appear so profound that we struggle to grasp it. However, this enduring presence of God is the central message that resonates from the Bible's pages. In the beginning, in the book of Genesis, we learn about the "presence of the Lord God amongst the trees of the garden." From there, we discover that God frequently engages in familiar and daily interactions with His people.

In Exodus, we find Him requesting the construction of a sanctuary, so He might "dwell among them." He journeyed with them in the wilderness, and chose to reside with them in the Promised Land. He encouraged His people to view Him as a constant friend and helper, to consult Him in all matters, and to entrust their lives to His guidance.

Ultimately, in the form of Jesus Christ, He walked the Earth as a man among men. He became bone of our bone and flesh of our flesh, embracing our human nature. He illustrated in the most tangible way that He intends to be with us always, until the end of time. Anyone who truly believes this will discover a resolution for all life's trials within this revelation.

I remember from my childhood, whenever trouble or perplexity arose, the arrival of my father or mother brought immediate relief. As soon as I heard one of them say, "Daughter, I am here," my burdens eased and anxieties quieted. Their mere presence brought comfort. They did not need to pledge assistance, nor share their plans for my relief. Their presence alone assured me that everything would be well, and I waited eagerly to see their solutions unfold.

Perhaps my parents were exceptional to inspire such confidence in their child. I believe they were. Yet, our God is undoubtedly extraordinary, and His constant presence is genuinely all we need. It would suffice even if we lacked any specific promise or understanding of His plans.

Repeatedly in the Bible, He quiets all questions and fears by simply declaring, "I will be with thee." Who among us can deny that these words signify His assurance that all His wisdom, love, and omnipotent power will be engaged in our favor?

In conclusion, the name Emmanuel, "God with us," not only describes God's personal presence in our lives, but also stands as a testament to His enduring love and guidance. His constant presence is our refuge, our guide, and our assurance that we are never alone. His promise to be with us is a beacon of hope, instilling us with confidence and peace as we navigate the journey of life.

"The Constant Comfort: God's Unceasing Presence"

As a child, the reassuring words, "Look, there's Mom!" provided immediate comfort and solace. And as I grew older, a similar phrase, whispered with reverence, "Behold, God is here!" offered a more profound deliverance. God's presence assured me, there was no reason to fear. The scriptures assure us of His constant presence, for He has promised, *"I will never leave thee, nor forsake thee" (Hebrews 13:5, KJV).* This gives me the boldness to declare, *"The Lord is my helper, and I will not fear what man shall do unto me" (Hebrews 13:6, KJV).*

I still recall the overwhelming feeling of safety my

earthly father's presence brought. Fear was a stranger when he was around. In a much grander sense, with my Heavenly Father close, fear finds no place. It's for this reason I want to underscore the beautiful reality of "Emmanuel, God with us". Regrettably, many of God's children seem to doubt this truth. While they verbally acknowledge His presence, a lingering "but" often follows their affirmations, casting a shadow of doubt.

However, there are no "buts" for the soul that fully embraces the literal presence of God. Such a soul overcomes fear and doubt, joyfully proclaiming God's presence as a sufficiency. His presence is their security and provision, at all times, for all things.

Let's delve into *Psalm 139 (KJV),* a treasure trove that beautifully unravels this truth. Verses 7 to 12 resoundingly declare:

"Whither shall I go from thy spirit? or whither shall I flee from thy presence? If I ascend up into heaven, thou art there: if I make my bed in hell, behold, thou art there. If I take the wings of the morning, and dwell in the uttermost parts of the sea; even there shall thy hand lead me, and thy right hand shall hold me. If I say, surely the darkness shall cover me; even the night shall be light about me. Yea, the darkness hideth not from thee; but the night shineth as the day: the darkness and the light are both alike to thee. For thou hast possessed my reins: thou hast covered me in my mother's womb."

This passage assures us that there is no corner of the universe where His presence does not reach. While people strive to step into His presence, it's clear they can never step out of it. Neither heaven, nor the depths of the sea, nor the darkest night can hide from Him. He exists within us, guiding us wherever we may venture.

Thus, when Jesus assured us, *"Lo, I am with you alway, even unto the end of the world" (Matthew 28:20, KJV)*, it wasn't mere sentiment but an indisputable truth. We may find ourselves in the thickest darkness, unable to perceive Him, yet it doesn't mean He can't see us. The darkness may conceal Him from our sight, but we are never hidden from Him. Even when we find ourselves spiritually distant or lost, His presence never leaves us.

In conclusion, no matter where we may roam or the darkness we may encounter, we remain under His loving watch. There is never a moment or place where His care doesn't reach us. This is the divine promise and comfort of our Heavenly Father's ceaseless presence.

Understanding His Everlasting Presence

At certain moments in our lives, the fog of confusion can envelop us, making us oblivious to those who care for us deeply. A child in the throes of a fever may call out for its mother, stirring her heart with its pleas, even as she tenderly holds the child's hand, caring for it with a mother's deep love. The child may not recognize her due to the disorientation of illness, but the mother never loses sight of her child.

Similarly, we can relate this situation to our relationship

with God. At times, doubts, fears, sorrows, despair, or even sins cast shadows, preventing us from sensing God's presence, but they never make us invisible to Him. He assures us in the Holy Scriptures, in the Book of *Psalms 139:12 (KJV): "Yea, the darkness hideth not from thee; but the night shineth as the day: the darkness and the light are both alike to thee."* Believing in this, we can navigate the darkest times, certain that even when we can't see or feel Him, God cares for us and will never abandon us.

However, our perception of God's presence can bring either comfort or dread, depending on our understanding of His nature. If we imagine Him as a stern ruler, focused only on His own glory, we may fear His unending presence. But if we view Him as a loving Father, concerned primarily with our welfare and joy, we would be grateful for His constant company. The presence of genuine love can only be a blessing for the one loved.

Psalm 139:1-5 (KJV) wonderfully illustrates God's loving presence: *"O Lord, thou hast searched me, and known me. Thou knowest my downsitting and mine uprising; thou understandest my thought afar off. Thou compassest my path and my lying down, and art acquainted with all my ways. For there is not a word in my tongue, but lo, O Lord, thou knowest it altogether. Thou hast beset me behind and before, and laid thine hand upon me."*

Our Father in Heaven knows us, understands us, and is familiar with all our paths. In this world, we are often misunderstood, our actions misjudged, and our motives misinterpreted. Our inherent traits and genetic predispositions might be overlooked. Often, no allowances are made for our health struggles or the battles we face. But God comprehends all. He understands us perfectly, taking into account every element that shapes our character and guides our actions.

Only an all-encompassing love can judge justly, and our God is just. It brings to mind the words of the hymn writer, Frederick William Faber:

"There is no place where earth's sorrows
Are more felt than up in Heaven;
There is no place where earth's failings
Have such kindly judgment given."

Some of you might fear His justice, thinking it will be against you. However, you must understand that it stands in your favor, just as a mother's justice does. As *Psalm 103:14 (KJV)* states: *"For He knoweth our frame; He remembereth that we are dust."* God's understanding of us is a precious comfort. Sometimes, we might feel lost, as if our inner world is a jumbled mess. But then we remember that God, who has searched and knows us, comprehends even the thoughts that bewilder us, and we can entrust the intricate puzzle of our lives to Him to unravel.

In conclusion, the presence of God is not a mere abstract concept, but a tangible reality. His presence is an embodiment of His immense love and understanding for us. When we are clouded by our trials and tribulations, we should remember that the same cloud that obscures our vision of Him does not obstruct His sight of us. God's knowledge of our condition is complete and His understanding is perfect.

The love of our Heavenly Father is not a conditional love that wanes in the face of our missteps or diminishes in the shadows of our despair. Rather, it is an all-encompassing, steadfast love that embraces us in our entirety – our strengths, our weaknesses, our triumphs, and our failures. Just as a mother's loving care for her child is not deterred by the darkness of sickness, so is God's love for us unyielding in the face of our struggles and shortcomings.

In our life's journey, there may be moments when we feel misunderstood, judged, and unfairly treated. However, it is during these trying times that we must remember the comforting truth of God's unwavering love and understanding. Our God knows us intimately, He understands our deepest thoughts, and He is acquainted with all our ways. The Psalmist declared in *Psalm 139:16 (KJV), "Thine eyes did see my substance, yet being unperfect; and in thy book all my members were written, which in continuance were fashioned, when as yet there was none of them."*

Even when we feel we are in an inextricable tangle, we can trust that God will bring order to our chaos. Because He knows and loves us entirely, we can safely entrust our lives to Him, assured that He will guide us through our most challenging circumstances.

In this realization, we find a profound sense of comfort

and peace. The awareness of God's constant, loving presence can be a source of immeasurable joy and reassurance. His justice, stemming from an all-comprehending love, is always on our side, making allowances for our human frailties. As stated in *Psalm 145:8 (KJV), "The Lord is gracious, and full of compassion; slow to anger, and of great mercy."*

As we navigate the path of life, let us remember that we are never alone, never misunderstood, and never without divine guidance and love. Our Heavenly Father, in His infinite wisdom and unending love, is always with us, leading us gently towards His light. He holds our hands, just like a loving mother, even when we are not aware of His touch, guiding us, supporting us, and embracing us with His endless love.

In the end, the knowledge of God's constant presence and unyielding love for us is a wellspring of peace and comfort. When we feel overwhelmed by life's challenges, we can find solace in the truth that He is always with us, ever understanding, infinitely caring, and ceaselessly loving. It is in His presence that we find our greatest strength, our deepest peace, and our truest joy.

Loving Watchfulness of our Divine Shepherd

In my heart, I find myself engulfed in a sense of peace, akin to sinking onto the softest of pillows, a sanctuary of absolute serenity. How comforting it is to know that God understands our every need, aware of when we sit down and when we rise, attuned to our journeys and our resting periods. This divine love mirrors the selfless devotion of a mother for her precious, sometimes thoughtless, and unaware children.

Just as a mother prioritizes her child's comfort, ensuring they are safe from the cold draft, their paths smooth and secure, God does the same for us. A mother will accept personal discomfort to provide the finest for her children - comfortable chairs, warm blankets, and safe paths, even if she must endure the rough and dangerous paths herself.

Our God, in His infinite love and sacrifice, is surely greater than any motherly love on this Earth. As stated in the (KJV) of the Bible, **Psalm 139:2-3, "Thou knowest my downsitting and mine uprising, thou understandest my thought afar off. Thou compassest my path and my lying down, and art acquainted with all my ways."** Hence, we can rest assured that even in the minor details of our lives, His wisdom, power, and love guide us towards the absolute best.

I wish to stress that God's caring extends to our literal seats and beds, providing us exactly what is most beneficial for our overall development. Here, God's love surpasses a mother's because His love is wise, understanding the future outcomes and prioritizing our ultimate good. Unlike a mother's gentle love focusing on the child's present comfort, God's robust, insightful love tolerates present discomfort for the future glory it would yield.

Whether at home or traveling, let us trust God with the selection of our seats, our beds, and every mundane detail of our everyday existence. As written in **Psalm 139:5 (KJV), "Thou hast beset me behind and before, and laid thine hand upon me."** God lovingly 'besets' us, remaining unwaveringly by our side despite our reluctance or indifference. He surrounds us with His presence, much like a mother tidying up after her children, removing the detritus they leave behind.

In conclusion, the everlasting love and self-sacrifice of our Divine Shepherd, aware of our every action and need, are sources of immense comfort. While His love may sometimes allow for present discomfort, it is always with the view of a glorious future. In every detail of our lives, God's wisdom, power, and love provide for us, surpassing even the selfless love of a mother. His unyielding presence, that 'besets' us from all sides, is a testament to His enduring love for us. Let us welcome His loving watchfulness, safe in the knowledge that He seeks our highest good.

"God, Our Loving Shepherd "

As a mother, I've been nurturing my children since their infancy. My heart leaps with joy when they laugh, and it aches when they cry. It's my lifelong mission to tidy up the mess they leave behind, straightening the crooked lines and untangling the knotted threads. Sometimes, their carelessness leads to these knots and tangles, but even then, my love for them encourages me to gently unravel each one. This love is what makes every challenge worthwhile. After all, which mother could turn her back on a tearful child with a muddled toy, or a lively boy struggling with tangled kite strings?

This is a reflection of how God cares for us, starting from our birth and throughout our lives. He's always present, even when we aren't aware. He yearns to correct our errors, free us from our entanglements, and constantly atone for our mistakes. Indeed, if any regrets or anxieties plague our past, let's trust in God's promise to make things right. Even our blunders and missteps can serve a greater good if we entrust them to Him. God's encompassing love is truly marvelous.

Consider these comforting words from *Psalms 139:14-16, (KJV): "I will praise thee; for I am fearfully and wonderfully made: marvellous are thy works; and that my soul knoweth right well. My substance was not hid from thee, when I was made in secret, and curiously wrought in the lowest parts of the earth. Thine eyes did see my substance, yet being unperfect; and in thy book all my members were written, which in continuance were fashioned, when as yet there was none of them."*

At times, we might question our unique make-up. Perhaps we think we're too impulsive or not enthusiastic enough. Maybe we wish we were more like someone we admire. We might even believe that our personal traits prevent us from serving God in the best possible way. Such doubts can lead us to feel that we can't please God with who we are.

But if we truly understand that God Himself created us, we'll realize that these doubts are baseless. Sometimes, we might feel like our characters have been formed randomly, without God's hand. We might accept the concept of creation in general, but struggle to apply it personally.

Yet, the Psalm teaches us that God has supervised every detail of our creation. As if writing in a book, He determined our individual traits even before we were born. Therefore, we are exactly as God intended us to be. He crafted us meticulously for a specific purpose.

In conclusion, it's crucial to remember that, like a loving mother, God is always ready to help us straighten the crooked paths of our lives. We are His perfect creations, specifically designed to fulfill His divine plan. Even if we stumble and create knots along the way, God stands ready to help us unravel them. His infinite love is a testament to His desire to transform even our mistakes into a part of our journey toward His greater good.

A Divine Manifestation of God's Creative Power

Allow me to clarify, beloved children of the Lord, I am referring to our innate traits, and not the distortion of these traits brought about by sin in our lives. This perspective illuminates the splendor of our Creator. Just as a genius craves for various means and forms to express its creativity, so does our heavenly Father. An artist in true spirit never replicates his creations, every painting or sculpture he crafts is a unique display of his artistic prowess.

Think of it this way, when we visit an art exhibition, we

would consider it a diminishment of the art if two pieces were identical. It is the same with us, as we are "God's workmanship". Ephesians 2:10 says, "For we are his workmanship, created in Christ Jesus unto good works, which God hath before ordained that we should walk in them." His creative power manifests differently in each one of us. Our unique 'make-up', which often perplexes us, is nothing but His power manifested uniquely in us. Without it, the grand exhibition, where each one of us is a praise to His Glory, would be incomplete.

God seeks that since He shaped us, He should also manage us, as He is the only one who fully understands us. The creator of a complex machine is best suited to manage and repair it, as interference by others may cause damage. Reflect upon our intricate inner machinery and the constant failure of our self-management, and rejoice in surrendering it all to the one who crafted us, leaving it in His capable hands.

Trust in the Lord, for He will then craft the best out of us. Yes, even we, with our unique temperaments and seemingly unfortunate characteristics, will be molded into vessels of honor, sanctified and fit for the Master's use, ready for every good deed. In the words of an old Quaker writer I once read, "Be content to be just what thy God has made thee." This wisdom has helped me grasp the point I'm trying to make: being content with our own 'make-up' is as vital to our surrender to God as being content with any other circumstance of our daily life.

Should we exist any differently than we are by nature, one expression of God's creative power would be absent, and one aspect of His work would be incomplete. Moreover, to lament about ourselves is essentially to lament about our Creator, which undeniably grieves Him. Therefore, let us be content, and ensure that we allow the Divine Potter to mold us into the best we can be, and use us according to His holy will.

Psalms 139:17-18 articulates another aspect of God's constant presence with us. "How precious also are thy thoughts unto me, O God! how great is the sum of them! If I should count them, they are more in number than the sand: when I awake, I am still with thee." Many are tempted to believe that God is indifferent to them. They perceive their interests and matters as being too insignificant or unworthy of His notice. However, such thoughts grossly misjudge Him.

Consider a mother's love; she cares as much for her smallest infant as for her older children, and is as attentive to its little needs and joys as she is to theirs. A mother's thoughts often revolve around the one who needs them most. Our Father, who created the mother's heart, would certainly not be less attentive to the needs and pleasures of the least and most helpless of His creations. "Are not two sparrows sold for a farthing? and one of them shall not fall on the ground without your Father." (Matthew 10:29). If even a sparrow cannot fall without Him, surely we, who are worth more than many sparrows, need not fear being overlooked for even a moment.

Indeed, the responsibility of creation necessitates continual care from the Creator. It is the glory of His omnipotence that He can attend to both the smallest details and the grandest operations simultaneously. He hears the cry of the young lions and cares for every sparrow, so we, His precious creations, can trust that He will not neglect us.

In conclusion, each one of us is a unique manifestation of God's creative power, made with purpose and intricacy. As we navigate the ups and downs of life, we should always remember that we are God's masterpieces, His precious works of art, each molded differently for a specific purpose. This realization invites us to submit ourselves entirely to our Divine Potter, trusting in His wisdom and care as He shapes us into vessels fit for His use. We must learn to be content with who we are and to embrace the peculiarities of our 'make-up'. It's a fundamental part of our journey with God. Just as a mother never neglects her child, God will never neglect us. His thoughts towards us are precious and beyond count. Therefore, let us rejoice in the knowledge that we are never alone, but forever in His sight and under His loving care.

" Embracing of Divine Presence: A Journey of Faith"

"Behold, I am with you always, even unto the end of the world." (Matthew 28:20 KJV). With these words, I am reminded of the majesty of the Almighty's infinite greatness. His love, so boundless, accommodates all things within its fold. A greatness less than infinite, I am certain, would be overwhelming.

I've often pondered why we, as humans, label someone as weak if they manage grand affairs yet overlook smaller details. Then, paradoxically, we criticize our Heavenly Father as if He would do the same. If any of my readers have formerly succumbed to such erroneous thinking, let it cease. Instead, firmly hold onto the belief that the Lord constantly thinks of you. *"Many, O LORD my God, are thy wonderful works which thou hast done, and thy thoughts which are to us-ward: they cannot be reckoned up in order unto thee: if I would declare and speak of them, they are more than can be numbered." (Psalms 40:5 KJV)*

Delving further into the Psalm, we encounter a beautiful harmony between our souls and God, born out of an earnest, simple faith. Once we grasp the transformative reality of God's ever-present care and attention, our souls merge with Him so profoundly that we start to love what He cherishes and despise what He detests. We beg Him to scrutinize us, testing our hearts, to ensure no trace of discord remains. In the divine light of His presence, shadows of doubt must scatter, and our hearts begin to yearn for every corner to be touched by His illumination. For, *"in His presence is fullness of joy; at His right hand there are pleasures forevermore." (Psalm 16:11 KJV)*

Consider the story of an elderly woman in a remote part of England who earned her livelihood selling ale and beer to passing travelers. Although she sought Christian salvation and eternal bliss, she felt uneasy about her trade. She yearned to follow the path of Christ but was reluctant to abandon her source of income, causing her deep turmoil.

During one religious gathering, a visiting preacher spoke of the divine joy that comes from acknowledging God's constant companionship. The woman's soul was stirred by the promise of such a gift. She forgot her concerns about the beer business and eagerly started to trust in the presence of the Lord. Her heart echoed the preacher's words, expressing surprise and joy, "Lord Jesus, I didn't realize you were always with me! How wonderful to know you are with me always, caring for me! I'll never feel lonely again!"

As she returned home that night, her heart sang with joy, "Lord Jesus, you're going home with me. I won't let you go, Lord, now that I know you are with me!" Her faith in His presence sparked such happiness that upon reaching her home, and seeing the large pot of ale prepared for sale, she instantly felt, "The Lord won't approve of this ale in His dwelling place." Without hesitation, she committed to remove the ale. She prayed for strength to overturn the heavy pot, and God answered her plea.

Once the task was done, she thanked God for His strength, promising Him, "Lord, if there's anything else in this cottage you don't like, reveal it to me, and it shall be removed."

In conclusion, understanding and accepting the constancy of God's presence can be transformative. It opens our hearts to align our desires with His and strengthens our commitment to eliminating any element discordant with

His divine will. As we walk in faith, we must remember that in His infinite love, "there are pleasures forevermore.

Knowing the profound truth of God's enduring presence and His unending care, we are inspired to walk a path aligned with His divine will. Just as the elderly woman surrendered her trade in ale to better welcome the Lord into her home, we too must have the courage to abandon those aspects of our lives that run counter to God's teachings. His love and grace grant us the strength to face such challenges. As the Apostle Paul stated, *"I can do all things through Christ which strengtheneth me."* *(Philippians 4:13 KJV)*

The woman's story demonstrates that God's presence doesn't merely provide comfort in loneliness, it also helps us to better discern right from wrong. Her faith led her to realize that the beer trade was incompatible with a Christian life, prompting her to choose God over worldly gain. She allowed the Lord's love to fill her life and her home, replacing what was lost. Indeed, our lives can only be enriched by His presence, for He promises, *"But seek ye first the kingdom of God, and his righteousness; and all these things shall be added unto you." (Matthew 6:33 KJV)*

In our daily routines, in the hustle and bustle, it can be easy to overlook God's constant presence. But let us take heart from the old woman's example and strive to keep our faith simple and sincere. Let us invite God's presence into every corner of our lives, not just our houses of worship.

Moreover, we should ask God to reveal the things in our lives that displease Him, just like the old woman did. It may require strength to remove these things, strength that we may feel we lack. But rest assured that God can provide that strength, just as He did for the woman tipping the ale pot. We only need to ask and believe in His power. *"Ask, and it shall be given you; seek, and ye shall find; knock, and it shall be opened unto you" (Matthew 7:7 KJV).*

In conclusion, recognizing and embracing God's eternal presence in our lives is a transformative journey of faith. It aligns our desires with God's divine will and empowers us to remove anything that stands in the way of this divine harmony. As we tread this path of faith, let us hold onto the comforting words of our Savior, *"I am with you always, even unto the end of the world." (Matthew 28:20 KJV).* Indeed, the pleasure and joy that spring from His presence are boundless and forevermore.

"Emmanuel, God with Us"

"Isn't this just like the end of the Psalm I was reading? *'Do not I hate them, O Lord, that hate thee? and am not I grieved with those that rise up against thee? I hate them with a perfect hatred; I count them mine enemies. Search me, O God, and know my heart; try me, and know my thoughts; and see if there be any wicked way in me, and lead me in the way everlasting' (Psalm*

139:21-24, KJV). Like a candle flickering against the night, God's presence drives away sin from our lives. When we stand firm in our faith, we feel a fantastic freedom and deliverance.

You might be wondering, 'How can I make God's presence real to myself?' Let's explore some straightforward steps. First, you must persuade yourself through God's words in the Bible that His presence is a real, unchanging truth. Our feelings don't create this truth; instead, the truth stirs up our feelings. So, what every one of us needs, more than anything, is a firm belief, rooted in God's word, that His continual presence is a fact.

Once this is settled, it's time to make it real by 'practising His presence,' as a wise person once said. This means recognizing His presence at every moment, in every place, and in every action. Obey the Bible's command to *'acknowledge Him in all your ways' (Proverbs 3:6, KJV)*. Remind yourself throughout each day, 'The Lord is here.' Carry out your daily tasks—eating, drinking, and everything else—as if He were there with you, because He is. In fact, *'Whether therefore ye eat, or drink, or whatsoever ye do, do all to the glory of God' (1 Corinthians 10:31, KJV)*.

Practicing His presence regularly will build a strong faith habit. Eventually, it will feel natural to believe in His presence. You don't need to make any giant leaps, just maintain steady faith. It's not about complex arguments or profound meditations, but about simple faith that God is always present and then having constant chats with

Him about everything in your life. He isn't asking us to do anything grand, just to remember Him and show our love for Him as we go about our daily life.

When we remember to live with a sense of God's presence, our hearts can relax and find peace. Even the tiniest act of remembering Him is precious and helps us to feel His presence. If you faithfully follow this practice, you'll soon understand the rich truth I've been sharing and more that words can't capture. It will all make sense, just like when the Bible tells us, *'They shall call His name Emmanuel, which being interpreted is, God with us' (Matthew 1:23, KJV).*

In conclusion, the presence of God is not a concept to be grasped intellectually but an experience to be lived daily. As we embrace this daily practice, we embody the essence of 'Emmanuel'—God with us. His divine presence accompanies us every day, in every task, at every moment. Our hearts can take comfort in His nearness, and His unfaltering presence becomes a guiding light for our paths. Let us cultivate this recognition of His presence in our lives, dwelling in His love and guidance, and growing in faith, hope, and love.

ABOUT THE AUTHOR

Dr. Michael and Kathleen Yeager have served as pastors/apostles, missionaries, evangelists, broadcasters and authors for over four decades. They flow in the gifts of the Holy Spirit, teaching the Word of God with wonderful signs and miracles following in confirmation of God's Word. Doc has authored over 200 books. In 1982, they began Jesus is Lord Ministries International, Biglerville, PA 17307.

Websites Connected to Doc Yeager

www.docyeager.com

www.jilmi.org

www.wbntv.org

Some of the Books Written by Doc Yeager:

"Living in the Realm of the Miraculous #1"

"I need God Cause I'm Stupid"

"The Miracles of Smith Wigglesworth"

"How Faith Comes 28 WAYS"

"Horrors of Hell, Splendors of Heaven"

"The Coming Great Awakening"

"Sinners In The Hands of an Angry GOD", (modernized)

"Brain Parasite Epidemic"

"My JOURNEY To HELL" - illustrated for teenagers

"Divine Revelation Of Jesus Christ"

"My Daily Meditations"

"Holy Bible of JESUS CHRIST"

"War In The Heavenlies - (Chronicles of Micah)"

"Living in the Realm of the Miraculous #2"

"My Legal Rights To Witness"

"Why We (MUST) Gather!- 30 Biblical Reasons"

"My Incredible, Supernatural, Divine Experiences"

"Living in the Realm of the Miraculous #3"

"How GOD Leads & Guides! - 20 Ways"

"Weapons Of Our Warfare"

"How You Can Be Healed"

Made in the USA
Middletown, DE
28 June 2023

33978270R00225